Contents

THE MEDIA IN QUESTION

THE MEDIA IN QUESTION

Popular Cultures and Public Interests

edited by
Kees Brants, Joke Hermes
and Liesbet van Zoonen

SAGE Publications
London • Thousand Oaks • New Delhi

For Denis

Editorial selection and Introduction © Liesbet van Zoonen,
Joke Hermes and Kees Brants 1998
Chapter 2 © Peter Golding 1998
Chapter 3 © Karen Siune 1998
Chapter 4 © Els de Bens 1998
Chapter 5 © Jan van Cuilenburg 1998
Chapter 6 © Jay Blumler 1998
Chapter 7 © Cees J. Hamelink 1998
Chapter 8 © Ien Ang 1998
Chapter 9 © Peter Dahlgren 1998
Chapter 10 © Jan Wieten 1998
Chapter 11 © Liesbet van Zoonen 1998
Chapter 12 © Kaarle Nordenstreng 1998
Chapter 13 © George Gerbner 1998
Chapter 14 © Andrew Tudor 1998
Chapter 15 © Joke Hermes 1998
Chapter 16 © Kees Brants 1998

First published 1998

SAGE Publications Ltd
6 Bonhill Street
London EC2A 4PU

SAGE Publications Inc.
2455 Teller Road
Thousand Oaks, California 91320

SAGE Publications India Pvt Ltd
32, M-Block Market
Greater Kailash – I
New Delhi 110 048

British Library Cataloguing in Publication data

A catalogue record for this book is available
from the British Library

ISBN 0 7619 5722 7
ISBN 0 7619 5723 5 (pbk)

Library of Congress catalog card number 97–061883

Typeset by Mayhew Typesetting, Rhayader, Powys
Printed in Great Britain by The Cromwell Press Ltd,
Broughton Gifford, Melksham, Wiltshire

Contributors

Ien Ang, Research Centre in Intercommunal Studies, University of Western Sydney, Nepean, Australia.

Els de Bens, Department of Communication, University of Ghent, Belgium.

Jay Blumler, Emeritus Professor, University of Leeds and University of Maryland.

Kees Brants, Department of Communication, University of Amsterdam.

Jan van Cuilenburg, Department of Communication, University of Amsterdam.

Peter Dahlgren, Media and Communications Studies, Lund University.

George Gerbner, Temple University, Pennsylvania.

Peter Golding, Department of Social Sciences, Loughborough University.

Cees J. Hamelink, Department of Communication, University of Amsterdam.

Joke Hermes, Department of Communication, University of Amsterdam.

Kaarle Nordenstreng, Department of Journalism and Mass Communication, University of Tampere.

Karen Siune, Analyse Institute for Forskning, Denmark.

Andrew Tudor, Department of Sociology, University of York.

Jan Wieten, Department of Communication, University of Amsterdam.

Liesbet van Zoonen, Department of Communication, University of Amsterdam.

Acknowledgements

This book is for and, in a way, about Denis McQuail. All the chapters have been written in honour of him and his work on the occasion of his retirement from the University of Amsterdam. The authors share his interest in and concern for the performance and accountability of media and their practitioners, which culminated in his seminal *Media Performance* (Sage, 1992). They all have met and worked with Denis in some way or another, and were invited to write a strong normative chapter on pressing and/or neglected questions with regard to media and public and popular interests. A core theme was of course what exactly these interests are and should be in today's fragmented world.

A book like this, which tries to cover a vast array of current and enduring issues of media at the turn of the century, is bound to be incomplete. We would have liked to take up in more detail issues such as multiculturalism and ethnicity, media structures in Eastern Europe and media audiences. They do turn up in various chapters, but would have needed a more encompassing attention. So be it.

In the groundwork for and editing of this collection we have had an enormous intellectual input from colleagues who unfortunately do not turn up in the list of contributors. We name and thank particularly Brenda Dervin, Marjorie Ferguson, Renaldas Gudauskas, Wolfgang Hoffmann-Riem and Karl-Erik Rosengren. We also thank our editors at Sage, Stephen Barr and Julia Hall, for their enthusiasm and support. Most of all we thank Denis McQuail for being his stimulating, generous, funny and adorable self. Denis, you have been a truly wonderful colleague.

1

Introduction: of Public and Popular Interests

Liesbet van Zoonen, Joke Hermes and Kees Brants

The terms 'public' and 'popular' in all their varied and fluid meanings are inseparably linked to the study of contemporary mass media. Although both 'public' and 'popular' exist outside of the media environment, media cannot exist without a public or a popular dimension and should preferably contain both. The idea of responsible media, however, has mainly been discussed with respect to their public dimension. The suggestion is all too often that 'popular' is synonymous with political disinterest and wanton consumerism. At best popular culture is seen as mere entertainment and irrelevant to society's wider concerns. In this book, we and many other authors argue differently. We will suggest that nowadays the distinction between public and popular, between information and entertainment, between citizens and consumers is impossible to maintain. We will therefore discuss 'responsibility' in relation to both popular and public media and we will assume their complementarity rather than their mutual exclusion.

How are 'public' and 'popular' intertwined nowadays? 'Public' in its literal and self-evident sense pertains to media publications of events, issues, affairs, stories, myths, fairytales and other kinds of narratives. 'Public' thus refers to accessibility for everyone, regardless of time and space. But 'public' has other inflections as well which are also related to mass communication. 'Public' can also mean of concern to everyone and pertaining to a common good or interest, as for instance in the Habermassian notion of the public sphere as a space between society and the state in which people can freely discuss and evaluate matters of public concern. 'Public' then implies a more normative stance on the general interest as opposed to particular interests, and is articulated with mass media in questioning how the media operate in the public sphere or how they can and should contribute to the public interest. The European public broadcasting model is one historic answer to these questions, invoking yet another aspect of 'public' which refers to state-related means of organization and financing.

As a classic theme in mass communication, the relation of mass media to publicity, public concerns and the public interest concerns a number of key questions that reflect the various meanings of 'public': how accessible are the mass media? Do mass media publish and circulate matters of concern to all and do they show the variety of concerns and perspectives in society? How do mass media function in relation to the public interest? And how should the mass media be organized, legally and financially, in order to realize its potential as a carrier of public values? Traditionally, these questions have been raised mainly in the context of news and other forms of information, focusing among other things on roles and values of journalists; the quality of news performance; the accessibility of news media for diverging opinions; the role of the media in political campaigns; the way citizens process news and information; public opinion; how public broadcasting should fulfil its public role; how market forces can be countered, and so on. Popular media genres have been largely ignored in these debates with the exception of considerable concern over pornography and popular representation of forms of violence and its effects on audiences, youth and children in particular.

As a result, especially the performance of journalism in relation to the public interest has been subjected to normative theorizing, as expressed for instance in the various reformulations of the classic study *Four Theories of the Press* (Siebert et al., 1956), which has been part of the simultaneous development of ethical and professional codes. However, social normative thinking on other aspects of media performance has been relatively rare and the frameworks developed for the press apply uneasily to other genres. As Denis McQuail, key thinker in contemporary normative media theory, argues:

> The frameworks offered . . . have failed to come to terms with the great internal diversity of mass media types and services and changing technologies and times. There is, for instance, little of relevance in any of the variants of the theory which might realistically be applied to the cinema, or the music industry, or the video market, or even a good deal of sport, fiction and entertainment on television, thus to much of what the media are doing most of the time. (McQuail, 1996: 67)

But it is not only the failure of existing normative theories to cover popular media genres, that necessitates new directions in normative thinking, it is also the profound transformations of the media landscape taking place: the changes in journalism, the increasing relevance of popular culture in public life and the changed nature of 'the public'. Any debate on media and the public interest thus has to take into account this general popularization of the public domain, and although this has been subject to considerable and strong criticism, the most productive starting point for its evaluation seems to be an acknowledgment of the irreversibility of these developments. As Dahlgren (1991: 8) says:

> While much in the contemporary situation is troubling to say the least . . . we live in an age of electronic media and mass publics and cannot turn back the historical clock. We can only go forward.

In looking forward then, we have tried to engage four interrelated normative debates on the responsibility of public and popular media. The first section covers the classic and well-known topic of media regulation of broadcasting, which has become all the more pressing with the enormous changes in technology, financing, content and media law. The following sections are set in motion by the conditions of late modernity and contain a rethinking of the core value in normative media theories, namely 'the public interest', the ethics of popular journalism and the politics of popular culture.

The first section of the book covers the classic debate on media regulation. Whereas the printed press has always had considerable freedom from government intervention, broadcasting has been the domain *par excellence* where the state has made its mark. Broadcast media institutions, texts and technologies are now changing rapidly: diminishing technological constraints, growing economic importance and loss of legitimation of the public service project have led to an explosion of commercial broadcasting stations in Western Europe. In addition, the emergence of new information and communication technologies, such as the Internet, has the potential to diminish the importance of mass media (commercial and public) as intermediaries of public life. These technologies can revitalize forms of communication that broke down with the present top-down forms of mass communication. On the other hand they can also reinforce existing inequalities with respect to the availability and user-friendliness of technology. As a result of both commercialization and fragmentation of media channels, not much has been left of the erstwhile grand projects of public broadcasters in Western Europe. They can be said to be in deep crisis; a crisis that is much debated among communication scholars, who take positions varying from a staunch market justification to a persistent defence of the public broadcasting model. In Part I of the book both extreme positions are defended. Els de Bens and Karen Siune adamantly favour the public broadcasting project and abhor the market logic that has come to poison public broadcasters in Western Europe. On the other hand Jan van Cuilenburg is a fervent supporter of the free marketplace of ideas. Since it is impossible to assess media content in a satisfactory way, we should at most regulate access to that market, he claims. Peter Golding's contribution to this section takes a middle position from which he gives a highly useful sketch of the history of this debate.

Part II of the book searches for the answer to the fundamental question underlying all media debate, namely: what is the public interest. The idea of a 'public' as a more or less unified group of citizens that belong to a well-defined nation state which forms the anchor-point of much writing on media and the public interest has never been in concord with social reality and has lost its relevance completely under contemporary western conditions of migration, statelessness and multiculturality. As several authors have shown, notions of the public interest as a general interest have concealed its articulation with particular values (e.g. Fraser, 1992). Critical analyses of the development of the public sphere for instance, have shown that the public allowed to take part in public debate consisted of white male middle-class men (Calhoun, 1992); women, workers and blacks historically were excluded from public debate, a situation one can easily recognize today when looking at, for instance, access to the media of these groups. In addition, there are groups of citizens who have constructed their collective identities as different from 'the public at large' such as feminists, the elderly and homosexuals who are similarly excluded from public debate. Most important, however, in present-day Europe, for the recognition of 'the public' as fragmented rather than unified, are migration patterns which have constructed 'publics' that cross the boundaries of nation states, thereby undermining the taken-for-granted unity of any nation. 'Publics' therefore, rather than 'the public' should form the core of a debate on media and the public interest, or better 'public interests' rather than 'the public interest'. All authors in this section acknowledge the need to think of the public as a plurality, but they differ in their provision of alternatives. After a close inspection, Jay Blumler concludes that social and media turbulence are not quite as upsetting to the notions of the public interest as is often assumed and he convincingly retains the basic values of quality and diversity in media output. Cees Hamelink acknowledges the postmodern fragmentation of norms and values, but sees a strong universal framework for the public interest in human rights. Ien Ang takes the most radical position here and argues that whereas general assessments of the public interest can never be made, particular evaluations at particular times can and should be made.

The two remaining sections of the book articulate the public with the popular, in Part III by looking at changes in journalism. Commercial broadcasting and the attractions of popular television culture for audiences have produced new journalistic genres, such as infotainment, reality television and the talk show in which traditional distinctions between information and entertainment have collapsed. Journalism in its broadcast but also in its print form has become market driven and guided by – as it is sometimes called – what is interesting rather than what is important, by an audience orientation rather than an institutional logic. As a result of these developments themes formerly hidden from the public eye have become generally visible; this is clear, for instance, in the obsessive search of contemporary journalism for scandal in the private lives of public officials, or in the incredibly intimate confessions of people appearing in talk shows, or in the sensationalist reality genre. The once more or less taken for granted social responsibility of journalism has been undermined and a pressing question is whether market logic allows for an ethical journalistic practice. This issue is addressed from different angles. Peter Dahlgren looks at the changes in television journalism, the countermovements of civic journalism in the United States and what this can mean for European television. The paradox of seemingly normlessness and at the same time lived ethical standards of producers of reality television and gossip journalists is discussed by Jan Wieten and Liesbet van Zoonen. Kaarle Nordenstreng examines which general codes could still bind all genres of journalism and argues for a more 'people-centred' and less technocratic approach.

Not only has journalism become popularized, non-journalistic popular genres have also gained importance for public life (these trends for that matter build on existing tendencies within journalism and popular culture and do not represent a complete change of direction), as is argued by the three authors in Part IV on the politics of popular culture. Social movements such as the black and the women's movement find in popular culture genres like music and books strong means of expression and identification not offered by official journalism, as is clear in Joke Hermes' contribution on women's crime writing. Popular culture genres bind their fans into interpretive communities sharing certain frames of references, which can have an emancipatory potential. Andrew Tudor's chapter on sports journalism, however, shows that the community of soccer fans that soccer reporters are can be utterly conservative in their nationalism and racism without even realizing it. In a more general sense, George Gerbner states in this section that mediated popular culture deeply affects the way people experience their immediate environment, thus providing another example of the importance of public interest in popular culture as well as in the public dimension of popular culture itself.

In a summary of the issues brought forward by all authors, Kees Brants looks back at the problems they raise and forwards as to what these and other issues mean to the changing role of that hybrid landscape of media in twenty-first century democracies.

With these chapters we intend to contribute to an agenda for a debate on media and the public interest that will meet the challenges offered by the postmodern condition in western industrialized societies; which takes into account the ubiquity and predominantly commercial orientation of mass media; which looks at the variety and range of popular genres and discourses that have become relevant for contemporary public life; and which assumes the fragmentation of the public interest into public interests. In the face of such overwhelming requirements it is not surprising that explicit normative media theorizing is no longer a usual practice within the community of communication scholars. Much communication research of course is implicitly normative by accepting the current status quo; administrative and market-oriented research (which has come to dominate the universities as well) does little to rethink a socially responsible role for the media today. By definition, we would expect critical media studies to offer more of a change-oriented perspective, but here the field is fragmented into the particular concerns of, for instance, ethnicity, gender, homosexuality and class. In fact, the postmodern recognition of difference and plurality that typifies much of today's critical media studies appears to have made the search for an overall perspective unfashionable and naive and has paralysed the possibility of strong normative stances that would make a difference to contemporary media practice. That field is now left to conservative forces which are not bothered by variety and are driven more by moral panics than by notions of liberty and freedom, unless of course where they concern the market.

There are, however, some examples of critical and progressive counter-movements, both practical and theoretical. A practical example is the Cultural Environment Movement, initiated some years ago by a group of communication scholars who claim the preservation of culture to be as important as the preservation of the environment (see George Gerbner, Chapter 13, for more detail). A strong theoretical and normative counterpoint to conservative and market logic on the one hand and critical fragmentation on the other, is offered by Denis McQuail's ground-breaking work *Media Performance* (1992). Here all the issues of developing and measuring media performance, questions of economic and political dominance, diversity, access, objectivity, solidarity, culture and identity are placed within the media's role and responsibility in 'the' public interest. In locating these principles, he too is confronted with the fragmentation and diversity of today's societies that thwart such an enterprise (see Ien Ang, Chapter 8). Nevertheless, McQuail's normative project is inspiring for its agenda and challenges its critics to come up with alternatives and additions. This is precisely what this current volume is aimed at: to build on to existing normative theory, to refine and to revitalize it, to add to its agenda and to invite the community of communication scholars to rethink their own normative positions.

References

Calhoun, C. (ed.) (1992) *Habermas and the Public Sphere*. Cambridge, MA: MIT Press.

Dahlgren, Peter (1991) 'Introduction', in P. Dahlgren and C. Sparks (eds) *Communication and Citizenship: Journalism and the Public Sphere*. London: Routledge, pp. 1–26.

Fraser, Nancy (1992) 'Rethinking the public sphere: a contribution to the critique of actually existing democracy', in C. Calhoun (ed.) *Habermas and the Public Sphere*. Cambridge, MA: MIT Press.

McQuail, Denis (1992) *Media Performance. Mass Communication and the Public Interest*. London: Sage.

McQuail, Denis (1996) 'Mass media in the public interest: towards a framework of norms for media performance', in J. Curran and M. Gurevitch (eds) *Mass Media and Society*, 2nd edn. London: Edward Arnold.

Siebert, Fred S., Peterson, Theodore B. and Schramm, Wilbur (1956) *Four Theories of the Press*. Urbana: University of Illinois Press.

2

New Technologies and Old Problems: Evaluating and Regulating Media Performance in the 'Information Age'

Peter Golding

Mass communication matters. That axiom has been fundamental to the academic exploration of the modern mass media, and especially to the sociological inflection given that enterprise by such distinguished exponents as Denis McQuail. Thus the links between media structures and products on the one hand, and public policy for the management of the communications process on the other, have been at the heart, however implicitly, of the investigation of mass communications from the outset. In one of his earliest interventions McQuail points out that the enormous potential power of the media demands such a framework. 'Because of this potential, formal and informal mechanisms develop for the control of those who operate mass communications and who take part in the selection and editing of content. The result is to ensure that the latter process is guided by the prevailing laws and social norms . . .' (McQuail, 1969: 13).

Inevitably that train of thought takes us to an assessment of the social role of the mass media, and the notion that social analysis of the media cannot be divorced from some understanding of the contribution of such analysis to the public evaluation of their role. 'The starting point for the kind of sociology recommended here', wrote McQuail in the introduction to a seminal collection published a quarter of a century ago, 'is thus, inevitably, some fundamental thinking about the purpose and objectives of mass media institutions in society' (McQuail, 1972: 16). Without any hint of an unavoidable functionalism in this formulation, the analysis of mass media is set inextricably in a normative context, and thus, seamlessly we move on to the search for criteria of performance which might allow us to assess the contribution of the media to the public interest, that 'complex of supposed informational, cultural, and social benefits to the wider society which go beyond the immediate, particular and individual interests of those

who participate in public communication, whether as senders or receivers'
(McQuail, 1992: 3).

In this chapter I wish to review this analytical ambition in the context of
technological change, to ask whether the questions which have arisen from
past research are adequate to the supposed fundamental changes in our
media environment now in train.

A history of tension: liberty and licence

It is ironic that our current high interest in questions of performance
evaluation emerges at a time when 'deregulation' would appear to signal a
retreat by the state from a close interest in how the media perform. Why
search for measures of media success or failure if the state is less interested
in controlling or policing communications in the public interest? But, of
course, this retreat is no such thing, and as many have pointed out,
'deregulation' is more nearly 're-regulation', as statutory intervention in the
media tackles new problems and responds to new pressures. It was ever
thus. The standard history of media–state relations constructs a narrative
of gradual emancipation, in which occasional eruptions of heroic defiance,
coupled with the awakening liberalism of late modernity, have steadily
withdrawn the shackles of state control and oppression from liberty of
expression. Journalism is especially vulnerable to this seductive myth, but
the hard reality is a little different.

The emergence of printing in very early capitalism reveals from the
earliest days the tension between governments' sensitivities to potentially
uncontrolled and dissident expression and the requirements of an expanding liberty of expression. Taking over from where the Church *Index* of
banned books had led, the emerging states of Europe sought regularly to
curtail the independence of the printing press. Licensing of printers,
especially when 'news' became the subject of the printers' art, was rigidly
enforced in the England of the early seventeenth century, and only
weakened for a period in mid century before being reinforced with the
restoration of the monarchy. It was the emerging commercial security of
the press more than anything which was to provide the platform from
which its ringing declarations for liberty of expression could be proclaimed.
The imposition of numerous taxes, from the Stamp Act of 1712 to the
various 'taxes on knowledge' in the early nineteenth century, represented
but the fiscal skirmishes of a continuing war of attrition between commercial viability and statutory regulation (Collet, 1933; Cranfield, 1978).

Crucial to this period was what Habermas has influentially construed as
the emergence of a public sphere. Uninhabited by women, the propertyless,
or the uneducated, this was a limited realm, a distinctly bourgeois space. For
Habermas it is 'understood as the sphere of private individuals assembled
into a public body, which almost immediately laid claim to the officially
regulated "intellectual newspapers" for use against the public authority

itself' (Habermas, 1979/1962: 199). England provided an especially propitious breeding ground for this development, and the coffee houses of London became the archetypal locale of the rational debate and critical forum which are the core of Habermas' model (Garnham, 1986; Thompson, 1995: 69–75). Leaving aside for the moment debate about the accuracy of Habermas' historiography, what emerges is a struggle for independent thought and expression, in which the state seeks to contest the surging independence of the new media for the public voice.

Yet, as James Curran has reminded us, the notion of social control of the press rather disguises the extent to which the press has itself been an agent of social control (Curran, 1978). Thus, in examining the history of state intervention or regulation of media performance, we need to stand back a little from a model which inevitably focuses our attention on the contrary ambitions of state and media, to assess to what extent regulation by the state may be in the interest of the media themselves as much as in the public interest. Curran's point is to note how the press has been a carrier for dominant ideas and values, as, in the early nineteenth century, it was the emerging middle-class press which was the key vehicle for the final suppression and burial of the radical and working-class newspapers.

Thus we can recast the notion of a tension simply between liberty and licence. McQuail rightly suggests that in the 'basic matter of conflict between authority and freedom' a picture of historical progression towards unfettered liberty of the press is too simple, since contemporary media display a mix of different elements (McQuail, 1992: 9). A second tension needs to be introduced into the equation, that between social order and diversity of expression. The state has always had to juggle with both these sets of imperatives, so that the notion of the public interest, far from being a clear and cogent objective of statutory intervention into communications, has been a complex ideological field, in which different parties have had varying ability to impose their definition of where the 'public' interest lies.

The twin imperatives of media regulation

Whatever their intentions, governments seek to regulate the media in two ways. First, they are anxious to ensure that the media do not propagate messages or values they consider not conducive to the public good. This might include material they consider harmful to public order, or to the sensibilities or vulnerability of minority or weaker groups, whether children, ethnic minorities, linguistic groups or religious communities. Equally, of course, this concern just might extend to material the state considers unconducive to its own well-being, and no regime, however liberal, has been utterly selfless in this regard. The other side of this coin is the concern all governments share of promoting as positive a picture of their own activities as possible, often treading a fine line between the unacceptable exploitation of the media for propaganda and the reasonable demands of public information. This line has been policed with growing uncertainty and friction in many countries in recent years. In Britain, for example, the emergence of what I have termed the 'public relations state' (Golding, 1994, 1995) has fostered an explosion of state activity in this direction of unprecedented scale and energy. At the same time the sophistication of state information management has left many dubious about the capacity of the media to provide the range and depth of material necessary for informed citizenship. Even the publication of commitments to open government, that are the common rhetorical currency of the modern state, can be a little soured by actual practice. In 1994 the UK government published a long-awaited Code on open government, yet its eventual features left many commentators aghast. As Birkinshaw points out, the Code 'does not give access to documents but to information which is filleted by officials, and this is subject to exemptions which take up four and a half pages of the nine-page Code; the information to which access will be given covers one page' (Birkinshaw, 1997: 169–70).

The second aspect of the media states seek to regulate is their structure. This includes the licensing of production and distribution, the most ancient form of state regulation of communications. It also includes intervention in the economic and financial structures of the media, by controlling patterns of public subsidy, if any, by statutory controls over revenues, special taxation arrangements, monopoly restrictions, and cross-ownership or foreign ownership controls. The reason regimes are involved in both these forms of regulation is that the media are at one and the same time cultural institutions providing major and core features of the symbolic and normative environment in which we live, while also being industries of enormous and growing significance in the changing industrial landscape, with substantial command of both the centres of key industrial growth, and of large proportions of consumers' disposable spending power.

Governments thus have a double dilemma in regulating the media. Firstly, they must take account of their peculiar standing as cultural institutions, serving the political and cultural needs of the community in unique fashion, while at the same time they must consider the contribution of the media as industries at key nodes in the nation's economic fabric. Secondly they have to recognize that their populations confront the media in two roles, as consumers and as citizens. In these two roles their needs, and their demands for government action, may well be incompatible. The twin roles of government in regulating both structure and content are summarized in Figure 2.1 (Golding and van Snippenburg, 1995). The figure shows that, schematically, there are four possible stances in the form of government intervention in communications. Interventionism in both content and structure implies an authoritarianism which seeks to regulate all aspects of cultural production and distribution. A liberal approach to structure coupled with an interventionist approach to content emerges from governments keen to foster the freedoms of the market place and the industrial expansion of their communications industries, but with considerable

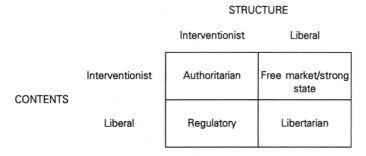

Figure 2.1 *Government intervention in communications*

sensitivity to the political potency of moral regulatory groups, perhaps religious or otherwise significant sections of their communities. Regulatory regimes concern themselves with structure, but are quite happy to withdraw from too active a role in policing content, while libertarian regimes see no significant place for government in either direction.

States find themselves on the horns of a dilemma in assessing where in this array to situate themselves. This is true at both national and international level. The EU, for example, has been anxious to protect European culture from the incessant waves of imported American materials, especially film and television. Yet these are popular with audiences, and it is not at all clear quite what the indigenous European culture being protected might comprise. Equally the EU is devoted to the encouragement of European audiovisual and information industries and their successful competition with Japanese and American giants. Material designed primarily for universal consumption and export might not, however, be identical to that designed to serve the parochial needs of the European citizen. The twin policies, of cultural protection and industrial expansion, do not always sit easily with each other.

Regulatory uncertainties: in whose interest?

In Europe generally there are two quite different legacies detectable in the apparatus and culture which provide for state intervention in the media. In most countries the press has grown out of a party political system from whose embrace, formally at least, it has almost completely escaped. With scattered exceptions, the modern press is a fully commercial enterprise, largely selling to local or at least national readerships, and little encumbered with significant statutory controls. In some countries subsidies attempt to ensure some equity in the circulation of newspapers supporting different political factions, while others have controls over regional or sectoral monopoly. However, the press represents a medium at some distance from the apparatus of the state.

By contrast, broadcasting in Europe has evolved with one dominant model, that of public service broadcasting, as the cornerstone of most systems, even where subsequent commercial alternatives have become significant, or indeed dominant. Rooted in the exemplary model of the BBC, they provide entertainment, information, and education to high standards, in what they presume to understand as the public interest, and within a legislative and fiscal framework designed to place them both a some remove from the state, yet independent of commercial sponsors or ownership. The relationship between such broadcasters and the state has become problematic in recent years as new technologies and the intensifying competition that comes with them, rising costs (with the corollary embarrassment of rising licence fees or taxation burdens), and often ideological scepticism about the place of broadcasting in the public sector, have cumulatively undermined the special role and statutory location of this unique configuration. Public service broadcasters have thus found themselves losing audience shares, and obliged increasingly to pay their way in a competitive market.

One feature of this twin legacy is the somewhat convoluted and contradictory apparatus that has evolved to provide a regulatory framework for the media. This varies from country to country, but in all the contrary inclinations to regulate broadcasting and the press, and the often contradictory directions of industrial policy and cultural policy, have bequeathed a diverse and awkward statutory apparatus. In Britain, for example, the relevant bodies are a mix of the statutory and the non-statutory, and have a wide array of powers, while each being restricted to a single medium. The Broadcasting Standards Council was formed in 1988, and receives complaints about matters of taste and decency (largely the usual suspects of violence, sex and bad language) on which it pontificates and publishes judgements. It has no authority to enforce its decisions. The Broadcasting Complaints Commission was established in 1981, and its powers now derive from the 1990 Broadcasting Act. It is a quasi-judicial body which receives and adjudicates on complaints about unfair treatment by broadcasters, infringement of privacy, and similar concerns. It is accountable to the Department of National Heritage, the ministry which has somehow inherited responsibility for broadcasting (well, some aspects of it). These two bodies are due to merge in the near future. Commercial broadcasting is controlled and regulated by statutory bodies, the Radio Authority and the Independent Television Commission.

The press comes under the jurisdiction of the Press Complaints Commission, established in 1991 following the closure of the Press Council. It 'continues to be funded generously by the newspaper and magazine publishing industry' (Press Complaints Commission, 1996), and receives about 2000 complaints a year, of which just 28 were upheld in 1995. The PCC has no statutory basis, and much of the debate in the UK in recent years has been about whether the increasingly recurrent bouts of sensationalism associated especially with the tabloid press, as it pushes back the boundaries of 'infotainment', will propel the government into erecting a statutory regime for press monitoring and regulation. Despite much sabre rattling no government has felt so inclined thus far, given the political inclinations and electoral potency of the press. Films and advertising each have their own industry-based structure of self-regulation. Telecommunications is another story, being monitored by a regulatory watchdog, OFTEL, which is nicely described as a non-ministerial government department, formally independent of ministerial control, but accountable to the Secretary of State for Trade and Industry.

This extraordinary mix of structures, some regulatory and interventionist, some statutory some not, with a variety of relationships to the industry, consumers, and parliament, is an unholy mess reflecting no clear philosophy whatever about the role of the media or communications in public life. It is normally assumed that regulation reflects the perception of communications as a utility rather than a commodity. It is seen as in some sense more akin to health or education than to, say, foodstuffs or consumer electronics. Thus statutory intervention is justified as in the public interest, even where this may infringe the freedom of individual producers or distributors. That principle, however, has always been only partially accepted, and as the variety of statutory provision in the UK illustrates, is far from uniformly applied across the range of communication industries. Sometimes this variety is justified in terms of the particular features of the medium. Broadcasting, for example, was said to have special characteristics – it 'came into the home', or frequencies were a scarce resource which would thus require allocation by some judicial body. However, the ideological opposition to regulation comes from two quite different positions. The libertarian position requires that freedom of expression be unfettered, and that any inhibition on such a right is a greater mischief than the possible harmful effects of uncontrolled distribution. From a more economistic, and perhaps less fundamentally principled position, comes the alternative justification that communications are a good in the market place, over whose distribution and consumption the only proper control is that of free choice in that market place. That mechanism in itself will guarantee the best standards of quality and availability.

With such a variety of philosophical and administrative apparatuses, it is no surprise, therefore, to find that much intervention by the government has been more properly understood as in the private rather than the public interest. Lack of clear political direction has inevitably meant that pressure, power, and influence have played their usual part in the affairs of state. Three examples from the UK make the point. The introduction of commercial television in the early 1950s was widely promoted by a number of significant pressure groups, including a small number of Conservative backbench MPs and manufacturers, advertisers, and performers' unions. Public opinion was not a major factor – the public interest remained unarticulated, and other major forces – the trade unions, the press, the church – remained adamantly opposed (Briggs, 1979: Part VII; Wilson, 1961).

Secondly, in 1981 the franchises awarded to the regional television companies who make up the commercial network were due for renewal, leading
to a major exercise in judgement over their allocation by the Independent
Broadcasting Authority, established by law for that purpose. Forty-two
companies competed for the existing 15 franchises plus the new breakfast-
time slot. With virtually no recourse to public consultation, and with little
apparent rationale to the decision-making, a set of decisions was made,
which its chroniclers describe as arbitrary, despite the 'atmosphere of
contrived drama' (Briggs and Spicer, 1986: 219–20).

Thirdly, and inevitably, we bring Rupert Murdoch on to the scene.
Murdoch has elevated to an art form the ability to persuade regulatory
regimes of the exceptions appropriate to his own enterprises, not least by
reminding them of the value of his organs for their political prosperity.
Murdoch acquired the *Times* newspaper group in 1981 from the Thomson
Organization. What should automatically have required a reference to the
Monopolies and Mergers Commission was dismissed on the grounds that,
but for Murdoch, the newspapers would have closed. A similar contrivance
was erected when Murdoch acquired the *Today* newspaper from the
Lonrho group. Murdoch's subsequent ingestion of satellite broadcasting in
the UK and elsewhere drove further coaches and horses through the wholly
ineffective and selectively applied monopoly legislation, and the equally
compliant cross-media ownership restrictions. The FCC in the United
States has been similarly pliable in waiving cross-ownership rules as
Murdoch bought up big city television stations in the mid 1980s. In the UK
the benign interventions of Margaret Thatcher on Murdoch's behalf were
legion and legendary, her admiration for his buccaneering entrepreneurial
style forcefully buttressed by the evident political return in the support
given her by Murdoch's newspapers. This clearest evidence of regulation in
the private interest would be hard to improve on (Evans, 1994).

These three examples thus illustrate the role of intervention and regulation as potentially as much in the private as in the public interest. That
regulation can be of uncertain direction in this way is becoming more
problematic with the emergence of new technologies and the innovative
questions they pose for regulatory regimes, and it is to that issue we finally
turn.

Regulation in the information age: of what, by whom?

In assessing how we might address the problem of media performance in the
light of changing technologies McQuail has rightly noted that we may have
radically to rethink familiar models. He points to the change from an 'old
model' in which limited supply of broadly homogeneous content is delivered
to a passive audience with undifferentiated effects. In its place is a 'new
model' in which variegated sources provide material through diverse
channels to a fragmented and active audience with varied and unpredictable

effects (McQuail, 1992: 312). This may, however, be to overstate how far the new technologies are indeed prompting and demanding new approaches to questions of performance evaluation and regulation.

Essentially four key changes are usually cited in elaborating the 'model change' succinctly outlined by McQuail. First, the arrival of cable and satellite especially has facilitated an explosion of channels for distribution of audiovisual material, creating far greater diversity of expression than hitherto possible. Certainly, the carrying capacity of such technologies is increasing exponentially. However, the shift from multiplicity to diversity is an important one, and a distinction that is sometimes elided. The castigation of early cable systems as 'one hundred times the same old junk' may readily come to characterize newer technologies whose carrying capacity vastly outstrips the capacity of production systems to provide both diverse and voluminous contents. Secondly, new technologies provide for consumer autonomy of an unprecedented potency. We can all be our own television scheduler, arrange for the newspaper of our own design and complexion to be constructed via the Internet for daily downloading, exploit video on demand to evade the leisure diktats of the distribution chains. Well, maybe, up to a point. As yet there is little sign of new technologies being quite so benign in the control they offer. Moreover the range of choice available depends directly on the traditional and familiar medium of consumer sovereignty, namely affluence. Thus choice increases with disposable spending power, and diminishes without it. The notion of information poor and information rich is perhaps a cliché, but it is born of clear and growing evidence of just such a divide (Golding, 1994).

The third feature we are directed to is interactivity. Transcending the traditional defining characteristic of mass communications, new forms of digital delivery facilitate everything from the electronic referendum to instant audience feedback. The problem with such visionary utopias is that the systems are not designed for that purpose, and are not being developed for such uses (Golding, 1996). Aside from the limited, technically literate and economically upmarket community who will have access to this on-line polity, the implications of such political systems are not entirely auspicious, with inherent tendencies towards the individualization of politics and the degradation of representative institutions. The presupposition of universal access, itself illusory, is also based on a fiction about the nature of interactivity. Interactivity on the World Wide Web, far from a mechanism for democratic debate and influence, will descend to the ability to fill in on-screen questionnaires and to remember the password which goes with your credit card number.

Fourthly, the new technologies reflect the globalized nature of communications, which indeed poses severe questions for the practicalities of both performance evaluation and for regulation. As the EU has found, what transnational regulatory bodies may believe to be in the 'public interest' may not convincingly be so from the perspective of the nation state. And, as we have observed earlier, the nation state may not always see the public interest as distinct from that of major multinational private sector players. Globalization itself may have become a little overstated (Golding and Harris, 1997: 7–8). Both the realities of capital location and the resilience of culture and politics at national level suggest that globalization may yet be a chimera in the analysis of international communications.

In terms of Figure 2.1 it might seem that the new technologies encourage a move towards the libertarian, or at least purely regulatory regime. Yet, as the periodic moral panic over Internet pornography has illustrated, there remains a sense that an unstructured medium requires some new apparatus of regulation, however impractical or unrealistic. But the truth is that the new technologies do not, in fact, pose wholly new questions, because the questions that matter are not primarily about communications apparatuses. Indeed as lawyers have pointed out, as they gradually get to grips with the new technology, the idea of some wholly different 'cyberlaw' is utterly misleading. Existing legislation on communication, exchange, and information retrieval remains pertinent, however the complexities of the conflict of laws increase in practice (Gringrass, 1997).

The search for criteria of media performance presupposes some sense of the public interest. Communications media are unique in providing both goods that command a critical place in the modern economy as well as providing the vehicles by which the symbols and values that people deploy in making sense of their lives are delivered and disseminated. That is to say, they resource citizenship. That claim lies behind the attempts by successive bodies to articulate the need for evaluation and regulation. The postwar Royal Commission on the Press in Britain put it thus:

> The democratic form of society demands of its members an active and intelligent participation in the affairs of their community, whether local or national. It assumes that they are sufficiently well informed about the issues of the day to be able to form the broad judgements required by an election, and to maintain between elections the vigilance necessary in those whose governors are their servants and not their masters. . . . Democratic society, therefore, needs a clear and truthful account of events, of their background and their causes; a forum for discussion and informed criticism; and a means whereby individuals and groups can express a point of view or advocate a cause. (Royal Commission on the Press, 1947: 101)

What is crucial to this clarion call is that it takes us beyond the media. Performance evaluation, as carefully unpacked by McQuail, needs a number of dimensions to assess the character and adequacy of what the media do and provide. However that will never be enough. Whatever the technologies of delivery and consumption, questions of access and equity will remain central. The 'means whereby individuals and groups can express a point of view or advocate a cause' will require not merely the technical capacity for such actions, but the material resources and equity for it to become a reality. This means that media regulation can only go hand in hand with other forms of intervention in public life, whether through the education, social security, or economic systems. This takes us on a longer journey than that on which we embarked. But it is the essential starting point on the road to the better-ordered society to which social research contributes. As McQuail (1992: 316) insists, 'Knowledge without action is not enough.' But it is a start.

References

Birkinshaw, P. (1997) 'Freedom of information', *Parliamentary Affairs* 50 (1): 166–81.

Briggs, A. (1979) *The History of Broadcasting in the United Kingdom. Vol. IV: Sound and Vision*. Oxford: Oxford University Press.

Briggs, A. and Spicer, J. (1986) *The Franchise Affair: Creating Fortunes and Failures in Independent Television*. London: Century Hutchinson.

Collet, C.D. (1933) *History of the Taxes on Knowledge*. London: Watts & Co.

Cranfield, G.A. (1978) *The Press and Society from Caxton to Northcliffe*. London: Longman.

Curran, J. (1978) 'The press as an agency of social control: a historical perspective', in G. Boyce, J. Curran and P. Wingate (eds) *Newspaper History: From the 17th Century to the Present Day*. London: Constable.

Evans, H. (1994) *Good Times, Bad Times*. London: Phoenix.

Garnham, N. (1986) 'The media and the public sphere', in Peter Golding, Graham Murdock, and Philip Schlesinger (eds) *Communicating Politics: Mass Communications and the Political Process*. Leicester: Leicester University Press.

Golding, P. (1994) 'Telling stories: sociology, journalism, and the informed citizen', *European Journal of Communication* 9 (4): 461–84.

Golding, P. (1995) 'The mass media and the public sphere: the crisis of information in the "information society"', in S. Edgell, S. Walklate, and G. Williams (eds) *Debating the Future of the Public Sphere*. Aldershot: Avebury.

Golding, P. (1996) 'World wide wedge: division and contradiction in the global information infrastructure', *Monthly Review* 48 (3): 70–85.

Golding, P. and Harris, P. (eds) (1997) *Beyond Cultural Imperialism: Globalisation, Communication, and the New International Order*. London: Sage.

Golding, P. and van Snippenburg, L. (1995) 'Government, communications, and the media', in O. Borre and E. Scarbrough (eds) *The Scope of Government*. Oxford: Oxford University Press.

Gringrass, C. (1997) *The Laws of the Internet*. London: Butterworths.

Habermas, J. (1979/1962) 'The public sphere', in A. Mattelart and S. Siegelaub (eds) *Communication and Class Struggle*. Paris: IG/IMMRC.

McQuail, D. (1969) *Towards a Sociology of Mass Communications*. London: Collier-Macmillan.

McQuail, D. (1972) 'Introduction', in D. McQuail (ed.) *Sociology of Mass Communications*. Harmondsworth: Penguin Books.

McQuail, D. (1992) *Media Performance: Mass Communication and the Public Interest*. London: Sage.

Press Complaints Commission (1996) *Annual Report 1995*. London: Press Complaints Commission.

Royal Commission on the Press (1947) *Report*. Cmd 7700. London: HMSO.

Thompson, J.B. (1995) *The Media and Modernity*. Cambridge: Polity Press.

Wilson, H.H. (1961) *Pressure Group*. London: Secker and Warburg.

3

Is Broadcasting Policy Becoming Redundant?

Karen Siune

In Western Europe there are several traditions of media policy. Some take the form of political regulation, often formulated in specific media laws, others are characterized by minimal political interference; to decide not to regulate is also a kind of policy. Print media have in principle in most countries in Western Europe been private, and combined with their struggle for press freedom and against state interference in public opinion this explains why we find so little political regulation here. In contrast, national broadcasting has been policed since its very beginning and the logic behind political regulation of the electronic media is very indicative of the expectations attached to them.

Radio and television have everywhere been perceived as playing a significant role in democratic political systems. Ideally they have access to the overabundance of information, from which they select on the basis of professional norms. In their role as channel and sender they are able to inform and thus more or less have an obligation towards the citizenry. With knowledge about the array of relevant issues and policies, citizens can form opinions and, if they feel like it, actively participate in the political discourse. Media seen as such are a cornerstone of parliamentary democracy: they have to inform about and give meaning to the chaos of happenings in the world, to give a platform to the plurality of expressions and interests that form the heart of the political process, and to evaluate critically the decision-making process and the political actors that participate in this. Not only do such media need protection from those trying to interfere in their independence, they need some form of regulation to guarantee their democratic functioning as well.

Some might call this an idealistic view, void of the acceptance of present-day realities: a broadcasting system in flux, a multiplicity of channels, an abundance of programmatic choice, and a public which is less and less interested in that democratic role and just wants to enjoy the realities of fiction instead of the facts of reality. This chapter deals with the changes in broadcasting, and of television in particular. It raises the question whether media policy concerning broadcasting has become redundant as a result of an increased number of broadcasting channels. Or, as is my position, whether broadcasting politics is still a salient issue which has all but lost its urgency and necessity? But let me first play the devil's advocate, which is not too difficult and even tempting, because those who claim the obsolescence of broadcasting policy have a strong hand of cards, their trump being 'the end of scarcity'.

The case for redundancy

The existence and the character of given physical facts – only limited availability of frequencies – has since the beginning of broadcasting in the 1920s made media policy natural and political regulation legitimate. Scarcity prompted policy, accepted and acceptable in the form it was initiated by many national parliaments in Western Europe. By definition, an authoritative allocation of scarce goods with validity for all in a given nation is politics, so the limited number of frequencies for broadcasting was a natural object for some form of political regulation. Public broadcasting monopolies, some attached to state authorities, others more independent but with some form of public accountability and stated responsibility, became the general pattern.

During the last decade the situation in television land has changed dramatically. Today, audiences in all Western European countries have access to more than one national and usually many foreign television channels. The majority are received either by satellite dishes or via cable networks, sometimes a combination of the two. Terrestrial broadcasting is just one of many ways from sender to receiver and ongoing digitalization will open up new and manifold ways of reaching audiences. At the end of the century it seems the general perception that there is no longer scarcity of frequencies. The increase in the number of channels offered to the European households gives every citizen the feeling that there is enough to zap along and to choose from. And judging from audience ratings of the new commercial stations, they like it a lot and are generally glad that they have a choice. No longer do the public broadcasters know and decide what the public needs; the latter knows for itself what it wants and goes for it. The logic in regulating broadcasting, based on scarcity of goods, has vanished and so should regulation. It is redundant.

Over the years regulation based on the scarcity argument has taken the form of certain arrangements and prescribed roles, because if goods are scarce one has to define the prerequisites for their allocation, the distinguishing factors why the one is allowed access and should get the money to perform and the other not, why it should be paramount to hear one voice and to be devoid of another. And if one is going to ask the public to pay a licence fee, one has to have good grounds to say that the programmes of these broadcasters are in the public interest and should thus be provided by the state as a universal service and paid for by all via a general levy. This is exactly what private stations and their (political) supporters are protesting about. 'We are the real and only legitimate public broadcasters', they claim. 'We know and give what the public wants.' 'With so much to choose from', many viewers add, 'why should we pay for something we did not ask for, but got prescribed by the cultural-pedagogic logic of the paternalistic do-gooders?'

But there is another, related, reason for political regulation, which is based on the widespread belief in the intrusiveness and powerful influence of television: how it can mould and form the morals of the young, lure audiences into the temptations of the consumer society to the detriment of public health and, certainly not least, how private ownership or organizational freedom might, paradoxically, lead to unacceptable interference in the free flow of communication and the potential domination of one political view over another. In its own logic, but also technically, the electronic media were directed towards potential mass audiences and belief in their power was for some exactly the main reason for trying to get access. The conviction that these mass media had a great impact has persisted, albeit several empirical studies already in the early days of television showed limited impact on attitudinal change and on (voter) behaviour (Lazarsfeld et al., 1944).

The result of this view of media power was that either in law or in forms of self-regulation, certain content, notably the portrayal of pornography and the promotion of smoking in advertising, was prohibited in most countries, and openness of the broadcasting system, diversity and balance in the voicing of opinions existing in a given society were safeguarded. It took the form of the cultural-pedagogic logic, so criticized for its paternalistic arrrogance, whereby public broadcasting was expected to contribute to the well-being of society and should thus, in the public interest, present a palette of information, culture and education, and also – as relaxation was considered a legitimate element of well-being – entertainment. As long as it was original and of high quality, of course. One hears the moaning and groaning of the proponents of the redundancy argument.

Regulation in the public interest

This body of principles concerning what media ought or ought not to do, laid down in laws, regulations, commission reports and, more and more, (international) court rulings, one way or the other builds upon some notion of 'the public interest'. It is here that the work of McQuail is of particular interest. In his search for norms for media performance in the public interest, he starts with a view, to which I wholeheartedly subscribe, that 'public communication, as carried out mainly by way of the mass media, has a significant contribution to make to the general welfare of society and carries a corresponding "social responsibility"' (McQuail, 1992: 11). His basic communication values not surprisingly coincide with the core values of modern western society: freedom, justice/equality and order/solidarity. I will discuss them here, because they very much correspond with the norms that I deem relevant for public broadcasting organizations and which are so much criticized by the free-market enthusiasts.

Freedom of communication has a dual aspect based on supply and demand: offering a variety of voices and responding to a wide-ranging demand. It thus makes a connection between

> structural conditions (legal freedom to publish); operating conditions (real independence from economic and political pressures and relative autonomy for journalists and other 'communicators' within media organizations); opportunities for 'voices' in society to gain access to channels; benefits of quality of provision for 'receivers', according to criteria of relevance, diversity, reliability, interest, originality and personal satisfaction. (p. 70)

Equality has of course many links to freedom but calls, first, for an absence of discrimination or bias in the amount and kind of access available to senders or receivers. Secondly, equality refers to diversity of access and content.

> Media provision should proportionately *reflect* the actual distribution of whatever is relevant (topics, social group, political beliefs, etc.), or just reflect the varying distribution of audience demand or interest. The differentiation of media provision (content) should approximately correspond to the differences at source or to those at the receiving end (the audience). (p. 72)

Finally, equality as an evaluative principle finds a communication 'translation' in the notion of objectivity, operationalized as: neutrality, fairness and truth.

Order, as an ambiguous concept in discussions of media and society, belongs, as McQuail notes, to a more general and higher level of analysis than either freedom or equality. But in the media performance context he uses it in a much more limited sense of 'cohesion' or 'harmony'. Positively formulated, mass communication can, and in my opinion should, contribute to forming and maintaining personal identity and group cohesion, while the media are expected 'to promote education and traditionally valued culture, or to promote cultural autonomy and authenticity for social groupings based on language, region or nation' (p. 74). It should be noted, of course, that media might have not only centripetal but also centrifugal effects, in that they disrupt the normal order of the society, by not only centralizing and unifying, but also differentiating and individualizing.

With McQuail I believe that the idea of public interest connotes one particular form or media arrangement, that of 'public service broadcasting', and that in fact the idea of public interest is invoked in defence of that system. If diversity, (e)quality, balanced programming, access for all, broadcasting to all, independence, if all these requirements were fulfilled, I would be the first to support the advocates of regulation redundancy. If not, should we then rid ourselves from the regulatory prescriptions for these values?

Public service: a concept under change

The traditional form for regulation of access to broadcasting has been that those interested in becoming broadcasters had to apply to a public authority for permission to do so. Those who wanted a licence should fulfil some requirements, defined by the authorities. In most countries of Western Europe it was required that they should show public service responsibility, based upon four elements:

1   a commitment to balanced scheduling;
2   broadcasting institutions as public bodies with financial independence from governmental and commercial sources;
3   the service should be provided to all in return for a basic payment usually in the form of a licence fee;
4   political content was obliged to be balanced and impartial.

Ideally all the items from this list should be fulfilled, but the request for balanced and impartial political content was the issue studied most often, and it is the issue that has been given the greatest political concern. Commercialization and privatization have changed the picture. Much of these changes were allowed within the frame of a given national media policy, albeit such changes challenged the old system. In most countries a new pattern with a dual structure consisting of both private and public broadcasting organizations has been established.

The intended or unintended 'overspill' from satellite-transmitted broadcasting put an end to the idea at the beginning of the 1980s about coherent national media policies. Instead, deregulation was on the political agenda. Nevertheless, Europe saw a huge number of media laws presented in parliaments during the 1980s and into the 1990s. The conclusion is once again that, in spite of the rhetoric, it was not deregulation we saw in Europe, but rather re-regulation that took place (McQuail and Siune, 1986). It is, however, of great relevance for the answer to the question raised in the title whether the changes in the broadcasting landscape will lead us to answer 'yes': media policy has become redundant, because the policy so far has not been able or willing to protect the old national media structures and its virtues.

One first question of relevance is: Did the national broadcasting organizations themselves want to be protected, and did the national political actors want to protect their national media systems at all? The answer to this is a double one. There is no doubt that broadcasting organizations of the old monopoly type wanted to remain in a privileged position as long as possible. Being locked in a sort of administrative logic, their prime recommendation in a situation where new, particularly digitized, technologies allowed for the expansion of frequencies, was to ask for the extra channels to be added to the ones for which they already had responsibility. However, broadcasting organizations in most European countries were not very powerful media policy makers. They were in a way too involved, and the logic they used was too obviously aimed at self-protection.

The fundamental paradigm for public service broadcasting has itself been under change for the past 10 years, partly because broadcasters in an increasingly competitive environment almost everywhere have tried to show their ability to compete with the private broadcasters. At the same time, public broadcasters chose to adapt more than they purified their performance (Hultén and Brants, 1992). Partly because of that, private stations have become a socially and politically accepted element in the European media system; moreover, they were eager and willing to run risks as they offered to broadcast for free. New private stations were generally popular among bourgeois political parties too, since they represented a break with the old monopoly system and their success could be used as proof of the validity of a market philosophy and government at a distance.

The concept of public service responsibility has changed. If you cannot evade the burden of responsibility you can always try to redefine the concept. And so it has been. The newest version of the social responsibility attached to public service broadcasting institutions has not much to do with public service in the old sense and is a far cry from the four criteria mentioned above. The element of democracy and the focus on viewers as active citizens and knowledgeable participants is no longer the prime issue in the media political debate. Citizens are not the target group any more, only as consumers; public service is more than anything else to give the public what it wants (Syvertsen, 1992). Commodification is the magic word and the goal is to find the majority of a potential audience, to get them to listen, to watch, to buy. Indeed, redefining the concept of public service in broadcasting has been one of the alarming issues of late, which has taken place almost without public discussion.

The case for regulation

For many, politicians as well as ordinary citizens, the overall support for the idea of public regulation is vanishing; in some parts of the population, for that matter, the support for any kind of political regulation is dwindling or has already totally disappeared. Instead, we hear an increasing number of citizens and political actors talk about the need for protection *from* government, an argument which always has been a fundamental part of liberal ideology. Since (neo-)liberal values in general are spreading all over Europe, it is not surprising to hear it repeated with regard to media structure.

The main argument for an end to interference in communication has been the disappearance of scarcity of frequencies. From that flowed a whole range of advantages for audiences and political actors alike: an abundance of choice, a greater chance for independence, more control from 'below' and thus freedom for sender as well as receiver, room for both mainstream and originality, for fact and fiction, for authenticity, solidarity and attachment. It is heaven on earth, or, to put it more bluntly, someone has been reading a summary of McQuail's performance norms. But is the scarcity issue settled? Is there broader access, more diversity? And does the multiplicity of channels favour a sense of community, does it advance cohesion or has the technological communication explosion, the so-called Information Society, a notably one-sided character which sooner fragments than binds, and individualizes more than it socializes?

The irony in my tone might have made clear where I stand, but there is more to it than emotion or staunch belief in the state's role in the makeability of society. To begin with, the technological scarcity, the limited number of frequencies, has not totally disappeared, but the issue has changed its influence. With satellites and cables, and more than ever with the increased digitalization the scarcity problem is reduced, but it is nevertheless still there, since access might well become a money problem (look at the elitist participation on the Internet!). But also more and more actors want to get access to broadcasting; not only to broadcast but also access to control the electronic media.

Secondly, I foresee developments and problems in the form of financial control, new forms of monopolies, concentrated and media cross-ownership, and on the content side, information reduced to the saleable and digestible, increased entertainment and eventual political dominance by financially strong actors. Some argue that national culture is under attack or even at stake (Bakke, 1986). This issue has to some extent been a driving force behind media-political initiatives in the form of the establishment of new national channels and demands for a certain quota of national programmes. Not very much is heard with reference to this issue, now close to the turn of the century. The quota talked about in Europe are for European programmes, not for national ones. It has become almost illegitimate to protect the national within the Single Market.

While on the one hand we see a deregulatory rhetoric with regard to media economics, there is a restrengthening of regulation of immaterial values. New forms of regulation recently presented for public discussion have been legal attempts to put some kind of responsibility in the content transmitted by the Internet. Network providers bringing, or at least not prohibiting, more sex and pornography than anything else, are potential objects for new policy initiatives. In a way that story is a repetition of former episodes with reactions to sex and pornography on television. How it is possible to regulate Internet activity is under discussion; some argue that it is not at all possible to do it by laws, since legal regulation is meaningless if it cannot be controlled and eventually sanctioned. The issue is still up for debate. But media policy is not obsolete!

The future of broadcasting regulation raises a series of questions. Is any kind of regulation needed in a democratic society with a large number of channels of communication? Shall we see government intervention as a threat or as guardianship? The answer according to the author of this chapter is that regulation is still needed to make sure that the criteria defined as public service are fulfilled; I perceive government intervention as guardianship! We still need normative prescriptions, but we need more than that. We need a kind of control over the fulfilment of these demands. We can of course raise the issue, whether these requests should be defined by governments or by listeners and viewers directly, for that matter. But politics is about the authoritative allocation of values in a society, in the public and not the individual interest, and political parties and governments have traditionally been entrusted with this task as representatives of the *volonté générale*. So it is easy enough to argue in favour of letting national parliaments continue to formulate demands in exchange for funding licence fees. We can have doubts whether governments at a national level are at all capable of defining performance criteria more than in the abstract. The norms themselves might come from public debate among concerned citizens. A thorough discussion of all the aspects of media performance is still needed. Public service accounts as recently discussed within the Scandinavian public service organizations may be the answer, albeit that basing arguments on measures of content is a difficult exercise.

A concluding plea

I would argue for an ongoing discussion of what is needed in the sort of societies we want, since only an ongoing awareness of what we need in democratic societies that build upon participating citizens can raise the public awareness of a need for media policy. To arrive at such a public discourse and public opinion necessitates an infrastructure, an audiovisual space for such debate, and professional journalists who can transform the public agenda into a media agenda and that into a political agenda.

Habermas (1962) may have sketched a rather gloomy picture of the twentieth century, with a lack of rational discourse, an abundance of publicity as public relations and social engineering in the media, but in the end independent and critical mass media would still have a relevant role to play in the future of European democracies. Sadly, however, the concept of democracy has suffered under inflation as well. Today it is argued that it is a democratic right to be able to watch sports on public channels, a discussion which has dominated both media and public platforms for some time. There seems to have been less room for the 'traditional' debate related to politics, for information needed to make one a participant in democracy, not just a client or consumer.

The debate about the need for a national and European media policy has disappeared too quickly. That does not mean that consumers are satisfied, and it certainly does not mean that citizens are satisfied, let alone that democracy's needs are satisfied. The idea is that there are so many channels that it is only a matter of time before you have found the right one, the one that could satisfy your instant needs. Blinded by choice one might forget that in the end it might not be there, unless we continue to have some form of normative framework, a sort of remote control based on values. Media policy is not redundant!

References

Bakke, Marit (1986) 'Culture at stake', in Denis McQuail and Karen Siune (eds) *New Media Politics*. London: Sage, pp. 130–52.

Habermas, Jürgen (1962) *Strukturwandel der Öffentlichkeit*. Neuwied: Luchterhand.

Hultén, Olof and Brants, Kees (1992) 'Public service broadcasting: reactions to competition', in Karen Siune and Wolfgang Truetzschler (eds) *Dynamics of Media Politics*. London: Sage, pp. 116–29.

Lazarsfeld, P., Berelson, B. and Gaudet, H. (1944) *The People's Choice*. New York: Columbia University Press.

McQuail, Denis (1992) *Media Performance: Mass Communication and the Public Interest*. London: Sage.

McQuail, Denis and Siune, Karen (1986) *New Media Politics*. London: Sage.

Syvertsen, Trine (1992) *Public Television in Transition*. Trondheim: Norges allmennviten-skaplige forskningsråd.

4

Television Programming: More Diversity, More Convergence?

Els de Bens

The convergence hypothesis revisited

'More channels. More choice' is a euphoric feeling often expressed by the proponents of commercial television. Supporters of a strong public broadcasting system tend to make a more sombre prediction when they claim that 'more channels' will lead to 'more of the same'. McQuail (1992), who has repeatedly expressed his concern about the public role of the mass media and their task of offering quality and diversity, confirms that, on the one hand, the 'market model' can stimulate the growth of new channels. On the other, he is afraid that the market mechanism may boost convergence between the kind of programmes and the sort of schedules private and public broadcasters produce. Moreover, because of growing commercialization, the quality criterion is increasingly being threatened. As commercial stations try to satisfy as many tastes and needs as possible, quality and diversity are not exactly their prime targets.

The two must not be equated. Diversity is a precondition for quality (Schenk and Gralla, 1993: 10) and undoubtedly the most important of the criteria that can be used to judge it (Schatz and Schulz, 1992). According to McQuail (1992: 144), the mass media can contribute to diversity in three ways: 'By reflecting differences in society; by giving access to different points of view and by offering a wide range of choice.' In taking this 'wide range of choice', or the structural diversity of the supply as our starting point, the question is whether the launching of numerous new television channels in Europe over the past decade has increased or decreased structural diversity. The available research uses different methods of measurement. One of the earliest and most popular has been developed by Dominick and Pierce (1976). A much-used method is the well-known Herfindahl index (e.g. Litman, 1992). More recently a number of studies also apply the so-called Relative Entropy method (Hillve, 1995; Ishikawa, 1996; Kambara, 1992). Many stick to the traditional quantitative method (cf. De Bens and Tanghe, 1993; Hellman and Sauri, 1994; Krüger 1996). Most of these authors have been dealing with longitudinal research, so that shifts in programme categories were revealed over time.

There seems to be agreement among these researchers that by the extension of the number of channels broadcasting time is also extended, but this has not been a stimulus for more diversity. On the contrary, due to competition from new commercial stations we see a convergence of programmes between commercial and public channels, especially at prime time. Yet it can be observed that the range of programmes offered by public channels is more varied and that they carry more educational and arts programmes than their commercial counterparts. Drawing on our longitudinal study of Flemish television supply, we will analyse the development of the convergence process in a highly competitive situation. We will also raise the more normative question how to assess these developments in light of the public role of television. Can and should something be done about this? Some authors (e.g. Gates, 1995; Gilder, 1992; Negroponte, 1995) claim that in the near future the digital era will result in hundreds of new television channels which will focus on fragmented smaller audiences. According to these authors this so-called 'narrowcasting' will be to the benefit of diversity. How real is this 'digital dream'?

The Flanders example

Flanders offers an interesting case study, because of its special television situation. Belgium has had the highest cable-penetration in the world for the past 20 years (93 per cent of television households). Apart from the five Flemish and three Walloon channels, some 15 to 20 general interest foreign channels are supplied (Germany, UK, Italy, Spain and the Netherlands) together with about five thematic channels (Eurosport, MTV, ARTE, CNN and Canal Plus).

The substantial foreign channel supply obviously increased structural diversity, but it also boosted competition between the home channels and the foreign ones, at a moment when in most European countries the public television stations still had an absolute monopoly. It was not until the end of the 1980s that Belgian commercial channels entered the scene. Until then, Luxembourg's RTL was the only commercial channel supplied through the Belgian cable network. Because of competition by the substantial foreign channel supply, home channels moved their more serious programmes to earlier and later hours, outside prime time, and inserted more entertainment and especially fiction. However, these shifts were not very significant: the number of programmes on education and the arts remained practically unchanged in terms of total broadcasting hours, and Flemings and Walloons alike showed great loyalty to their home channels. Language and cultural barriers turned out to be decisive in the selection of foreign channels (De Bens, 1985, 1986, 1988; Geerts and Thoveron, 1979/ 1980).

In 1989 Flanders got its own commercial channel, VTM, which was immediately immensely popular; in 1995 the Scandinavian Broadcasting

System followed suit with another initiative, VT4, which prompted VTM to set up a second channel of its own, Ka2. The result of all this is that Flanders now boasts three commercial channels. In spite of the many channels available on the Flemish cable network, Flemish channels are watched even more than in the past (De Bens and Van Landuyt, 1996). As the public broadcasting corporation is solely financed by public funds, it came under increasing pressure because of shrinking viewing figures. It was felt that these dwindling figures might be used against the public broadcasting system and might eventually lead to cuts in public funding. Consequently this situation meant that the public broadcasting corporation was more than tempted to imitate the commercial channels' 'success story'.

A quantitative content analysis over a period of eight years (three months per year) shows first of all that channel competition has expanded the total number of broadcasting hours, especially in the morning, the afternoon and late at night (De Bens et al., 1997). By expanding the number of broadcasting hours, the commercial channels try to attract and hold viewers earlier and later in the day. Obviously this extension is meant to allow for more commercial breaks and thus extra profits. Likewise, the public broadcasting corporation is forced to expand its broadcasting hours but in the case of Flanders this does not yield any extra income from advertising and therefore in fact represents an additional financial burden for the public system.

Looking at the different programme categories we get a clearer picture whether competition has led to programmatic convergence.[1] The version of the category system we developed uses a rudimentary subdivision based on programmers' intentions. Apart from the three main categories – entertainment, information and education – we have also used two other important categories – arts and children's programmes – because these are perceived to be different programme genres by the viewer. Moreover the important category *arts* will allow us to optimize the degree of diversion between public and commercial broadcasting systems. The term 'arts' has been used to describe the 'culture' category, especially for the purposes of this research. We have deliberately avoided the term 'culture' because of its vagueness which can be confusing and ambiguous. With 'arts' we are referring to types of arts performance such as classical music, theatre and ballet, fine arts, literature, aesthetic photography, film, architecture, etc. This programme category, together with the category education (educational and scientific programmes, documentaries, service and consumer programmes), is often neglected due to the channel competition by commercial stations.

The public broadcasting corporation in Flanders has two channels: BRTN-TV1 and BRTN-TV2, of which BRTN-TV1 has by far the highest audience share (19.3 per cent in 1996). This implies that competition mainly takes place between BRTN-TV1 and VTM, the commercial station with the highest audience share (32.8 per cent in 1996). The increase of *entertainment* for BRTN-TV1 is dramatic: from 48.7 per cent in 1988 to 60.6 per cent in 1995. In prime time it amounts to 74.1 per cent in 1995. The entertainment share is of course very high as well for the commercial stations: 82.5 per cent for VTM in prime time (1995) and 86.7 per cent and 97 per cent for the two smaller commercial stations, VTM-Ka2 and VT4 respectively. The increase of entertainment on the public television station BRTN-TV1 shows that public and commercial stations are growing closer.

As far as the category of *information programmes* is concerned, we see again that BRTN-TV1 and VTM are getting very close: 13.1 per cent for BRTN-TV1 and 12 per cent for VTM in 1995. For the public broadcasting station the information share of the first channel has remained almost unchanged; in absolute value it has risen by only one minute when examining the entire research period. For the commercial channel VTM the news share is equal to that of the first public BRTN-TV1 channel. Yet it should be noted that VTM's news broadcasts do not increase proportionally to the overall increase in broadcasting time. News programmes are expensive and the commercial channel's management has announced it intends to invest more on 'infotainment' and reality shows (De Bens and Tanghe, 1993: 40). Research abroad has confirmed that information is the public channel's stronger point but that the commercial channels have been seriously catching up lately (Krüger, 1996: 424). Obviously, differences in news quality can only be demonstrated through more refined analysis. It is often claimed that commercial channels pay more attention to human interest topics, are more sensation-minded, present more 'parochial' news, but hardly any empirical quality research is available to support this hypothesis.

The *arts* programmes and *education* are an important parameter for the convergence hypothesis. As far as the commercial channels are concerned, the figures confirm our expectations: no arts programming! The BRTN-TV1 arts programmes have decreased from 4.9 per cent in 1988 to 2.1 per cent in 1995, and during prime time the arts programmes have been reduced to zero. The same goes for educational programmes: for BRTN-TV1 from 17.7 per cent in 1988 (12 per cent in prime time) to 14.5 per cent in 1995 (7 per cent in prime time). On VTM the supply of educational programmes is of course limited, with only 2 per cent in 1995 (0 per cent in prime time). For the first public channel BRTN-TV1, one cannot deny that competition has caused convergence instead of diversity.

But the public broadcasting corporation also has a second channel, BRTN-TV2 (audience share in 1996: 5.7 per cent), and the question is whether this second channel has been used as a tool for safeguarding diversity. The programme makers have at any rate tried to give this second channel BRTN-TV2 a complementary profile, but as they have constantly changed the programme strategy, they did not succeed. In 1996 the management announced that all present arts programmes would be deleted and replaced by programmes with a 'lighter' approach. Most of the newspapers reacted using expressive headlines such as 'culture slaughtered on the second channel'. The channel's complementary character is at stake and diversity may in the future be even more threatened. The corporation is constantly turning its policies upside down, which makes it look more like a panic reaction than a well-thought-out strategy. The only successful counterattack that BRTN-TV2 made was the introduction in 1994 of a successful new news magazine.

We can conclude that public and commercial stations are growing closer. Diversity is clearly in a defensive position and convergence is on the offensive. This trend seems to be more manifest in Flanders than in other foreign countries. The public broadcasting system in Flanders does still show more structural diversity than the commercial one, but there is a clear reductionist trend.

More European television fiction, more cultural diversity?

Many authors (cf. Biltereyst, 1995; De Bens et al., 1992; Dorfmann and Mattelart, 1975; Pragnell, 1985; Schiller, 1976; Sepstrup, 1990; Silj, 1988; Varis, 1985) have shown that the main share of fiction programmes is of American origin and that the omnipresence of American fiction on European channels stimulates convergence and undermines the cultural diversity of the European programming industry. All these studies also pointed out extensively that viewers invariably prefer home-made fiction which also yields the highest ratings. One of the consequences is that all European channels have made major financial efforts in recent years to produce more home-made fiction. Because of the extension of broadcasting time, however, they are forced to rely on foreign imports to fill the many programming hours. The scenario is the same everywhere: American productions are cheaper than the European ones and on top of that they ensure high ratings.

Yet the European Commission has set up a quota system in which 'a majority proportion of broadcasting needs to go to European works' (Art. 4 of dir. 89/552/EEC). The problem with this new guideline is that all programmes may be counted (except news, sports, games and advertising) which does not allow for the origin of fiction to be assessed separately. The results are therefore misleading and according to the latest report of the Commission (European Commission, 1996) practically all channels comply with the norms set by Art. 4. If, however, one was to calculate the fiction category separately one might come to a totally different conclusion and indeed admit that the imports of American fiction are still immense.

Ultimately this guideline was meant to stimulate the audiovisual programming industry and more specifically television fiction. By merely adding up all programmes this measure has proved counterproductive: even before the guideline came into force, most channels had already complied with the norms of Art. 4. In 1991 the home and foreign share of the total programming supply of 53 European channels had a majority of home-programming. Home-made fiction scored lowest in terms of share and

American imports turned out to be the highest, considerably higher than all imports from all other European countries (De Bens et al., 1992).

Within the entertainment category, fiction is the dominant category: during prime time, almost half of the broadcasting time goes to fiction, both on the public broadcasting channels and on the commercial channels. The launching of VTM-Ka2 and VT4 has boosted fiction: almost 80 per cent of the entire programme supply consists of fiction. These hours are filled in mainly by American fiction. Flanders is not alone here; a recent study revealed that all over Europe the amount of American television fiction import has increased (De Bens and De Smaele, 1997).

In spite of the fact that public and commercial stations have made substantial efforts to produce more home-made fiction, round-the-clock television will have to rely on cheap and successful (measured by audience ratings) American television drama imports. The overwhelming presence of American fiction and feature films on both public and commercial stations stimulates convergence in the long run. It would be very useful if the EC would impose quotas for European television series and films. Such a strategy would enhance more diversity on the European television channels.

More diversity with digital television?

From what we have seen so far it turns out that the market model is evolving towards convergence. However, a number of authors feel that soon, in the digital communication era, hundreds of television channels will invade the living room which will induce the viewer to become more selective and to choose à la carte. To put it differently: broadcasting will be replaced by narrowcasting and even 'bitcasting' (Gilder, 1992). Bitcasting means that the viewer will only select bits, that is, certain programmes, so viewers will in fact compose their own programmes and make a kind of do-it-yourself package. Programme schemes will disappear and the viewer will choose from a menu with unlimited programme choice. One of the most important features of such a fragmented television market would obviously be its diversity. Is this optimistic scenario a realistic one? Will television viewers become so active overnight? Will they be able to compose their own à la carte programme every night?

The viewer will have to choose from an electronic menu, but these menus are not always very user-friendly or convenient. Perhaps only a small minority of white-collar viewers will develop the need for more quality and will be able to choose adequately (Schulz, 1992: 34). We should also not forget that for most viewers it is the programme schedules which are the decisive element. These schedules are also important for the television channel to develop a specific channel strategy, namely stimulating viewer loyalty, inserting new programmes between two popular familiar programmes, etc. Commercial stations know all too well that programme schedules are one of the main reasons for success. They not only give an identity to a channel, they also stimulate fixed viewer habits as they create a kind of bond between viewer and channel (Dagnaud, 1991). Programmers have become very important people and in the United States they are being head-hunted by competing channels. Both vertical and horizontal programming have proved the importance of binding the viewers. In Flanders commercial channels have especially used horizontal programming strategies to stimulate viewer fidelity.

Moreover, advertisers have also turned out to be more in favour of traditional programme schedules. They have their doubts about narrowcasting. According to advertisers and marketeers, the consumer market will never be as fragmented as some authors would have us believe. The erosion of the advertising market in the digital era would represent a mortgage on the survival chances of many channels: 'a 500 channel world is one in which 490 services will fight each other over even smaller audience fragments' (Jankowski and Fuchs, 1995: 161). Indeed, many authors have their doubts whether an extension of the channel range will drastically alter viewers' habits. The Flemish case is interesting because even after more than 25 years of major cable penetration with some 30 television channels available, the Flemish viewer has remained extremely loyal to his/her own Flemish channels. Achille and Miège (1994: 43) also use the Belgian situation to illustrate that market penetration does have its limits, simply because the market quickly reaches a saturation point in terms of segmentation.

Finally, we must not forget that in the digital communication era, while technology does provide the means to offer hundreds of television channels, in essence nothing has changed in terms of the production process: the time and costs involved in making a quality programme remain unchanged; the creativity needed is the same whether used for a digital or an analogue production. Consequently many authors fear that hundreds of new television channels would end up presenting countless reruns and repeats of old programmes. As far as television is concerned, the digital era might simply lead to even more convergence.

Conclusion

It seems that the commercialization of the broadcasting landscape has become a spiral movement and that the convergence trend is irreversible. At the same time it is clear that European broadcasting policy has had no results: the import of American television fiction continues to increase and stimulates cultural globalization. In the digital communication era little or nothing changes for the average viewer; only a small number of white-collar viewer groups will probably be able to choose their own programmes à la carte and they will obviously have to pay for that privilege. While only the structural diversity was studied, further qualitative research would reveal an increasing trend of converging pulp. To ensure viewer loyalty, the channels disregard their own rules of decorum: blind dates, television confessions, reality shows, etc. speculate more and more often on the viewers' sense of voyeurism. These kind of programmes originated in the United States and are imitated by all channels.

The obsession for ratings is one of the main reasons for this increasing reduction in quality. For the commercial channels it is an inevitable evolution: high ratings mean more income through advertisements. For the public broadcasting system this is not the case: the majority of the funds still originate from public licence fees. All viewers pay and have certain expectations, wishes and interests. Therefore the mainstream strategy of the commercial channels should not be applied indiscriminately to the public ones. A public channel has to take into account its variety of viewers and has to be a social platform at the same time. All programme categories have to have their place on the public channel. Commercial channels cannot be obliged to broadcast educational and arts programmes. However, it is the task of the public channel to schedule them. Diversity ought to be the motto of the public channels. Imitating the programme strategies of the commercial channels is a risky policy, because convergence eventually takes away the public channel's reason for existence.

Nobody can deny that television is in the first place an entertainment medium, which also holds true for the public channel. However, the public channel can transcend the pulp of the commercial channels by being more creative. Creativity and amusement will keep the viewers interested in the long run. Information and public affairs programmes especially are incredibly important for the public channels because, as research has shown, such programmes lead to an increased score for the public channels in terms of their image of credibility and quality.

The problems are clearly with the educational and arts programmes, because ratings are especially low here. But they are relative too: they only indicate the number of viewers, but give no information about appreciation and evaluation by the viewers concerned. Furthermore, educational and arts programme categories obviously attract fewer viewers. The ratings of an arts programme have to be interpreted differently than those of an entertainment programme. Why is it that the Flemish public channel decides that a number of 100,000 viewers is too small whereas an independent newspaper like the Flemish *De Morgen* only sells 35,000 copies? When *De Morgen* experienced financial difficulties a few years ago, an animated public debate ensued, which was linked to various initiatives to save the newspaper. Numbers are therefore relative and merely measure quantity.

A public channel which bans most of its educational and all of its arts programmes from prime time, creates a void. McQuail (1992: 284) has stressed the potentially important role of television in making arts programmes accessible to a wider audience: 'The popular media may be the only effective means of bringing some of the arts (e.g. opera, ballet, classical music and drama, art photography and film) to the wider public. They can also serve generally as a gate for awareness of all the arts.' It sounds like a mission statement for the public channels.

The educational and arts programmes should obviously consider the specific characteristics of television, that is, it is artificial, fleeting and essentially an entertainment medium. Arts programmes have to be produced as closely as possible to the public: understandable, accessible and attractive. This is often forgotten and one ends up with bombastic rhetoric and intellectualist jargon. The 'package' is important because the viewers have to get interested. That is why the programme makers have a huge responsibility; instead of alienating the average viewer they should capture his or her interest. In other words, television is the most suited medium to bring arts to a wide public. Postmodernists and cultural studies proponents are often wrongly inclined to speak of paternalism in this respect. This is unwarranted, however. It is extremely arrogant and snobbish to ban all educational and arts programmes from the public channel by making use of arguments such as 'everybody chooses for himself', 'let only wealthy people pay for culture', 'the average public does not need culture', etc. (cf. De Meyer, 1991).

We therefore strongly oppose a separate second public channel exclusively devoted to serious, educational and arts programmes. This would create an elitist, cultural ghetto channel, in which the public broadcasting system would forgo its social function. In order to decrease the pressure of ratings and the market model on the public channels, we believe that financing public channels exclusively by public funds is a sensible solution. The BBC model, free of advertising, remains the target goal. Pursuing funds through advertisements, and in competition with commercial channels, leads to a battle for the viewer and stimulates convergence. Should public funds be insufficient, then the government has to provide extra support. The viewer cannot be expected to be prepared to pay more. For certain programmes, such as sports, the viewer will have to pay in the future anyway. It is up to the government to show its social responsibility by giving the public broadcasting system sufficient financial means in order to fulfil its task correctly.

In many Western European countries the government spends millions of (British) pounds annually in indirect support for newspapers (no or low VAT, reduced mail and telephone fees, interest-free loans, etc.) and in some countries there is even direct financial support (especially in the Scandinavian countries and the Netherlands). Newspapers have, next to their economic role, a social role. They are more than a mere commodity, and this is even more true for the public broadcasting corporations: the viewers are not only consumers, they are citizens too. The public channels will in future have to be unlinked from the mercantile market model in order to become independent, broad, social forums, complementary and different from the commercial channels; instead of convergence more diversity.

Note

1. The research was carried out over a period of eight years: from 1988, one year before the launching of the first commercial television station, until 1996. For each year, three months were examined: February, August and November. After analysing a number of category systems we have opted for our own. We intended to develop a handy tool which would allow us to place each programme unequivocally in one category and which would be geared to the differences between programmes that viewers tend to make themselves. We feel it is senseless to look for differences which are not observed by the viewers. This is one of the reasons why we did not use the EBU-escort system. Another reason was that it is a code system tailored to the programming of the public broadcasting systems.

References

Achille, Y. and Miège, B. (1994) 'The limits to the adaptation strategies of European public service television', *Media, Culture & Society* 16: 31–46.

Bens, E. de (1985) 'L'Influence de la cablodiffusion sur le comportement télévisuel des Belges et sur les stratégies de programmation', *Actes des 7es Journées Internationales de l'IDATE*: 318–29.

Bens, E. de (1986) 'Cable penetration and competition among Belgian and foreign stations', *European Journal of Communication*: 478–92.

Bens, E. de (1988) 'Der Einfluz eines grossen ausländischen Programmangebotes und die Sehgewohnheiten. Belgische Erfahrungen mit einen dichten Verkabelung', *Publizistik* 33: 352–65.

Bens, E. de and van Landuyt, D. (1996) *Video on Demand. A User Oriented Study. National Survey*, study commission by Belgacom, Brussels.

Bens, E. de and de Smaele, H. (1997), *Dallasification Revisited*, Research Report, Department of Communication, University of Ghent.

Bens, E. de and Tanghe, K. (1993) 'Televisie in Vlaanderen: de invloed van de commercialisering op het programma-aanbod. Een longitudinale structurele programma-analyse voor VTM en BRTN 1989-1992', *Communicatie* 23 (3): 28–48.

Bens, E. de, Janssens, H. and van Landuyt, D. (1997) *Longitudinal Programme Analysis (1988-1996) of the Public and Commercial Television Stations in Flanders*, Research Report, Department of Communication, University of Ghent.

Bens, E. de, Kelly, M. and Bakke, M. (1992) 'Television content: Dallasfiction of culture?', in K. Siune and W. Truetzschler (eds) *Dynamics of Media Politics*. Euromedia Research Group, London: Sage, pp. 75–100.

Biltereyst, D. (1995) *Hollywood in het Avondland: over de afhankelijkheid en de impact van Amerikaanse televisie in Europa*. Brussels: VUB-Press.

Dagnaud, M. (1991) 'L'Art de construire la grille de programmes', in Jean-Marie Charon (ed.) *L'Etat des Médias*. pp. 57–9.

Dominick, J.R. and Pierce, M.C. (1976) 'Trends in networking prime time programming 1953-1974', *Journal of Communication* 26: 70–80.

Dorfmann, A. and Mattelart, A. (1975) *How to Read Donald Duck: Imperialist Ideology in the Disney Comic*. New York: International General.

European Commission (1996) *Communication from the European Commission to the Council and the European Parliament on the Application of Articles 4 and 5 of Directive 89 552/EEEC, Television without Frontiers*, Brussels, 15/07/1996.

Gales, B. (1995) *The Road Ahead*. London: Viking.

Geerts, C. and Thoveron, G. (1979/1980) *Television offerte au public, television regardée par le public: une enquete internationale*. Bruxelles: RTBF.

Gilder, G. (1992) *Life after Television*. New York: W.W. Norton & Co.

Hellman, H. and Sauri, T. (1994) 'Public service television and the tendency towards convergence: trends in prime time programme structure in Finland 1970–1992', *Media, Culture & Society* 16 (1): 47–71.

Hillve, P. (1995) 'After research, measurement or perhaps vice-versa?', *Nordicom Review* 1: 23–36.

Ishikawa, S. (ed.) (1996) *Quality Assessment of Television*. Luton: University of Luton Press.

Jankowski, J. and Fuchs, D. (1995) *Television Today and Tomorrow*. New York: Oxford University Press.

Kambara, N. (1992) 'Study of diversity indices used for programming analysis', *Studies of Broadcasting* 28: 195–206.

Krüger, U.M. (1996) 'Programm-analyse: Tendenzen in den Programmen der grossen Fernsehsender 1985–1995', *Media Perspektiven* 98: 417–40.

Litman, B.R. (1992) 'Economic aspects of program quality: the case of diversity', *Studies of Broadcasting* 28: 121–56.

McQuail, D. (1992) *Media Performance: Mass Communication and the Public Interest*. London: Sage.

Meyer, G. de (1991) 'VTM in het cultuurdebat', *Communicatie* 20 (1): 38–52.

Negroponte, N. (1995) *Being Digital*. London: Hodder & Stoughton.

Pragnell, O. (1985) *Television in Europe*. Media Monograph No. 5. Manchester: European Institute for the Media.

Schatz, H. and Schulz, W. (1992) 'Qualität von Fernsehprogrammen. Kriterium und Methoden zur Beurteilung von Programmqualität im dualen System', *Media Perspektiven* 11: 690–712.

Schenk, M. and Gralla, S. (1993) 'Qualitätsfernsehen aus der Sicht des Publikums', *Media Perspektiven* 1: 8–15.

Schiller, H. (1976) *Communication and Cultural Domination*. White Plains, NY: International Arts and Science Press.

Schulz, W. (1992) 'European media systems in transition, general trends and modifying conditions', *Gazette* 44 (1): 23–40.

Sepstrup, P. (1990) *Transnationalised Television in Western Europe*. London: Libbey.

Silj, A. (1988) *East of Dallas. The European Challenge to American TV*. London: BFI Publishing.

Varis, T. (1985) *International Flow of Television Programmes*. Paris: UNESCO.

5

Diversity Revisited: Towards a Critical Rational Model of Media Diversity

Jan van Cuilenburg

Diversity, public opinion and democracy

'Truth is not manifest.' This famous dictum by Karl Popper expresses in essence the rationale for information and opinion diversity in democratic societies. It is only because of the epistemological impossibility of establishing truth without ambivalence and unquestionably, that diversity of information and opinion makes sense. This applies to all forms of knowledge, notably of course knowledge of social and political affairs. In societies claiming to know ultimate truth diversity of opinion is not appreciated. So former communist regimes preferred media like *Pravda*. However that may be, Popper in his *Public Opinion and Liberal Principles* recommends the search for political truth in democracy by way of imagination, trial and error and critical discussion. Here diversity and variety come in, for the quality of the civic debate 'depends largely upon the variety of competing views. Had there been no Tower of Babel, we should invent it' (Popper, 1968/1963: 352).

Of course, the idea of diversity as a crucial value is not new. More than 2000 years ago diversity as a means to truth-finding was the background of the Socratic dialectic of thesis, antithesis and synthesis. In history Socrates' line of reasoning was reiterated innumerably by philosophers, writers, journalists and often even by politicians. One highlight was, of course, John Milton's 1644 plea for freedom of the press and for diversity: 'Let (truth) and falsehood grapple . . . in a free and open encounter' (Milton, 1644). In the nineteenth century John Stuart Mill once again underlined the value of opinion diversity; in his famous *On Liberty* Mill argues that truth in the great practical concerns of life is a 'question of reconciling and combining of opposites'. Diversity is advantageous because even for a true opinion 'a conflict with the opposite error is essential to a clear apprehension and deep feeling of its truth' (Mill, 1972 (1859): 107 and 105 respectively).

Diversity, freedom of expression and democracy are, of course, closely connected. Democracy guarantees freedom of expression as a fundamental human right for all, which freedom fosters diversity of information and opinion. In promoting diversity of opinions, democracy foremost is a way of truth-finding in society. The relationship between these three concepts has been established in numerous normative theories, and even in court decisions – for example, in the Associated Press Principle (1943). In deciding against AP, the court stated that the First Amendment's underlying premise is to foster 'the widest possible dissemination of information from diverse and antagonistic sources'. According to the judge's opinion: 'this principle presupposes that right conclusions are more likely to be gathered out of a multitude of tongues, than any kind of authoritative selection. To many, this is and always will be, folly, but we have staked our all on it' (quoted in Dizard, 1994: 74, 75).

Next to the democratic framework for diversity, there is a clear and distinct relationship between diversity and tolerance. In our multicultural and multi-ethnic societies tolerance is of utmost importance. Diverse information on different cultures and different patterns of values, norms and ideas may contribute to mutual respect and acceptance. However, diversity and tolerance do not have an accord solely on their own. Diversity of information can only contribute to tolerance if people have a receptive mind and are willing to accept the fallibility of their own opinions and ideas. During the Vietnam War the Buddhist monk, peace activist and poet Thich Nhat Hanh formulated the Fourteen Precepts for a new Buddhist order, the Order of Interbeing. Two of those precepts precisely express what open-mindedness implies. They are worth quoting here: 'Do not be idolatrous about or bound to any doctrine, theory or ideology; even Buddhist ones. Buddhist systems of thought are guiding means; they are not absolute truth.' And 'Do not force others, including children, by any means whatsoever, to adopt your views; whether by authority, threat, money, propaganda, or even education. However, through compassionate dialogue, help others renounce fanaticism and narrowness' (Thich Nhat Hanh, 1993/1987: 17).

Many theorists suggest that diversity best flourishes in a free market place of ideas: if people can freely enter this market place to exchange information and opinions, then we may expect cultural variety and diversity to happen. Of course, this notion is based upon classical economic market theory: if there is full competition in the market place, then the market mechanism will most efficiently produce the best quality of products against the lowest price possible. The assumptions of the full competition market model are being described in every introductory economic textbook: the number of sellers should be very large, so that no one seller is able to dominate the market. Also the number of buyers should be large and buyers and sellers should be fully informed about the market structure and about supply and demand. Then and only then, the market will *ceteris paribus* produce highest benefits at lowest costs and lowest prices.

In transplanting this market model into the free market place of ideas, we have to operate on the basis of comparable assumptions. Diversity will only result from a market place of ideas if the number of different providers of information is great and competition between them is full and fair, so that power domination does not exist. We also have to assume that 'buyers' of information are fully and rationally informed about the market place. Then, and only then, will there be a balance of power between providers and users of information. And then, and only then, maximally diverse information will be supplied, exchanged and used by all people in the market of ideas.

We all know that the classical market model often is too simplistic a description of economic reality. Frequently situations of oligopoly and monopoly occur. This usually leads to some kind of government inter-vention and regulation of market entrance, competition and market conduct. According to Coase the free market place of ideas is no exception to this rule. He puts it even more strongly:

> (The) distinction between the market for goods and the market for ideas is (not) valid. There is no fundamental distinction between these two markets and, in deciding on public policy with regard to them, we need to take into account the same considerations. In all markets, producers have some reasons for being honest and some for being dishonest; consumers have some information but are not fully informed or even able to digest the information they have; regulators commonly wish to do a good job, and though often incompetent and subject to the influence of special interests, they act like this because, like all of us, they are human beings whose strongest motives are not the highest. (Coase, 1974: 389)

Many social scientists do not like economic models being applied to social, political and communication phenomena. In communication science there is a lot of criticism of the notion of a free market place of ideas: it is not a market place and if it is, it is certainly not free, runs the counter-argument. Social scientists prefer terms like *agora*, forum, public sphere, *Oeffentlichkeit* or *openbaarheid* instead of 'market place of ideas'. Accord-ing to Coase, however, we should take the free market place analogy seriously and use the same approach for all markets when deciding on public policy. Coase even goes as far as to posit: 'it is apparent that the case for government intervention in the market for ideas is much stronger than it is, in general, in the market for goods'. I tend to agree: in demo-cratic societies, opinion dominance, lack of political and cultural competi-tion and other forms of 'market failure' inevitably asks for governmental policy to enhance entrance of new, and rivalry among existing, ideas and opinions.

Diversity as a media policy goal

The notion that government has to play an active role vis-à-vis com-munications and media in society has always been very strong in the Netherlands. In this context the Dutch government asked Denis McQuail and me in the early 1980s to conduct a study into the diversity of the Dutch media system, notably television and the press (McQuail and Van Cuilenburg, 1982; McQuail and Van Cuilenburg, 1983; Van Cuilenburg and McQuail, 1982). In addition to freedom of the press and freedom of broadcasting, media diversity is the main goal of media policy in the Netherlands. The Dutch cabinet at that time needed a new conceptual framework to assess and evaluate the state of the art of the media and to design and implement new communications policies aiming at diversity, or 'pluriformity'[1] as it is called in the Netherlands. The concept of 'media diversity' originates from the 1960s and 1970s. In Western Europe it is strongly related to 'culture policy' (*Kulturpolitik, cultuurpolitiek*), as that policy was then labelled. In the Netherlands the concept got its prominent position in media policy when a wave of press concentration happened in the late 1960s: parliament and cabinet at that time were afraid that press concentration would end up in information and opinion monopolies. This fear of concentration in 1974 resulted in founding the Netherlands Press Fund (*Bedrijfsfonds voor de Pers*), an independent governmental agency for subventions and low-rate loans to financially endangered newspapers and magazines.

In the study for the Dutch government McQuail and I defined 'media diversity' as a concept referring to media content, that is, the heterogeneity of media content in terms of one or more specified characteristics. This definition is not without policy implication, because it focuses on media content rather than on media market structure and media organizational conduct. This definition avoids a too easy equalization of the number of media outlets to media performance: highly competitive media markets may still result in excessive sameness of media contents, whereas one should at least theoretically not exclude the possibility of media oligopolies or even monopolies to produce a highly diverse supply of media content. It is precisely for fine-tuning media policy that a distinction between structure and performance should be made.

Often media practitioners and politicians think that more media diversity is 'better'. This, however, is not the case: media diversity always has to be externally gauged in some way. Gauging should be based on the existing social diversity on which media are reporting. Put another way, media diversity should always be compared with variations in society and social reality.[2] Two different normative frameworks present themselves. Do the media relate to society in such a way as to reflect, pro rata, the distribution of opinion, allegiance or other characteristic as it appears in the population? Or is the content distribution within the media such that perfectly equal attention is given to all identifiable streams, or groups, or positions in society? If the first, the media adhere to *reflection* as the norm for media diversity: media content reflects differences in politics, religion, culture and social conditions in society in a more or less proportional way. If the second, then media performance satisfies the norm of *openness*, that is, in arithmetically absolute terms, perfectly equal access to media for people and ideas in society. Both these normative frameworks may be applied at different levels of media performance. So performance in terms of informing the audience, as well as opinion-forming activities and entertainment by media, may be assessed and evaluated in terms of reflection and openness.

There is a dialectic relationship between diversity as reflection and diversity as openness, as perfectly equal access. Only if population characteristics and conditions are fully horizontally, that is, equally and uniformly distributed over society, reflection coincides with openness. This is, however, seldom the case. More often than not, population characteristics tend toward the middle, toward normal distributions, toward mainstreams, so to say. This inevitably leads to media reflecting society performing poorly with regard to openness to a great variety of different social positions and conditions, whereas perfectly equal media access harms majority positions in favour of minority beliefs, attitudes and conditions. There is no easy way out from this dilemma: reflection and openness can hardly ever both be fully realized at the same time. So, some media policy choice has to be made. In choosing, however, one has to be aware that both normative frameworks have their own advantage and disadvantage. The weakness of reflection as a sole criterion lies in its conservatism, since reflective media focus attention preferably on mainstreams and on the conventional, thus making them more mainstream and more conventional. Media openness certainly corrects this bias. Social change usually begins with minority views and movements. If minorities, in arithmetic terms, have the same access to the social communication channels as majorities, then social discussion and dynamics may be expected to get a positive impulse. That is why media policy often tries to balance both perspectives at the same time, targeting at a position halfway between reflective and access-diversity. However, as I will try to demonstrate, reflective or representative diversity is bound to lose its prominence as a media policy goal in favour of access as a more general objective of communications policy.

Diversity since the 1980s: the abundance paradoxes of diversity

As said before, diversity as a media policy goal became prominent in the 1970s and 1980s when, notably in Western Europe, media policy as cultural policy and public service broadcasting were at their peak. Since then the media landscape has drastically changed. Four trends fundamentally changed the context of media diversity. First, over decades there has been an explosive *informatization* of society. Information supply has been growing geometrically like compound interest in a bank account. Measuring information supply is not easy (Dordick and Wang, 1993: 31–85). However, several older studies, conducted before the mid 1980s, using different kinds of indicators, showed that since the Second World War the supply of information has grown by 10 per cent per annum (Anderla, 1973; Machlup, 1962; Pool et al., 1984). A recent study of Japan confirms the overall picture. Statistics from that country show that between 1985 and 1990 the volume of information supplied grew by 36 per cent (Van der Staal, 1994: 32–50). With the Internet at that time still to be launched, it is hardly imaginable that growth rates have dropped since then; on the contrary. One should not underestimate figures like these. It implies that information supply at present is at least 117 (approximately) times more than immediately after the War.

Second, there is *convergence*. Convergence has been on the agenda ever since the former US Office of Technology Assessment (OTA) published its pioneering study *Critical Connections* (Office of Technology Assessment, 1990). Convergence technologically means that boundaries between information technologies and communication networks are blurring. Computer and telecommunications are converging to telematics, PCs and television sets get more and more similar, and formerly separated networks become increasingly interconnected to render the same kind of services. Multimedia, integrating text, audio and video, is also an example of digital convergence. Economically convergence points to the merging of economic branches, that is computing, communications and content (publishing). The impact of convergence for senders and recipients is that formerly separated communications logics of encoding and decoding of messages will increasingly be mixed together. A multimedia world requires equal facility in word, image and sound. Some say that present-day society needs a kind of overall digital literacy, which includes print literacy. Multimedia creates a digital flexibility that is radical. According to Richard Lanham (1995: 160), multimedia 'recaptures the expressivity of oral cultures, which printed books, and handwritten manuscripts before them, excluded.' However that may be, it is clear that future generations may make obsolete different communication languages which are unlinked, linked or hyperlinked. The impact of multimedia can still not be fully estimated, but multimedia will certainly change how people gather, digest and use information.

The third trend influencing media diversity is *diversification* in content, carriers and channels. A large part of information growth in society stems from diversification in media content for specific target groups. Tailoring information has become a dominant trend with target groups getting smaller and smaller. In addition to content diversification, there is diversification in information-carrying technologies and diversification in channels and outlets. What we see is a kind of exponential diversification according to the 'formula': Diversification = Contents × Carriers × Channels. Diversification, of course, increases freedom of choice for consumers. However, there is also a downside to diversification, that is, the availability of more different communications technologies and more communication channels decreases informational communality and exchange in society. This makes up the fourth main trend in communications nowadays: an increasing *segmentation and fragmentation* of audiences.

Superficially, one might think informatization and convergence would promote diversity of media content, production and exchange. The production and supply of ever more information yields more chances and opportunities for innovative social, cultural and political information. In addition, technological and economic convergence of media channels bring along the possibility of immediately supplementing media diversity based on one particular media platform (e.g. the press) with diversity from another platform (e.g. the Internet). Yet not all forms of media diversity benefit alike from informatization and convergence. Though diversity in the information society has reached unprecedented levels, we are being confronted with three abundance paradoxes endangering media in democracy.

The first paradox is the *diversity paradox*: 'more diversity is less diversity'. This paradox was implicitly referred to before; it stems from the dialectics between diversity as reflection and diversity as perfectly equal access. With informatization of society, media diversity indeed has reached an unimaginable maximum: it is very difficult to specify types of contents which are nowhere available in media markets. However, media markets are far better in producing reflection of majority civic interests and consumer preferences than equal openness to political and cultural innovations stemming from minorities. So, more reflective diversity usually goes with less diversity in terms of equal access. This paradox is often referred to as 'more of the same'. It finds its basis in a general tendency of media towards a middle-of-the-road policy mainly serving mainstream audience preferences.[3] Ratings and research into audiences and readership usually reinforce this tendency and make Hotelling's Law from 1929 still a valid assertion today for predicting lots of media supplies (Hotteling, 1929).[4]

The second paradox may be labelled as the *information paradox*: 'more information is less information'. The continuing explosive informatization of society brings along waste and overload of information. Maybe John Naisbitt was right after all in his *Megatrends*: 'We are drowning in information but starved for knowledge' (Naisbitt, 1984 (1982): 17). Nobel laureate economist Herbert Simon puts it like this:

> What information consumes is rather obvious: it consumes the attention of its recipients. Hence a wealth of information creates a poverty of attention, and a need to allocate that attention efficiently among the overabundance of information sources that might consume it. (quoted by Varian, 1995: 161)

So the real media policy issue today presumably is not lack of information, but decline in information accessibility for audiences, particularly accessibility toward new and innovative ideas and opinions of small cultural minority groups.

The third paradox is closely connected to the second. Communications technology is abundant in society. In the global village the communications paradigm is the AAA-paradigm of big telecom operators: anything, anytime, anywhere (Negroponte, 1995: 174). Modern communications technology provides for those who can afford it complete time and space independence in communication and information: people may fully autonomously define their own social communications space anytime anywhere. Ultimately, however, the AAA-paradigm may result in a *communication paradox*: 'more communication is less communication', that is, the availability of more different communications technologies and channels decreases informational communality and exchange in society. Democracy is only sustainable with an ongoing exchange of information, viewpoints and opinions; communication is crucial to public debate and dialogue in society. The diversification of communication channels and technologies may have fragmenting effects on society, leading towards a diminishing common and socially shared platform for public debate and discussion. Ultimately this paradox makes diversity in information and opinion completely fictitious, a nearly mythical concept with no practical meaning, because exchange of information and opinion for public discourse in society is only performed at a very low level of collective, common and shared participation.

The impossibility of media diversity assessment

The paradoxes of abundance make it necessary to recalibrate media diversity as a media policy goal: particularly reflective diversity as a policy objective is becoming increasingly obsolete. However, there is more to be added. Governments striving for diversity in media performance, in theory, should have some kind of measuring rod to assess media diversity. In the above-mentioned study for the Dutch government, Denis McQuail and I developed a methodology to measure media diversity performance by way of content analysis (McQuail and Van Cuilenburg, 1983). Diversity performance analysis, of course, is quality assessment. Developing plausible and acceptable media quality indices is not an easy and unproblematic task, particularly for governments. Maybe the most difficult step to be taken is the theoretical notion of media quality itself.

With diversity being a characteristic of media content we are dealing with media performance quality. There is no need for extensive argument that media quality can take on very different faces. Rosengren et al. (1991) has already sketched four different faces of media quality. First, descriptive quality indicating whether media give a more or less representative image of reality. The second concept, sender use quality, relates to objectives of publishers and editors: good media are media serving their intentions. Opposite this concept we have a third quality indicator, receiver use quality, focusing on the receiver's wishes, preferences, uses and gratifications. Fourth and finally there is professional quality which may be measured in terms of professional standards adhered to by colleagues. These four concepts make media quality an extraordinary relative and consequently highly subjective concept. Let me be a little bit provocative: if media performance quality can only be assessed subjectively then it resembles the economic value of goods and services which cannot be rationally and unequivocally determined in advance. As a Dutch saying goes: 'Market price is the madman's price.' We all know that economists are quite good at studying what the madman is willing to pay, but not in determining his motives why. Perhaps media performance analysis runs into the same fate economists run into in understanding prices and values in the market place.

The subjective nature of media performance does not mean that media quality per se cannot be measured. In the Netherlands, for instance, Scholten (1982) conducted an extensive content analysis of daily newspapers assessing all kinds of performance standards like fullness and objectivity in political news. Also, media diversity may be satisfactorily operationalized and quantitatively measured, as McQuail and I demonstrated in the 1980s (McQuail and Van Cuilenburg, 1983). If one nominalistically starts from a clear-cut definition of media diversity and if one operationally specifies very concrete and detailed content analysis indicators of media content diversity, then there is no problem, except perhaps that content analysis always takes a lot of effort.

Although measuring media diversity for policy purposes is possible in principle, the question arises whether policy makers should do it. The answer is 'no!'. That is why, in retrospect, I consider the 1983 attempt by McQuail and me to measure content diversity for policy purposes as a sin of youth. There are several reasons for the 'no' option to diversity measurement. The first reason is rather pragmatic: every operationalization of 'media diversity' ultimately remains scientifically questionable. No basic agreement among scientists is to be expected if it comes to concrete definitions and measurement of media diversity.[5] We may add that performance analysis by way of content analysis is very labour intensive and consequently costly. The cost–benefit ratio in general is therefore unfavourable. There is, however, a far more principal counterargument against performance measurement for media policy purposes. Media diversity belongs to the realm of freedom of speech and the press. In civil societies democratic governments should avoid any appearance whatsoever of interference with First Amendment rights. Extensive governmental content analysis of media performance for policy purposes is not in harmony with this premise. So, however important media content diversity is from a theoretical perspective for media policy, it is of little practical value. Consequently, I want to plead governmental media policy to move from media diversity toward the more formal, not-content-related concept of media access.

Media policy: from diversity to access

Both the abundance paradoxes and the impossibility of a satisfactory media diversity assessment call for a new paradigm for diversity. I want here to suggest a media quality model based on Karl Popper's theory of open competition of ideas already introduced before. Let me rephrase Popper's dictum about truth: 'media quality is not manifest; the search for quality demands at least imagination, trial and error and critical discussion'. Both a contextual and a procedural model of media diversity and media quality best serves this search. Contextual media quality stresses favourable social, political, cultural and economic conditions for media to operate and perform. Such a context presupposes free, unhindered, easy and, above all, equal access of people and ideas to the social communication arenas. That is, arenas sufficing the classic-libertarian principle of the free competition of ideas. Phrased in present-day language, contextual media quality requires independent journalism, full and active competition between broadcasting organizations and publishing houses and the breakdown of dominant positions in media markets. If market failure happens, media policy in these markets should actively strive for favourable economic and cultural conditions for competitive press and broadcasting. Communication scientists could help here by developing media barometers indicating how favourable the economic and cultural climate is for open, non-dogmatic and high-quality media performance.

Next to the contextual model, a procedural model stresses the fundamental and ever-changing nature of media quality and media diversity. In a critical rational approach media quality is not a datum but a dynamic becoming. It presupposes ongoing public debate on media quality by professionals themselves and other people. Important here is the process, the public debate, and not so much the results from the debate. That does not mean that we should not care about the outcome of the debate. We should, however, be tolerant as long as we do not run the risk of falling victim to the paradox of tolerance, which states that unlimited tolerance eventually will lead to the disappearance of tolerance itself (Popper, 1962: 265).

A critical rational approach toward media quality inevitably leads to new perspectives on media diversity as a policy goal. The foremost change in perspective is from reflective diversity, generally serving mainstream market preferences, towards openness and perfectly equal access, access for people and access for ideas. To conclude, let me make some remarks on what this could imply for media policy.

Democratic governments should, of course, refrain from any intervention in media content, but not from intervention in media markets. Critical rational media policy aims at *perfectly equal access for people*, on the one hand for media professionals as senders, and on the other for citizens and consumers as audiences. At the supply side of media markets this implies policy focus on competition, that is, prevention of media concentration through setting maximum levels to media ownership. Where lack of access for suppliers occurs, governments should stimulate innovation by way of subsidizing unconventional experiments in media production, distribution and marketing. On the demand side, governments should continuously monitor accessibility for the public to information and communication in a context of abundance. This brings along a need for policies directed at establishing and preserving social meeting platforms (e.g. digital cities); at affordability of media products (if necessary, price cap regulation or even media consumer subsidies); and at provision of cultural and ethnic minority media.

Of course, media access for people is worthwhile in itself. Ideally, communications systems provide access to everyone and every group and institution in society. But even more important is *perfectly equal access for ideas*. From the perspective of democratic truth-finding and political and cultural innovation it is particularly the confrontation of ideas that is important, aside from whether social support is large or small. Mainstream should have no more opportunity to manifest itself than the unorthodox minority. It is especially mainstream that is being served very well by the present media abundance. Therefore, currently particularly minority media content is of utmost importance. That is what equal access for ideas is all about: open access for minority ideas and opinions. Already in the nineteenth century Mill promoted openness to the unconventional: 'Complete liberty of contradicting and disproving our opinion is the very condition which justifies us in assuming its truth for purposes of action; and on no other terms can a being with human faculties have any rational assurance of being right' (1972/1859: 81). Mill's condition is never and by nobody easily met:

> for while every one well knows himself to be fallible, few think it necessary to take any precautions against their own fallibility, or admit the supposition that any opinion, of which they feel very certain, may be one of the examples of the error to which they acknowledge themselves to be liable. (Mill, 1972/1859: 80)

Free, open and perfectly equal access to ideas in media and communications for every citizen, poor or rich, ignorant or educated, is perhaps the best 'precaution against our own fallibility'.

Notes

1. In the Netherlands the terms 'verscheidenheid' (variety), 'diversiteit' (diversity) and 'pluriformiteit' (plurality or pluriformity) are almost synonymous.

2. The model McQuail and I used was a little bit more complex, relating variations in media content to variations in society according to relevant dimensions of social pluriformity. In the model, account was also taken of different functions of the media and different levels of operations; assessments were made according to more than one critierion (cf. McQuail and van Cuilenburg, 1983: 149).

3. This observation is far from being new. Already Klapper (1960) found: 'Commercial mass communication in a free enterprise society has been widely claimed to be of necessity a force toward the reinforcement of dominant cultural values, and to be economically constrained from espousing any view which is questioned by any significant portion of its potential audience'.

4. Hotelling's Law predicts and explains why in competitive markets sellers offer nearly the same kind of products. According to this Law and the models based on it, competitive media markets tend to homogeneity more than monopolistic or public service media models (cf. Steiner, 1952; also Owen and Wildman, 1992: 64–100).

5. The lack of a universal standard for newspaper quality has brought Turner to a quantitative approach of quality (Turner, 1995).

References

Anderla, G. (1973) *Information in 1985: a Forecasting Study of Information Needs and Resources.* Paris: OECD.

Coase, R.H. (1974) 'The economics of the First Amendment', *American Economic Review* 64 (2): 384–91.

Cuilenburg, J.J. van and McQuail, D. (1982) *Media en Pluriformiteit [Media and Pluriformity]*. 's-Gravenhage: Staatsuitgeverij.

Dizard, William P. (1994) *Old Media/New Media: Mass Communications in the Information Age*. White Plains, NY: Longman.

Dordick, Herbert S. and Wang, Georgette (1993) *The Information Society: A Retrospective View*. Newbury Park, CA: Sage.

Hotelling, Harold (1929) 'Stability in competition', *Economic Journal* 34: 41–57.

Klapper, J.T. (1960) *The Effects of Mass Communication*. New York: The Free Press.

Lanham, Richard A. (1995) 'Digital literacy', *Scientific American* September: 160–1.

Machlup, F. (1962) *The Production and Distribution of Knowledge in the United States*. Princeton, NJ: Princeton University Press.

McQuail, Denis and Cuilenburg, Jan van (1982) 'Vielfalt als medienpolitisches Ziel' [Diversity as media policy goal], *Media Perspektiven* 681–92.

McQuail, Denis and Cuilenburg, Jan van (1983) 'Diversity as a media policy goal: a strategy for evaluative research and a Netherlands case study', *Gazette* 31: 145–62.

Mill, John Stuart (1972/1859) *On Liberty*. London: Dent.

Milton, John (1644) *Areopagitica*.

Naisbitt, John (1984/1982) *Megatrends*. New York: Warner Books.

Negroponte, Nicholas (1995) *Being Digital*. London: Hodder & Stoughton.

Office of Technology Assessment (1990) *Critical Connections: Communication for the Future*. Washington: Government Printing Office.

Owen, B.M. and Wildman, S.S. (1992) *Video Economics*. Cambridge, MA: Harvard University Press.

Pool, I. de Sola, Inose, H., Takasaki, N. and Hurwitz, R. (1984) *Communication Flows: a Census in the US and Japan*. Tokyo: University of Tokyo Press.

Popper, Karl R. (1962) *The Open Society and its Enemies*, vol. 1. New York: Harper & Row.

Popper, Karl R. (1968/1963) *Conjectures and Refutations: the Growth of Scientific Knowledge*. New York: Harper & Row.

Rosengren, K.E., Carlson, M. and Tågerud, Y. (1991) 'Quality in programming: views from the North', *Studies in Broadcasting* 27: 21–80.

Scholten, O. (1982) *Krant en Democratie*. Amsterdam: VU Boekhandel.

Staal, Peter van der (1994) 'Communication media in Japan: economic and regional aspects', *Telecommunications Policy* 18 (1): 32–50.

Steiner, P.O. (1952) 'Program patterns and preferences, and the workability of competition in radio broadcasting', *Quarterly Journal of Economics* 66: 104–223.

Thich Nhat Hanh (1993/1987) *Interbeing: Fourteen Guidelines for Engaged Buddhism*. Berkeley, CA: Parallax Press.

Turner, Geoff (1995) 'A quantitative approach to quality in Australian newspapers', *Gazette* 55: 131–44.

Varian, Hal R. (1995) 'The information economy', *Scientific American* September: 161–2.

II IN SEARCH OF THE PUBLIC INTEREST

6

Wrestling with the Public Interest in Organized Communications

Jay Blumler

Once upon a time, the public interest in media matters seemed (relatively speaking), 'clear as the sun'. Today in contrast, it is 'dark as a wolf's mouth'![1] Thus, when broadcasting first came on the media scene, its providers were everywhere regarded as trustees for a 'public interest' that could be more or less consensually accepted. Only the roles of ownership, organization and control were in dispute. In the United States, the regulation of broadcasting for this explicit purpose was effected, first by the Radio Act of 1927 and then by the Communications Act of 1934. In Europe, public corporations were endowed more fulsomely with such a remit. Broad agreement to bring this medium under a 'public interest' umbrella was due to its society-wide reception and impact – its unique characteristics of pervasiveness, limited access and socio-political-cultural importance.

Latterly, however, many developments in the organization of both society and communications have upset this once sturdy applecart. We waver uncertainly between four different ways of thinking about the public interest in mass communications: (1) to phase it out; (2) to hold on to as much of it as possible in more difficult conditions; (3) to adapt it here and there; or (4) to fashion a new version of the public interest, 'capable of encompassing new opportunities and hazards' (Wedell, 1995).

The following commentary approaches this subject from three angles. First, the main challenges to the public interest media tradition are diagnosed. Second, some of the problematics of the concept itself are considered. Third, its possible application in new media conditions is addressed. In all this, one is indebted to the groundwork laid down in Denis McQuail's (1992) *Media Performance*.

The public interest under siege

Two sets of forces threaten to unravel the old public-interest cloak for media governance. One is media-specific, the other societywide. Since these are irreversible, the question arises: How should we come to terms with them?

The explosion of communication abundance is the first major source of challenge. The modern media scene is being transformed by an ongoing multiplication of electronic channels (satellite, cable, digital), other newer communication facilities (tapes, discs, videogames, the Internet) and an expansion of longer-standing leisure outlets (magazines, cinemas, galleries, indoor and outdoor sports, etc.). If, in these conditions, broadcasting becomes narrowcasting, why worry about trying to direct its providers toward communication welfare and away from abuse? It also becomes more plausible to presume that, as services proliferate, 'viewer choice, rather than regulatory imposition, can and should increasingly be relied upon to secure the programmes which viewers want' (HMSO, 1988: 5). Moreover, regulatory efficacy becomes more problematic as the number of suppliers to be monitored and controlled increases. Much of this particular challenge, however, is more apparent than real.

For one thing, despite abundance, the present communications scene is still dominated by a small number of actual and would-be giants. Partly this is due to people's 'conservative' viewing habits. Even in heavily multichannel conditions, most people sample only a minority of what is available, and something like three to five stations attract the bulk of viewing time. Partly this is reinforced by media economics – the need to devote huge resources to the provision of highly attractive entertainment, the gathering of worldwide news and the promotion of one's wares in a more crowded bazaar. Partly this is bolstered by governments' concerns to facilitate the emergence of strong national 'champions' in the global media market place. Pervasiveness, limited access, socio-political-cultural importance and accumulations of communication power with a high potential for social harm or good have consequently not departed the media scene.

For another, the ability of an enlarged media market to deliver the values that public institutions were expected to serve in the past appears modest and patchy. However much we may welcome more movies, sports, news, popular music and talk shows, there is in the newer channels a great deal of recycling, duplication and low-cost formatting. It would be difficult to maintain that the sum total of their contributions to diversity, quality and imaginative creation has yet been all that exciting or substantial.

Moreover, the incentives inside many communication organizations to serve public interest goals (however defined) recede as competition intensifies in the new media market place. Power shifts from creative to managerial personnel, and more priority is given to strategies for sheer organizational survival and betterment.

From this standpoint the policy problem is somewhat less confused than media proliferation might suggest. It reduces to those public interest requirements which the big players – those who still help to shape our cultures, politics, social systems and leisure options – should be expected and perhaps constrained to observe.

The other source of major challenge is deeper and more subtle. Notions of a 'public interest' cannot be divorced from the fabric of the societies to which they are to be applied. And in recent decades most modern societies have been changing in ways that make the public interest in communication more difficult to discern and implement.

Six interlinked processes appear to have been transforming advanced societies in the postwar period, albeit to different degrees and in different ways. These include *individualization* (the elevation of personal aspirations, fragmentation of communal experience, reduced conformity to the traditions and demands of established institutions); *consumerism* (the increased channelling of personal goals toward the consumer role, and the pervasive encouragement of commercialism that results); *privatization* (more preoccupation with personal domestic pursuits and reduced involvement in public communal ones, a diminishing 'social capital' (Putnam, 1995); *specialization and social complexity* (increased differentiation of functions performed by societal subsystems and emergence of more subgroups with their own formed identities, goals and political strategies); *anti-authoritarianism* (increased scepticism about the credentials, claims, performance and credibility of authority holders in all walks of life); and *globalization* (increased awareness of and engagement with events, personalities, ways of living and cultures beyond one's national borders).

These processes seem to be here to stay, and nowadays most significant social and political movements are obliged to work within them, adapting them where possible to their particular objectives. This is understandable, since modern developments have enhanced many (though certainly not all) individuals' life chances, broadened their horizons and strengthened their sense of personal worth. They have also faced public authorities with more demanding expectations of service and fuelled vigorous new thrusts of identity politics.

Nevertheless, these trends also press against the public interest idea in two main ways. First, in downgrading public life, institutions and authority, they may also diminish concerns and capacities to realize the public interest in the media field. Second, they threaten past versions of the public interest with obsolescence – as if relevant to social conditions and needs that no longer exist and values that no longer apply. Should we, for example, regard sexier soap operas, shorter soundbites, aggressively emotional audience talk shows and slice-of-life documentaries (at the expense of social-issue ones) as lapses from public-interest grace or instead as appropriate adaptations to a more brash, free-wheeling and populist society?

And yet, for all of us as members of the whole society, residing within defined state borders, there are still important cross-group relations to be managed and cross-group claims to be settled; common services to be provided; normative standards to be upheld; ways of ensuring that those services and standards are not imperilled by pursuit of narrow commercial, bureaucratic, partisan and subgroup interests to be maintained; and certain civil liberties and democratic procedures to be operated so that what is collectively done is broadly in line with what we can reasonably accept. In general, something like this could be termed 'the public interest'.

And the media are crucial to its realization due to a peculiarity of their systemic position. The media of organized communication comprise one of 'those institutions whose function it is actually to address society as a general unit' (Alexander, 1980). Admittedly, their social task is limited in a sense. They have no responsibility for making laws, executing policies, undertaking social action. But the news, stories and talk which they provide can be understood as an endless stream of offered insights into all corners of social life, 'a chief means through which society observes and evaluates itself' (as Seymour-Ure, 1991, puts it) and hence the raw material of public opinion and of current notions of the public interest. Moreover, this role is even more vital now than in the past due to the increasing incursion of communications into people's lives. As Reimer (1994) has put it, 'late modernity is characterized by an increasing mediazation'. The process so termed entails not only the 'penetration of ever more sophisticated electronic media into previously non-mediated leisure activities and . . . interpersonal relations' (Livingstone and Gaskell, 1995), as well as the increasing dependence of organized groups on media-based publicity to promote their political ends, but also the increasing centrality of the media as society's most ubiquitous symbolic resource. As often remarked, our experience of society is based less on unmediated reality these days and more on representations of it.

Problematics of 'the public interest'

We should not be naive about this notion of the collective good. In concrete terms, the public interest can never be definitively pinned down. It is pursued rather than known, and democracy entitles all with a point of view on it to take part in the search. But it is something on which differences almost always arise, due to the application to it of differing ideologies, values, weightings of diverse relevant values, and assessments of circumstances that must be taken into account. It nevertheless does refer to a somewhat elevated plane of discourse on which those differences can be aired. Neither are notions of 'the public interest' ever finally settled; they are a moveable feast because circumstances, needs and perceptions of societal requirements continually change.

Perhaps three points about this difficult concept deserve further comment. First, why do we need to wrestle with 'the public interest' at all? At bottom, it is because *justifiable* social organization rests not merely on power but also on authority. In politics, the claims of governments to be using public resources suitably depend on their deployment for certain public interests. In communications, the major media are similarly placed. The justification for their freedoms, their wide-ranging roles in society, politics and culture, and their place in regulatory orders depends ultimately on the public interests presumed to be served thereby.

Second, a certain transcendant quality attaches to the notion of the public interest. It is different from and, in policy terms, superior to particular interests. This entails a longer-term perspective, in which the claims of successor generations and the future of society are included as well as people's immediate needs. It also envisages potential conflict between particular individual, sectional or organizational interests and the public interest at large (however conceived). At the very least, claims arising from the former sources must be placed against broader considerations of principle before they can find shelter under the latter. But particular interests may often be in direct conflict with the public interest – as when governments withhold information from 'the public' about its conduct of affairs simply to avoid inconvenience or political embarrassment. Most insidious from a public interest standpoint perhaps is the collusion of several different organizational or sectional interests. This is an ever-present danger in the communications field, since the main news media are continually drawn into structured linkages with elites based in other sectors of society.

Nevertheless, thirdly, notions of the public interest must work in an imperfect and impure world. For democracies, a tension between transcendence and immanence is inescapable. Although visions, ideals and appeals to principle can carry real force at all levels of social life – hence the possibility of talking about and trying to effect a public interest – neither governmental politics nor media politics will ever be waged on a fully disinterested basis. From this standpoint, both Rousseau's notion of a 'general will', arrived at by citizens shedding all particular ties, and the Habermassian idea of a public sphere, in which rationality undistorted by interested parties prevails, appear impractically utopian. Probably the best that can be hoped for is that the exchange between interest-compromised notions of the common good will help to clarify the distinction between better and less well-founded versions of the public interest in particular situations. Media of public communication that facilitate such a clarification would also be doing a splendid job in the public interest!

The public interest in mass communication revisited

How, then, should we regard 'the public interest' in the new media landscape? It is perhaps something of an advantage that a short chapter cannot pursue this question exhaustively and must concentrate on priorities. Those developed in the following sections stem ultimately from an Aristotelian notion of 'man' (and woman of course) as a social, cultural and political animal – with, moreover, special communication needs as she and he grow up to become as fulfilled a version of such an animal as possible. The institutional implications of these priorities are then briefly addressed.

Social knitting

Phasing out the public interest (the first option mentioned in the introduction to this chapter) hardly seems appropriate. Since in our communications-dependent society, the major media reach so formatively and persistently into all its nooks and crannies, there is clearly a public stake in how well they depict those different areas, how they represent them in fact and fiction to each other, and the breadth and forms of access which they afford to them. This recalls (but is perhaps more wide-ranging than) the emphasis on 'issues of order and culture' in McQuail's (1992: 310–11) revised agenda of public interest concerns.

A core value here, meriting more attention than it has so far received in media criticism and assessment, is that of *authenticity*, or the idea that media fare should aim to do justice to a subject or a problem or a situation or the aims and activities of a subgroup in terms of what it is really like, instead of being prepared to distort the picture just for the sake of holding attention, to heighten the drama or to confirm the existing impressions (even prejudices) of audience members (Blumler, 1991). This value is specially important in our now highly differentiated and complex social orders. In such hybridized societies, the media have a crucial part to play in intercultural relations, in 'negotiating' as Hall (1993: 36) has put it, 'the many points of interdependence and interconnection on which the quality of our general life together depends'.

Cultural democracy

More debatable, as continuing foci of active public interest concern about media performance, are the long-standing content criteria of quality and diversity. McQuail (1992: 306–7) notes that, 'The expansion of media industries of all kinds and the rise in consumer prosperity has reduced the pressure to subsidize (socially valued) cultural production and consumption on "public interest" grounds' – though he also recognizes that trends of media industrialization, commercialization and competition can put brakes 'on imagination, creativity [and] risk-taking' (p. 308). Some argue as well that the problem of diversity disappears as multichannel abundance advances.

Cultural democrats will differ from cultural elitists over these matters. To the former, keeping the options open for as many people as possible to appreciate a variety of ways of enjoying cultural fulfilment remains an important if vulnerable value. Television is crucial to its pursuit, because the medium is used so extensively by almost every member of society. It is also exceptionally well equipped to offer rich cultural experience in accessible forms. That capability is supported by the uses and gratifications research tradition, which has regularly highlighted concerns among viewers to find in programmes not only opportunities for diversion, escape, excitement, companionship and the like, but also materials to reflect upon their places in the world, their personal relationships and their personal and social identities (McQuail et al., 1972).

Regarded from this perspective, there is a broad public interest in ensuring the availability of programming which is worthy of such involvement, offering viewers something to chew upon and think about; that does not just go for the obvious, the cheap, slick and easy; that avoids clichés; and that is in some sense literate. That we are unable to 'state clear and widely agreed standards of cultural quality' (as McQuail, 1992: 307, puts it) is not a valid objection to this position. The point is not to enshrine any particular interpretation of cultural quality but rather to keep the media doors open to all serious attempts at and versions of such quality.

Political democracy

Even more troubling public interest concerns arise in democratic politics, into which 'mediazation' has marched dramatically in recent decades. Little seems to happen in politics these days without media-related considerations or influences playing some part. Thus, the media have gradually moved from the role of reporting on and about politics, 'from the outside' as it were, to that of being an active participant in, shaping influence upon, and an integral part of the political process (Blumler and Gurevitch, 1995). This is not entirely unfortunate. One consequence of the increasing intervention of journalism into politics has been the exposure of more of its daily workings to general public scrutiny than ever before. The media searchlight probes into more corners. More abuses of power are brought to light that might otherwise have been kept under wraps. It is decreasingly sensible or feasible for officials to assume that any of their dealings can for long be kept confidential or secret. In the long run, this should act as a powerful force for more open and accountable government.

It is hard to be positive, however, about certain other effects of 'mediazation'. It has bred a near-Machiavellian 'modern publicity process', in which politicians (and other would-be opinion formers), when mobilizing public support, are impelled not merely to respond reactively to journalists' news agendas, but to try more proactively to plant their own stamps on those agendas – and to beat their political rivals in an unceasing competition over this (Blumler, 1990). It has also led to: a profound professionalization of parties' publicity efforts; increased media coverage of those efforts; the adaptation of many political messages to presumed media needs; an endless 'permanent campaign'; the translation of electioneering into a process of political marketing; more negative campaigning; plus widespread revulsion against the artificiality and sterility of much of the resulting political discourse.

Such trends presumably explain McQuail's (1992: 307) view that 'the communication conditions for healthy democratic politics' now 'require special attention'. Others even write of a 'crisis of public communication', since so little of it nourishes the citizen role and so much of it is tailormade to foster cynicism, disillusionment and alienation (Blumler and Gurevitch, 1995; Entman, 1989).

Although this state of affairs has attracted much attention in a burgeoning literature from scholars, thoughtful journalists and concerned politicians – as well as some practical reform efforts at community level (see Dahlgren, Chapter 9) – it is difficult to be very hopeful about the prospects for betterment, for reasons well summarized by McQuail (1992: 308): 'the chances of the [older] media contributing to informed debate and citizen involvement seem to diminish rather than to grow and the "new media" are not yet sufficiently developed to make up the deficiency'.

It is true that in technologically advanced societies more people are obtaining wordprocessors and can look forward to the prospect of downloading stores of political information and of engaging in interactive exchanges with political leaders and each other. In digital circles, more active ways of seeking information and holding political conversations do seem to be emerging. But however worthwhile such developments may be, they are unlikely to displace and at best will probably only supplement the mainstream media of political communication. Most people will continue to follow politics predominantly through television, radio and the press, and competing politicians will continue to invest most of their publicity effort in materials for those media.

The fact is that the core problems of political communication through the older media cannot be resolved by superficial or facile solutions. They are deeply seated in the tangled, if not incestuous, relationships of leading politicians and journalists, for both of whom many of the least satisfactory practices are actually highly convenient – such as tersely crafted soundbites, constructed news spectacles, personified leadership and aggressively negative attacks on opponents that make for arresting headlines. In Swanson's (1992: 299) words, we face a situation in which:

> politics, government and news media are linked in . . . a kind of supra-institution, the political-media complex. Within this complex, particular institutional interests often conflict with each other in the battle to control the public's perceptions, but mutual cooperation is required for each institution to achieve its aims. . . . What is not represented in the political-media complex is the public interest *per se*.

We cannot expect to dissolve such a complex, however, simply by urging some particular set of political communicators unilaterally to mend their ways. To stand any chance of success, proposed reforms 'must have systemic relevance and be able to harness systemic support' (Blumler and Gurevitch, 1995: 7).

Children and media

There is probably more agreement in principle about a public interest priority to safeguard the welfare of children and juveniles in the new media environment. Three values could apply to this:

1 *Respect* for the whole child's personality and development needs and the many ways in which our all-embracing media environment can serve, restrict or ignore them. This implies the affordable and convenient provision of media materials that, in addition to entertaining, will foster creativity and imagination, broaden horizons, stimulate curiosity and critical awareness and encourage social, cultural and civic competence – not treating children, then, merely as escapists and consumers.
2 *Fairness* in the sense of setting limits on advertisers' powers to reach and influence children and the media content intended for them.
3 *Avoidance* of the exposure of children to harmful materials and overly adult fare before they are ready for it.

Much public discussion (for example about child uses of the Internet) has recently been dominated by the third focus – as if our overriding concern must be to shelter the young from pornography, violence and bad language. But such an approach ignores the very real difficulties of effectively shielding children living in media-saturated societies from materials that adults consume in any quantity. They can see the top shelves of newsagents' magazine displays. Tabloid newspapers enter their homes. Many stay up to view adult programmes after watershed hours or watch them on their own bedroom sets or on friends' videos. They can pretend eligibility to attend R-rated movies. Increasing numbers are adroit Internet surfers.

Such a preoccupation also tends to deflect attention away from two arguably more important problems. One is how to deal with an insidious threat to the second value itemized above. This arises from the efforts of marketers and advertisers to tap the large pool of spending power now in young people's hands. In the more traditional print and audiovisual media, a host of controls and codes were evolved to 'play fair' to children by regulating the amount and methods of advertising to them, including the erection of firm barriers between commercial and editorial content. But few if any such controls yet apply to the Internet and other on-line services, where advertisers enjoy an almost free hand to offer hybrid forms of content, to entice children to interact, through games, quizzes and other forms of play, with product-related materials and characters, and to obtain information about their own and their families' consumer preferences for use in follow-up marketing. Here is a public interest vacuum that urgently needs to be filled.

The other important problem in this field is how to sustain in new media conditions the programming traditions (based largely in public service broadcasting organizations) that have reflected the first value mentioned above. Media privatization poses a direct threat to this, since the children's services of unregulated commercial broadcasters have always tended to concentrate on 'cartoon programmes, featuring robots, animated and stuffed animals, dolls and a range of animated adventure characters, including space fantasy heroes' (Blumler, 1992a: 37). According to recent research, however, certain overall trends of broadcasting reorganization (competition, budgetary pressures, internationalization of programming markets) are threatening even the commitments of European public broadcasters to provision of a range of well-made domestic programming for children (Blumler and Biltereyst, 1997; Blumler, 1992b).

Public is as public does

At a time when the media play such a big part in personal fulfilment and social organization, all the public interest concerns outlined above are too important to be left to chance. Regulation is essential for laying down framework conditions within which media organizations must operate; to set terms of fair competition for a 'level playing field' of entrepreneurial combat; to block undue concentrations of media power and inhibit gross abuses of such power; and to enforce baseline standards of conduct for key media personnel, such as journalists and advertisers.

External regulators' abilities to influence media content, however, are normally indirect, limited and modest. This does not necessarily mean that private providers should be relieved of obligations and expectations to serve the public interest in the mainstreams of their output. But since there can be no guarantee that commercial offerings will be primarily shaped by such considerations, there must be well-organized alternatives to a media market. The public interest will wither on the vine unless it is served by public institutions.

That is why, despite the myriad services of a multichannel television system, we still need to sustain principled, amply resourced and purposefully directed public service broadcasting organizations. Only strong and committed public television bodies can be expected to serve the public interest 'from the inside' as it were, treating its values and needs, not just as imposed requirements for obligatory or token conformity, nor just instrumentally as means to audience maximization, but as ends in themselves.[2]

A useful illustration of what this can mean in practice is afforded by current BBC approaches to the extraordinarily difficult dilemmas of civic communication outlined above. Despite all the problems, it has decided to try, during and after the 1997 General Election campaign: to restore freshness to political talk by involving ordinary voters, experts, and people with relevant first-hand experience in discussions of major issues with politicians in a range of programme formats; to constrain the competing parties to address a wider range of issues than for tactical reasons they might be inclined to do; to design coverage specially suited to younger and less-interested voters for placement in programmes and outlets they find congenial; and to lace reporting of parties' daily campaign initiatives with background information and analysis. This is not to claim that these measures are bound to work well and will overcome the prevailing disenchantment with campaign communication. But it shows how a principled public broadcaster can wrestle with the public interest in an important field, instead of just 'going with the flow' as a more commercially motivated provider might tend to do. Indeed, the BBC has even signalled its intention to grapple with the systemic root of political communication problems by holding a post-election seminar with leading politicians to consider ways of overcoming the 'soundbite culture' in which they are both implicated at present.

To ensure a vigorous and influential public communications sector, however, two further conditions must be met. First, public broadcasting organizations must not be allowed to become mere museums of past excellence. In policy and programming, they must respond creatively and imaginatively to present-day conditions, not wedding themselves only to re-runs of past approaches. This requires: research to keep in touch with audiences' evolving interests, tastes and standards of programme quality; regular reviews of programme provision to keep it relevant and in line with public interest needs; and the deliberate establishment of mechanisms for enabling public interest groups and concerned members of the audience to hold them to account for how they are serving society.

Second, innovative institution-building ideas for creating a public presence on the information highways of the future should be explored. In part, this need arises from a public interest in universal access to the benefits of new information technology, aiming to avoid 'creating situations where better, more interesting, more rewarding, and, ultimately, more empowering services are on "higher" . . . tiers at prices which exclude users on the basis of ability to pay' (Raboy, 1996: 13). Partly, it stems from the future informational needs of democratic societies. As Graham (1996) has pointed out, information on the Information Superhighway is likely to fall into two categories – high-quality market-generated material to be paid for by consumers, and public domain information that may often be low-quality in reliability, coverage or presentation. As he concludes: 'Above all, neither of these categories seems likely to produce the good quality public domain information that a democratic society requires. There is, in effect, likely to be a "gap" which public policy has to fill.' In part, the need also arises from a risk that a range of high-quality materials for children may be in short supply on the Information Superhighway. How to organize and pay for public institutions to fill these gaps will have to be worked out. Existing public institutions could transfer to the new technologies. New ones could be created for specific purposes. Or perhaps something like a Public Communications Consortium, embracing a range of functions, might be established. At present, however, policy thinking lags well behind public interest needs on these matters.

In conclusion

Curiously, social and media turbulence seem not quite so upsetting to notions of the public interest in organized communications as we first supposed. At least many of the basic values which underpinned those notions in the past remain valid. But the challenge of realizing them is greater today, and considerably more thought is needed on their policy implications for the newer information services. Institutions that have served the public interest in the past need to be supported and revitalized, but new ones also need to be invented.

Notes

1. English folk-phrases.
2. The foregoing three paragraphs draw extensively from Blumler and Hoffman-Riem (1992).

References

Alexander, Jeffrey C. (1980) 'The news media in systemic, historical, and comparative perspective', in Elihu Katz and Tamas Szecsko (eds) *Mass Media and Social Change*. London: Sage.

Blumler, Jay G. (1990) 'Elections, the media and the modern publicity process', in Marjorie Ferguson (ed.) *Public Communication: The New Imperatives*. London: Sage.

Blumler, Jay G. (1991) 'In pursuit of programme range and quality', *Studies of Broadcasting* 27: 191–206.

Blumler, Jay G. (ed.) (1992a) *Television and the Public Interest: Vulnerable Values in West European Broadcasting*. London: Sage.

Blumler, Jay G. (1992b) *The Future of Children's Television in Britain: An Enquiry for the Broadcasting Standards Council*. London: Broadcasting Standards Council.

Blumler, Jay G. and Biltereyst, Daniel (1997) *The Integrity and Erosion of Public Television for Children: A Pan-European Survey*. Geneva: European Broadcasting Union.

Blumler, Jay G. and Gurevitch, Michael (1995) *The Crisis of Public Communication*. London: Routledge.

Blumler, Jay G. and Hoffmann-Riem, Wolfgang (1992) 'New roles for public service television', in Jay G. Blumler (ed.) *Television and the Public Interest: Vulnerable Values in West European Broadcasting*. London: Sage.

Entman, Robert M. (1989) *Democracy Without Citizens: the Decay of American Politics*. New York: Oxford University Press.

Graham, Andrew (1996) 'Evidence to the House of Lords Select Committee on Science and Technology', unpublished paper.

Hall, Stuart (1993) 'Which public, whose service?', in Wilf Stevenson (ed.) *All Our Futures: The Changing Role and Purpose of the BBC*. London: British Film Institute.

HMSO (1988) *Broadcasting in the '90s: Competition, Choice and Quality*. Cmnd 517. London: HMSO.

Livingstone, Sonia and Gaskell, George (1995) 'The changing media environment for children and young people: developing the research agenda', paper presented to World Conference on Re-inventing Television, Paris.

McQuail, Denis (1992) *Media Performance: Mass Communication and the Public Interest*. London: Sage.

McQuail, Denis, Blumler, Jay G. and Brown, Ray (1972) 'The television audience: a revised perspective', in Denis McQuail (ed.) *Sociology of Mass Communications*. Harmondsworth: Penguin Books.

Putnam, Robert D. (1995) 'Bowling alone: America's declining social capital', *The American Prospect* 23: 65–78.

Raboy, Marc (1996) 'Public service broadcasting in the context of globalization', in Marc Raboy (ed.) *Public Broadcasting for the 21st Century*. Luton: John Libbey.

Reimer, Bo (1994) *The Most Common of Practices: On Mass Media Use in Late Modernity*. Stockholm: Almqvist & Wiksell.

Seymour-Ure, Colin (1991) *The British Press and Broadcasting since 1945*. Oxford: Blackwell.

Swanson, David L. (1992) 'The political-media complex', *Communication Monographs* 59: 397–400.

Wedell, George (1995) 'The public interest in broadcasting: what price the public interest?', paper presented to Consultation on the Public Interest in Broadcasting, Leeds Castle.

7

World Communication: Conflicting Aspirations for the Twenty-first Century

Cees J. Hamelink

Die Philosophen haben die Welt nur verschieden interpretiert, es kommt darauf an, sie zu veraenderen.

(Karl Marx)

In one of the films about the *Titanic*, the ship's band plays 'Abide with me' as the great ship goes down. The community of communication scholars often reminds me of this image. With great dedication and apparently oblivious to the disasters of the world, the band plays on. There seems to be little concern about where the world is going and little effort to think about the lifeboats we may need to stock for future catastrophe.[1] Paraphrasing Karl Marx, my contention is that communication studies are so absorbed with their attempt to provide different interpretations and explanations of the world that they tend to neglect the pressing task of changing the world.

We obviously need interpretations and explanations of the world. We also need theoretical ideas to guide our interpretations and explanations. However, if one looks at the bulk of communication research (in the books and scientific journals of the field or the papers presented at the big academic conferences), the lack of ideas about changing the world is overwhelming. This is disquieting because – in the light of the very real risk of human extinction – the field cannot afford the luxury of disengagement (Beck, 1992; Leslie, 1996). We desperately need normative ideas and imaginations that provide guidance to preferred futures. Communication studies should distance themselves from complicity with the fashionable 'market-centred' approaches and move towards designing aspirational visions for a 'people-centred' future which is the only common future we have.

The failure of prevailing approaches

There are at least two serious problems with the continued attempts within the social sciences to interpret and explain reality. First, the ambition to interpret and explain the world is bound to fail, and secondly, even if it succeeded it would not generate knowledge that would help us to change the world in preparation for the future. An apt title for Denis McQuail's (1983) classic on mass communication theory would therefore have been 'The failure of prevailing theory'. Most of the theoretical work McQuail describes has been developed in support of empirical-analytical research; however, the essential contestability of such approaches makes their explanatory validity rather poor.

Understanding reality as 'actuality', reality is interpreted and explained within the confines of a 'being-as-such' that can be described in terms of logical connections among empirical data. The underlying ontological assumption is that these connections can be expressed in language categories that are isomorphic with the structures of reality. The problem with this position is that we have no knowledge about this assumed ontological correspondence between scientific categories and structures of reality. This creates a fundamental weakness in the validation of our observations and their expression. Moreover, this position also has to assume that the scientific expression of our observations cannot contain contradictions and that theoretical ideas are statements about unalterable regularities and certitudes that provide the scientist with an instrument to control the environment. The assumption suggests that there is stability and coherence in the reality under study, whereas on the contrary these theories are characteristically 'underdetermined', meaning that there are always several theoretical perspectives that concur with the empirical observations of reality for which the empirical analysis of data provides no decisive arbitration.

A painfully manifest case in point concerns the (rather popular) efforts to forecast future social effects of information-communication technologies (ICTs). These are largely based upon the assumptions that it is possible to produce a valid explanation of the modes of interaction between technology and society and that it is possible to extrapolate these interactions into the future. There is, however, no theoretical perspective available on technology–society interactions that could provide the basis for a solid prediction about their future articulations. Given the essential contestability of theory in the social sciences, there is no prospect of such a prediction emerging at some later stage either. This may be disguised by the sophisticated nature of forecasting techniques, but the basic theoretical flaw makes them no better than ancient astrology.

The insights of Ilya Prigogine are a helpful counterpoint to dominant academic approaches:

> Classical science emphasized stability and equilibrium. Today we observe instabilities, fluctuations and evolutionary trends on practically all levels, starting with cosmology and going through fluid mechanics, chemistry and biology to the large scale systems studied by the environmental sciences. Notions such as chaos and self-organization have become quite popular. (in Perez de Cuellar, 1995: 39)

If the field could accept that contradiction and chaos are indeed the very characteristics of reality, it could liberate itself from traditional epistemological constraints and begin to take the future seriously. It would have to move beyond the conception of its objects of description and analysis as merely 'being-as-such', and view reality also as 'potentiality', as 'being-information'. Reality would then be understood as the dialectical tension between 'what is' and 'what could be' and the social sciences (including communication studies) would have as its major assignment to help us to distinguish between possible futures. For such crucial issues as the organization of world communication in the next century, we need normative ideas instead of analytical and descriptive ones. With this requirement we stand in a good tradition inspired by such thinkers as Grotius and Kant and also – more recently – by scholars in various disciplines: 'The return of normative ethics responded to a sense that there was something badly wrong with the way in which the positivist-empiricist social science of the 1950s formulated the issues and problems of the day' (Brown, 1992: 196).

The field of communication studies requires the development of normative approaches in order to adequately formulate the issues and problems of contemporary communication realities, to design possible futures, and to actualize preferred possibilities. The social significance of communication studies would greatly increase if the field were able to move beyond its current theoretical constraints and to develop normative ideas as in normative disciplines such as law and moral philosophy.[2]

Normative ideas and human rights

What precisely is meant by the challenge that the field of communication studies be more normative? This obviously depends upon the way in which the concept 'norm' is used in the present argument. I follow Neville in his proposal to use the root meaning of norm as 'whatever makes the difference between better and worse things to do' (1995: 115). Therefore, communication studies should be inspired by 'normative ideas' that help us to distinguish between better versus worse futures.

As a normative science the field would not necessarily tell us how communication ought to be in the future or what future we should want, or what the best future is, but it would assist us in reasoning about preferred futures. Normative ideas help us to see what alternative future possibilities there may be and inspire the dialogue about which alternatives are better or worse. Actually, without normative ideas – in other words, without the judgement between better versus worse – reflection on our responsibility for the future has no meaning. Normative communication studies would produce 'aspirational visions' that bring together our ambitions, desires and ideals for preferred futures. Such visions should go beyond mere defensible arguments about preferred communication futures. They should also design ways for the actualization of these futures.

With the emphasis in contemporary academic discourse on the contextual and relativist nature of 'norms' the foundations for essential normative ideas have become much contested:

- Are these foundations divine revelations in which the gods reveal to us what is morally justified? Divine guidance though is only useful for those who accept the divine revelation.
- Are moral principles grounded in human nature? But there are different interpretations of human nature and different, even conflicting, principles are derived from such interpretations, and also different principles derived from similar interpretations. Moreover, is anything people are naturally inclined to do, morally justifiable?
- Can foundations be identified through ontology? This would imply that moral principles are based upon the specific category of being the human species represents. However, there is no uniform interpretation of this specific category and no uniform principles can thus be derived.
- Can morality be grounded in a social contract between free and equal people who conclude voluntarily an agreement on common morality? This argument implies that moral principles are socially based, but societies are stratified into groups with different interests. They are also usually inegalitarian, with the result that the social contract in most societies is concluded between unequal parties. Moreover, when the moral principles are community-based, as communitarian thinkers suggest, they reflect the positive morality of a community which more often than not tends to be very conservative.
- Can we adopt the position that moral rights and wrongs are determined by our personal intuition and that moral principles are self-evident? This would seem to render moral arguments largely a matter of subjective and arbitrary preferences which pre-empt serious dialogue with others.

This situation which seemingly leaves us at a loss, is in fact very fortunate. The contestability of foundations of norms forces us to engage in dialogue with different traditions and to explore what common ideas we may have. Rather than searching for philosophical foundations, the optimal way to discover what normative ideas people may share would seem the practice of dialogical reasoning. As Reinders argues, this would change the search for justification of normative ideas 'from a logical into a social and historical issue' (Reinders, 1995: 20). This practice would have to be conducted within the community of communication scholars as an effort to identify what fundamental normative ideas could guide communication studies.

This dialogue could be inspired by the historical fact that the world community – over the past several decades – has managed to achieve a political consensus around the set of normative ideas that constitute the international human rights regime. The world community has recognized the existence of human rights, their universality and indivisibility, and has accepted a machinery for their enforcement. Despite all the turmoil, the Vienna World Conference on Human Rights (1993) managed to reinforce that the norm of human rights is universal (Hamelink, 1994: 65).

A point that needs to be raised here concerns the democratic prospects for dialogical reasoning when dialogues (in whatever community) do not take place under social conditions of equality. In reality the search for common principles is likely to take place on an unlevel playing field. The question, however, is whether this necessarily determines adverse outcomes for the less powerful players. The historic irony is that more often than not the moral intuitions of a community that protect the less powerful players against arbitrary use of social inequality will be enacted in consensus instruments such as national constitutions. Actually, most constitutional provisions constrain the more powerful players. The existing inequality will obviously still determine – often decisively – the concrete enactment of these provisions. Yet, once the abuse of power is rendered 'ultra vires', a great many different logistical actions are at the disposal of the less powerful players for their 'empowerment'. Even if in today's highly unequal world, human rights remain a largely ineffectual set of moral claims, it should not be underestimated that these claims have been universally adopted as the basic rules for the playing field.

Basic to the human rights regime is the moral premise that the human being is entitled to respect for his/her inalienable dignity. This means that the human being is worthy of treatment in accordance with certain basic standards. The recognition of the dignity of the human person implies that human beings cannot treat each other arbitrarily in ways they see fit.

The standards of human conduct have evolved in a long history of different schools of religious and philosophical thought. The novelty of the international human rights regime – as it was established after 1945 – is the formulation of these standards into a catalogue of legal rights. Human rights standards have been formulated in the United Nations Charter of 1945, in the International Bill of Rights (the Universal Declaration of Human Rights, the International Covenant on Economic, Social and Cultural Rights and the International Covenant on Civil and Political Rights), in a series of international human rights treaties, regional instruments (such as the European Convention for the Protection of Human Rights and Fundamental Freedoms (1950)), the American Convention of Human Rights (1969), and the African Charter on Human and Peoples' Rights (1981), and in the Islamic declaration of human rights which was prepared by the Islamic Council of Europe in 1980 and presented to UNESCO in 1981.[3]

In the International Bill of Rights we find 76 different human rights. In the totality of major international and regional human rights instruments this number is even greater. With the tendency among human rights lobbies to put more and more social problems in a human rights framework, the number of human rights is likely to further increase. It is questionable whether this proliferation of rights strengthens the cause of the actual defence of human rights. Various attempts have been made to establish a set of core human rights that are representative for the totality. One effort concluded the existence of 12 core rights:[4]

The right not to be discriminated against.
The right to education.
The right to fair working conditions.
The right to life.
The right not to be tortured.
The right not to be arbitrarily arrested.
The right to due process of law.
The right to food.
The right to health care.
The right to freedom of association.
The right to political participation.
The right to freedom of expression.

These core rights are the legal articulation of three basic moral principles. First, the inviolability of human life which implies the standard that intentional harm against human integrity is inadmissible. This principle is firmly entrenched in international law and in practically all constitutional law. It also has a solid grounding in the most important religious and philosophical schools of thought across history and culture. Secondly, the principle of equality which implies the standard that discrimination is inadmissible. The prohibition of non-discrimination belongs to the per-emptory norms in international law (Hannikainen, 1988: 467–89). Thirdly, the principle of autonomy which implies the standard that external coercion or constraints that obstruct the self-determination of the human person are inadmissible. Although typical for the enlightenment tradition from Kant to Habermas, the principle is essential in international law and is found in the tradition of different cultures.

The defence of human rights requires active efforts to implement the international human rights regime. This needs the guidance from another normative proposition: democratic governance. The realization of human rights is impossible without the existence of democratic institutions, both nationally and internationally (Waart, 1995: 49). Democratic procedures are essential to inform people about the existence of human rights, to enable victims to expose violations and to bring perpetrators to justice.

Beyond the mere establishment of democratic institutions, the defence of human rights also requires democratic governance as a 'way of life'. This means that people adopt the need for accountability as an indispensable dimension of the distribution and execution of power in their societies and communities. In several human rights instruments the idea of a 'democratic society' plays a key role. Since no right can be absolute in an extreme sense, the 'limitation of limits' to human rights has become a critical issue in relation to the defence of human rights. There is a growing consensus in the international community that restrictions of human rights are only legitimate when they are necessary for the protection of democratic governance.

Given the reality of different and conflicting conceptions of morality in the world, human rights principles will not be actualized in precisely the same way in different moral communities. The recognition of a variety of cultural interpretations has provoked the question of the degree to which local cultural interpretations can be accepted. There is increasing support in the human rights community for the view that culturally determined interpretations reach a borderline when they violate the core principles of human rights law. Since this cannot always be unequivocally or unilaterally determined, the admissibility of interpretations should be judged by the world community in an ongoing dialogue based upon respect for axiological pluralism.

The foundation of cultural identity – in the sense of individual or collective self-definition – is to an important extent axiological. It is – among other factors – based upon the belief that the individual or group deserves respect for the specific moral aspiration they pursue. The basis of cultural identity is a moral ideal. Religious as well as secular cultures are inspired by moral aspirations ranging from the emulation of Christ to the sanctity of private property. In all the essential religious texts there are fundamental instructions about how human beings should live. The great stories about Buddha, Jesus or Mohammed contain basic normative concepts about human life (Vroom, 1995: 27). These moral aspirations reflect different preferential axiological orders. Some components of these orders may overlap, others may diverge and imply ultimate disagreement. It is unrealistic to expect social consensus on fundamental beliefs. More importantly, shared axiological orders are not necessary in a democratic society and may even be undesirable. Axiological disagreement forces all to reflect on the validity of their own normative views. It protects society from entrenching itself in complacent forms of orthodoxy and thus contributes to the creation of open societies.

There are good historical, legal and moral grounds on which one could argue that the defence of human rights should be adopted as a normative idea to guide aspirational visions for the preferred future of world communication.

The future of world communication

The question to be posed then is how we construct a world communication practice that is guided by the defence of human rights, democratic governance and axiological pluralism? World communication encompasses all those within and cross-border movements of information, opinions, ideas and cultural expressions; it thus affects the quality of the daily lives of all people around the globe. What aspirational vision for a 'people-centred' world communication could guide this construction and how could communication scholars contribute to world communication? These questions pertain, among other things, to ideals of *regulation, organization* and *performance*.

World communication is *regulated* by a robust regime for the promotion and protection of cultural rights as basic human rights. These rights encompass the right freely to participate in the cultural life of one's community and the right to the protection of cultural identity. The regulatory practice provides for means of access to cultural participation and promotes the socio-economic conditions that enable people to access cultural resources. To facilitate free access to the world's cultural resources, the international regime for intellectual property rights has been reformed to accommodate the cultural needs of local communities. Legislation provides for the deconcentration of the control over the means for production and distribution of cultural expressions and special measures are taken to ensure – in particular – women's access to the benefits of cultural developments.

A strong emphasis is put on the protection of linguistic rights and concrete measures against 'linguistic genocide' are in place. The rights of cultural property holders are balanced by obligations they have vis-à-vis the communities in which they operate. There are rules on the abuse of rights to cultural property and rules on liability in case of such abuse. The control over means of cultural production may not be used to damage others. There are provisions on adequate public funding for the promotion of cultural development and broad popular participation in cultural life.

Following the recommendations of the UNESCO World Commission on Culture and Development, an International Code of Conduct on Culture has been enacted that provides the basis for the adjudication of violations of cultural rights. Guiding principles of the Code are: 'the promotion of cultural co-existence, the maintenance of cultural diversity and the preservation of cultural heritage' (Perez de Cuellar, 1995: 282). Also the International Office of the Ombudsperson for Cultural Rights has been set up to hear complaints, investigate cases, suggest processes of arbitration and recommend legal remedies (Perez de Cuellar, 1995: 282–3).

The future practice is *organized* in such a way that it allows all people to participate in world communication. The intellectual and physical resources for this participation are equitably distributed across the world. The democratic process has moved beyond the political sphere and extends the requirement of participatory institutional arrangements to other social domains. Forms of participatory democracy have therefore been designed for policy-making in the sphere of the production, development, and dissemination of information, culture and technology. People now participate on a grand scale in areas of public decision-making formerly accessible only to elites. Forms of participatory democracy are in place for policy-making in the production, development and distribution of cultural expressions. Modalities of public control have been designed that do not constrain the input of individual independent creativity. Particularly in large and complex societies, decisions may be delegated to representatives of the people, but those entrusted with deciding for others have to provide a full and transparent account to those on whose behalf they are invited to act.

There are rules, procedures and institutional mechanisms to secure public accountability. The principle of accountability implies the possibility of remedial action by those whose rights to participation and equality are violated. If those who take decisions engage in harmful acts, those affected have unobstructed access to procedures of complaint, arbitration, adjudication and compensation.

World communication *performs* as the world's major vehicle to promote participation in cultural life, awareness and enjoyment of cultural heritage of national ethnic groups and minorities and indigenous peoples. World communication is also an active agency for the conservation, development and diffusion of culture, and for professional education in the field of culture. Through world communication, respect for the independence of creative work is strongly supported. World communication creates public cultural spheres, provides for the widest possible range of cultural expressions, and contributes to the social process of learning cultural pluralism. This process creates a viable cultural order which seeks forms of cooperation under conditions of disagreement. It teaches people to view cultural diversity as a critically important asset.

World communication contributes to a worldwide viable and democratic social order in which people adopt different 'ways of life', may even show levels of irritation and intolerance vis-à-vis dissidents, but refrain from attempts to control the common cultural space.

If this people-centred aspiration for world communication were realized it would mean that ordinary people would get a more diversified and reliable global flow of information on matters of public interest, they would have easier and more affordable access to international sources of information and global means of communication (such as computer networks), they would have access to complaints procedures and judicial review mechanisms in case their cultural rights were violated, they would be invited to participate more fully in cultural policy-making, and the languages they speak would not be threatened with linguistic genocide.

Alternative aspirations

One could obviously also project an alternative aspiration onto the future of world communication. This vision could be guided by the normative ideas of capitalist globalization, such as the defence of free markets, deregulation, and privatization. The ideal regulatory practice in this vision would be to have no regulation at all. Markets around the world should be opened up to the trade in cultural goods and services. The access to cultural life, the provision and protection of cultural products would be defined by the preferences of the market place, and the investments of cultural industries would be protected through a robust and enforceable intellectual property regime. The protection of intellectual property rights is more inspired by the needs of commercial entrepreneurs than by a vision of cultural pluralism. There is 'a subtle reorientation of copyright away from the author towards a trade-oriented perspective' (Perez de Cuellar, 1995: 244).

In many cultural domains the common heritage is submitted to the exclusive ownership of private operators on the market place. The rules of the World Trade Organization reinforce the commercialization of cultural production and the liberalization of markets for the distribution and sales of cultural commodities. There is a strong trend to incorporate cultural production into most regional free trade agreements which have only very limited provisions for non-inclusion of culture, and these are constantly under challenge.

The organizational practice would be left to the control of private operators. In order to maximize efficiency of serving the market place, there would be no burdensome public mechanisms of consultation and decision-making. Democratic participation in cultural production is seen as highly undesirable and unnecessary. Private players on free markets need no public control and accountability beyond their minimal responsibility towards the law. This vision may accept different axiological preferences, provided they are in the end subordinate to the normative standards of the 'market'.

Whereas one could argue that the vision inspired by human rights, democracy and pluralism very much projects a 'people-centred' aspiration, the alternative is 'market-centred'.[5] On very essential norms these aspirational visions are mutually exclusive. Actually, the most essential features of the people-centred practice are fundamentally undermined by the market-centred alternative. The market-centred practice reinforces the growth of income inequalities and thus actively deteriorates the socio-economic conditions that would enable people to access cultural resources. It promotes no measures against the practice of linguistic genocide which occurs in many educational systems around the world (Skutnabb-Kangas and Phillipson, 1997). For the market-centred practice Stavenhagen's observation holds true:

> the power structure of modern society, the economic structure, the way the mass media are controlled and used, and the way in which publications are produced and educational policies are carried out, all of these factors tend to destroy minority cultures, even when there is no wilful intention to do so. (Stavenhagen, 1995: 75)

Following the market-centred aspiration, culture is not likely to be freely accessible and available to everyone. As expressions of people's cultures become treated as private property, a public culture is destroyed. Consequently, people around the world are deprived of access to their common heritage. The market-centred practice does not share the human rights commitment to the normative idea of equality in the sense of equal entitlement for all people to the conditions of self-development. It actually enlarges socio-economic disparities. Developments in the European Union demonstrate time and again that deregulated and free, competitive markets do not diminish income inequalities. The core of the market-centred practice is inherently undemocratic since it does not account to a public constituency for its acts and rejects the burden of social responsibility. At best it offers (albeit under uneven conditions) the 'right to shop' (Barber, 1995: 17), but it does not support economic democracy.

The pet project of the market-centred practice is economic globalization which seeks the unobstructed trading of goods and services around the globe and the creation of a globally integrated market in which the same product can be made available globally. It is guided by the belief that entrepreneurial efficiency and effectiveness demand a global reach and perceives its interests optimally served if its preferred socio-economic standards are replicated across the globe. Economic globalization has an imperial interest in the creation of a coherent set of values and norms, discouraging divergent norms, and perceiving deviance from its standards as a threat to stability.

The people-centred practice adopts as key normative ideas the solidarity among people, the recognition that all people matter, the inclusion of all in the entitlement to basic resources, and a compassion with those who lack access to such resources. It aims at the redistribution of the world's wealth so that all benefit. This practice which puts people in the centre is driven by a deep sense of social responsibility and a respect for the diversity of people's aspirations and preferences. The alternative aspiration adopts as key normative idea competition, a game in which some win and others lose. Its core purpose is individual accumulation of money. Fellow human beings can be used in this aspiration as objects. All people have to fit into the unidirectional mould of a consumerist society. The major actors accept no public accountability for the social impact of their actions. Beyond the acceptance of a limited liability in the strict legal sense, they do not allow public control and intervention in their activities.

The responsibility of communication scholars

The challenge for communication studies is to help in making a choice between these alternative futures and then assist the actualization of the preferred future, which means assisting in the creation of a (world) communication order that actualizes the preferred normative ideas. To meet this challenge, the field will need sufficient intellectual space for creativity and independence. This space is unfortunately at present seriously under threat!

The devastating impact of capitalist market thinking is becoming increasingly manifest in the decreasing status and quality of academic teaching, and poses serious obstacles to independent and creative reflection. Most university departments face cuts in public funding and resulting commercial pressures that make serious attention to normative aspirational approaches to world communication (or for that matter to any other issue area) not a priority. The essential normative idea of capitalist globalization 'everything for sale' (Kuttner, 1997) has – around the world – begun a very successful migration into social domains that were conceived as 'res publica' and as 'common heritage'. Among the victims are health care, social security and education. With the substitution of 'outdated' notions such as civic solidarity and common good by aspirations such as profitability and greed, an aggressive mode of social Darwinism is introduced. Only the most powerful players will manage; the weaker ones have only themselves to blame.

If the community of communication scholars is not capable of protecting itself against this wave of global destruction of intellectual capital, there is no realistic chance it can usefully assist in preparing ourselves for the future of world communication.

Notes

1. The *Titanic* sank in 1912 and out of the 2206 passengers 1503 drowned, largely as a result of the decision not to stock a sufficient number of lifeboats. The ship's perfect technology made any preparation for future disaster superfluous.

2. The possible fear that normative theorizing would not be scientific and would amount to no more than highly subjective daydreaming, needs a reply. There is no reason why the normal scientific criteria could not be applied, such as the requirement of the scientific attitude that accepts that all theories are contestable. Normative theorizing should use – like empirical theory – a substantial and transparent argument in its defence. More important, however, is that suspicions about normative approaches are probably inspired by the expectation that these are highly prescriptive. This finds some ground in the fact that so-called normative theories of the media are usually presented as 'sets of ideas about how media ought to be related to their society' (McQuail, 1983: 65). These theories, like so much work in the area of media ethics, tend more towards 'moralistic studies' than 'ethical reflections'. The latter do not contain prescriptions or rules, but assist in the critical reflection on moral choices.

3. Universal Declaration of Human Rights in Islam. In *Encounter: Documents for Muslim–Christian Understanding*, No. 116, June 1985.

4. The 12 core rights are based upon a list developed by Donnelly and Howard (1988) and by the participants in a human rights seminar convened by PIOOM (Interdisciplinary Research Program on Root Causes of Human Rights Violations, University of Leiden) in 1991.

5. It is important to note here that by 'market' is meant a very specific type of market, that is, a market operated according to the normative ideas of capitalism. It is remarkable that most of today's writings on the state of the world fail to mention that the present international order is based upon a 'capitalist market economy' within which no 'free market' figures. The world market is the highly uneven playing field that is centrally controlled by a few monopolists who are not open to public accountability for their actions. This market is anything but free. Nor is it an economic arrangement that – as is often suggested by development professionals – is capable of supporting democratic processes. As long as we equate democracy with some level of transparency and control in the execution of power, the capitalist market demonstrates more autocratic than democratic features. Its core operators, the largest transnational corporations in the world, are to a great extent responsible for environmental destruction, growing unemployment, and widening income differences.

References

Barber, B. (1995) *Jihad vs. McWorld*. New York: Times Books.
Beck, U. (1992) *Risk Society. Towards a New Modernity*. London: Sage.

Brown, C. (1992) *International Relations Theory: New Normative Approaches*. New York: Harvester.

Donnelly, J. and R. Howard (1988) 'Assessing national human rights performance: a theoretical framework', *Human Rights Quarterly* 10 (2): 214–48.

Hamelink, C.J. (1994) *The Politics of World Communication*. London: Sage.

Hannikainen, L. (1988) *Peremptory Norms in International Law*. Helsinki: Finnish Lawyers Publishing Company.

Kuttner, R. (1997) *Everything for Sale. The Virtues and Limits of Markets*. New York: Alfred A. Knopf.

Leslie, J. (1996) *The End of the World. The Science and Ethics of Human Extinction*. London: Routledge.

McQuail, D. (1983) *Mass Communication Theory*. London: Sage.

Neville, R.C. (1995) *Normative Cultures*. New York: State University of New York Press.

Perez de Cuellar, J. (1995) *Our Creative Diversity. Report of the World Commission on Culture and Development*. Paris: UNESCO.

Reinders, J.S. (1995) 'Human rights from the perspective of a narrow conception of religious morality', in A.A. An-Na'Im, J.D. Gort, H. Jansen and H.M. Vroom (eds) *Human Rights and Religious Values*. Grand Rapids: William B. Eerdmans, pp. 3–23.

Skutnabb-Kangas, T. and Phillipson, R. (1997) 'Linguistic human rights and development', in C.J. Hamelink (ed.) *Ethics and Development*. Kampen: Kok, pp. 56–69.

Stavenhagen, R. (1995) 'Cultural rights and universal human rights', in A. Eide, C. Krause and A. Rosas (eds) *Economic, Social and Cultural Rights*. Dordrecht: Martinus Nijhoff, pp. 63–78.

Vroom, H.M. (1995) 'Religious ways of life and human rights', in A.A. An-Na'Im, J.D. Gort, H. Jansen and H.M. Vroom (eds) *Human Rights and Religious Values*. Grand Rapids: William B. Eerdmans, pp. 24–42.

Waart, P. de (1995) 'International order and human rights: a matter of good governance', in A.A. An-Na'Im, J.D. Gort, H. Jansen and H.M. Vroom (eds) *Human Rights and Religious Values*. Grand Rapids: William B. Eerdmans, pp. 45–61.

8

The Performance of the Sponge: Mass Communication Theory Enters the Postmodern World

Ien Ang

Denis McQuail once characterized himself to me as a sponge. What he meant by this was that he felt he did not have much original to say; that his strength lay in absorbing and synthesizing other people's ideas and insights. And indeed, what has made his voluminous and important work in mass communication theory distinctive over the years is its tremendous capacity to process and summarize novel information and ideas, whether these be new theoretical paradigms and perspectives, social trends, empirical findings, or recent developments in media policy, technology and culture. What makes a book such as *Mass Communication Theory* so unique – and so eminently useful – is the way it manages to integrate the enormous and enormously varied amount of scholarship which has been produced in more than 50 years of mass communication research. The performance of the sponge is realized by this propensity towards absorbing inclusiveness.

But the absorbing capacity of the sponge cannot be limitless. At one point the sponge will start to leak. McQuail's latest and, arguably, most ambitious work, *Media Performance*, demonstrates the paradox generated by his preoccupation with comprehensiveness in his examination of 'past and present ideas of what counts as being in the public interest, as far as mass media are concerned' (1992: 1). McQuail has embarked on this project out of a deep commitment to the advancement of the mass media's role in serving the public good, 'in the slow journey towards a more just and decent society' (1992: xvi). However, McQuail's encyclopaedic effort to produce as complete a picture as possible of what he calls 'media performance assessment' ultimately reinforces a deep realization of the complexity and, to a great extent, intractability of the project. I want to suggest that this realization is more than eerily in line with a postmodern sensibility – a characterization I suspect McQuail himself would only grudgingly own up to.

'Postmodernism' has developed a bad reputation in communication research circles. It is often dismissed as lacking in responsibility and seriousness, as irresponsible and indifferent towards truth, justice, and other morally respectable modern goals. For many communication researchers who consider themselves the guardians of accountable scholarship, the postmodern raises the spectre of ideological vacuousness, stylistic excess, playful irreverence, and uncritical celebration of commercial popular culture, as well as an 'anything goes' mentality, a nihilistic relativism when it comes to tried-and-tested values, standards and forms of knowledge. But this is a one-sided, and often facile, dismissal and characterization of the postmodern which, ironically, underestimates the seriousness and consequentiality of the so-called 'postmodern condition'.

At the very least, a distinction needs to be made between conservative and critical postmodernism as an intellectual attitude (as made, for example, by Huyssen, 1986): while the former does indeed succumb to an 'anything goes' attitude (and therefore indulges in a happy surrender to all the seductions of postmodern culture), I would argue that the latter, critical postmodernism, is motivated by a deep understanding of the limits and failures of what Habermas calls the 'unfinished project of modernity', and by the need to respond to these limits and failures not through a forced extension of modernist ways of thinking, but through a sceptical questioning of the certainties and absolutisms of those ways of thinking. In this regard the distinction between postmodern*ism* and postmodern*ity* is an important one: while one can refuse to be a postmodernist and remain loyal to the more secure convictions of modernism instead, one cannot, to all intents and purposes, deny or escape the reality of postmodernity, which, as an over-all term, describes some of the social, political and cultural quandaries of the current world-historical condition. As Zygmunt Bauman (1991: 272) rather dramatically puts it, postmodernity is modernity coming of age, modernity coming to terms with its own impossibility: 'Postmodernity is no more (but no less either) than the modern mind taking a long, attentive and sober look at itself, at its condition and its past works, not fully liking what it sees and sensing the urge to change.' The (critical) postmodern sensibility, in short, is a response to the failure of modernity to live up to its own ideals and ambitions (including those of 'progress' towards a more 'just and decent society'), not by discarding those ideals and ambitions altogether but by recognizing and accepting the profound ambivalence involved in their pursuit (Bauman, 1991). Seen this way, Denis McQuail's adoption of a postmodern perspective in his engagement with (the fate of) mass communication theory, if reluctantly, will turn out not to be so surprising at all.

The media as (defective) meaning machine

Anyone working in the field of mass communication scholarship knows how explosive its growth has been, especially since the late 1960s. In the last 20 years or so the field of communication studies has also become a highly quarrelsome one, as new players have entered the field with a baggage of concepts, theories, questions and methods which were rather alien, if not anathema to the predominantly social science-based establishment. In the American context for example, where the social science tradition has been dominant from the emergence of mass communication research as a specialist area of study in the 1930s (the word 'discipline' was never quite appropriate for it despite the ambitions of the 'founding fathers' to pronounce the field's status as one), the struggle over parameters and paradigms for doing communication research was highlighted with the appearance of a special issue of the *Journal of Communication* in 1983, significantly titled 'Ferment in the Field' – a ferment in which so-called 'critical' approaches (influenced by diverse forms of reinvigorated marxism, feminism and culturalism) played a key role.

In *Mass Communication Theory*, which has seen three revised editions (appearing in 1983, 1987 and 1994 respectively), McQuail, whose own intellectual background is generally in a pluralist and empirical kind of media sociology, exhibits a tireless attempt, sponge-like, to update the map of the increasingly diverse and complex field, that is, to absorb the differences of opinion and the struggle over the field's meaning by integrating them in an overarching and comprehensive overview. As a student and junior colleague of Denis, I benefited greatly from this sponge performance: its underlying generosity of spirit made it possible, for example, for me to write a thesis under his supervision working with theoretical assumptions and analytical interests which departed greatly from his own. I would also argue that it was to a large extent Denis' inclusive and democratic sponge ethic which enabled a group of lecturers in the Department of Communication of the University of Amsterdam to develop and teach a broad introductory course in communication studies together despite our virtually unbridgeable differences (the positions represented within the group ranged from that of a hardnosed positivist information scientist to that of a radically anti-positivist, critical-cultural theorist). In this context McQuail's *Mass Communication Theory*, the second edition of which we used as a textbook, could serve, by its sheer (ambition towards) comprehensiveness, as a more or less impartial middle ground. Indeed, I am pleased to see that the latest, third edition of *Mass Communication Theory* (1994) bears the clear marks of this odd meeting of minds: in comparison with the second edition, there is a much more balanced summary and synthesis of both 'dominant' and 'alternative' paradigms, of the contributions of both 'culturalists' and 'scientific-empiricists'. Yet the balancing act and open-mindedness needed to hold these different, often conflicting positions and perspectives together is not an easy one and, I would argue, it has not left McQuail's own take on things unchallenged and unchanged. In other words, the sponge cannot remain neutral; it is affected by what it absorbs.

For the sake of simplification, 'semiotics' can perhaps be identified as the position here – semiotics not defined as the structuralist 'science of signs' (which we can quite justifiably consider a failed project) but as a shorthand term for the fundamental *problematization of meaning* (its production, its politics, its power) which has revolutionized the study of media and mass communications. What a semiotic perspective generally foregrounds is that meanings are not fixed or natural, nor objectively determinable through some scientific method, but are continuously produced, negotiated and contested in the thick of social and political life (from which mass communication scholars are not extracted). Thus, the notion of 'struggle over meaning' has become central in the study of media and mass communications, especially in the 'critical' variety of the craft. In my own development as a media studies scholar, the British cultural studies tradition led by Stuart Hall had a formative influence, the gist of which is marked in the title of Hall's (1982) path-breaking article, 'The rediscovery of "ideology": return of the repressed in media studies'. While Hall's particular brand of theoretical (post)marxism may not find universal agreement, what is important in Hall's foregrounding of the 'ideological' is precisely that it launches the study of the media squarely (back) into the arena of social and political struggles over meaning. This meant not only that the study of media and communications could not be separated from the study of history, society and culture, but also, more importantly, that the role of the media was now explicitly theorized in terms of their importance as sites and vehicles of meaning, production and consumption.

In the third edition of *Mass Communication Theory*, McQuail expresses his appreciation for this perspective by characterizing the media, in characteristic succinctness, as a '(defective) meaning machine'. As he says:

> One of the least ambiguous results of revised or alternative paradigms is the conclusion that mass communication is centrally about the giving and taking of meaning, although the outcomes are enormously varied and unpredictable. (1994: 379)

It is important to signal McQuail's emphasis on the *defectiveness* of the media as meaning machine:

> In part this inefficiency stems from the multiplicity of purposes served by the mass media, but it also derives from the lack of fixed or unitary meanings in any media 'text' or 'message', whatever the intention of a sender might be, or the shaping by rules of language and discourse. . . . Most fundamentally, this uncertainty derives from the essentially creative, interactive, and open-ended nature of communication, in which meaningful outcomes are always negotiated and unpredictable. (ibid.)

Interestingly, the paradox of the sponge can also be described in terms of the defectiveness of meaning-making. After all, the inclusive logic of the sponge is also a communicative logic: as mentioned above, McQuail's work is a superb instance not only of the bringing together, but also the putting into dialogue of different paradigms and perspectives, with the implicitly anticipated promise of an integrative synthesis. But any attempt to be inclusive will sooner or later run into the problem of how to manage the diverse points of view so carefully brought together. This is because greater comprehensiveness will also lead to greater heterogeneity, to a more frequent occurrence of unprocessed (and unprocessable) differences, and therefore, of necessity, to an intensification of uncertainty of, if not struggle over, meaning. Here, then, the sponge confronts the contradictory limits to its performance: as the world becomes ever more complex and diverse, the very effort to be comprehensive and to include all becomes not only more herculean, but also beset with greater uncertainty, instability, contention.

In *Media Performance* McQuail himself is acutely aware of – and affected by – this, arguably very postmodern, predicament. Time and again he refers to the 'contestation' and 'confusion' which besets the enterprise of 'media assessment'. Even as McQuail's (modernist) ambition is to develop 'as comprehensive a framework of normative principle as possible' (1992: 17) by way of objective and systematic methods of research, he acknowledges 'the uncertainty and ambiguity of the enterprise of performance assessment' (1992: 11). There is not even a clear and solid set of definitions on which the enterprise can be securely based:

> On most matters, there is no objective way of determining the 'correct' identification and it is impossible, in general, to say when and where the activities of mass media belong to the public or the private sphere, and thus whether or not they are proper matters of public concern. This allocation can only be made in specific cases according to subjectively chosen criteria. (McQuail, 1992: 2)

The struggle over meaning presents itself very clearly here: there can be no objective, a priori assumption about exactly what needs to be assessed, what 'good' performance might be, even what specifically might count as 'in the public interest' (1992: 11). Issues of media 'quality' and 'diversity' for example, so routinely brought up in media policy discourse as stated aims to be pursued, are matters of public debate; how they come to be defined and made to mean in particular contexts is a matter of social construction, often the object of major disagreement and heated contestation among interested parties.

Take 'quality', arguably one of the vaguest but most powerful terms used in media policy discourse as 'a good thing'. It can be defined in traditional aesthetic terms (and thus related to concepts of 'taste'), in professional terms (e.g. related to 'production values'), in broader cultural terms (e.g. in terms of social representativeness) or, for that matter, in terms of audience appreciation (in which case 'quality' is articulated with 'popularity'). The fact that there are different ways of defining 'quality' and that different definitions are not innocent in their political and policy implications is not often explicitly acknowledged; in other words, the 'subjectively chosen criteria' McQuail refers to are not often made explicit as such. Instead preferred definitions are often presented in objectivist terms, as if they represented universal public truths. To put it another way, dominant discourses of 'quality' are often so taken for granted as 'true' in particular contexts that they appear to be natural.

For a long time this has been the case, of course, with the 'high culture' concept of 'quality'. European defences of public service broadcasting for example have often pivoted around the presumably absolute and universal superiority of what has been constructed as 'high culture'. This modernist stance – exemplified in the world of public broadcasting in the civilizing mission of the well-known Reithean ethos – has been increasingly eroded by the emergence of competing assertions of cultural value. The feminist work on soap opera and other forms of popular culture is a case in point. The issue in this work is not, as has been mistakenly argued by some of its modernist critics, to suggest that soap operas are 'as good as', say, Shakespeare, but rather that the value of soaps should be looked at within the context of viewers' experiences and understandings of their lives, and how particular soaps – they are not all the same – manage to articulate those experiences and understandings in particularly meaningful and astute ways. This is a discourse of 'quality' which emphasizes different criteria of value from the discourse of high culture, one that leads to different judgements and assessments.

The point is not that recognizing such differences will make us slide into a morass of cultural relativism and nihilism (as anti-postmodernists often argue), but that with the emergence of such alternative discourses of quality what counts or should count as 'value' and 'quality' has become explicitly politicized, the object of social contestation and negotiation. Accepting such a point of view emphatically does *not* imply a declaration of bankruptcy to the project of public service broadcasting as such (as is often suggested), but it does mean that its cultural legitimatization needs to be rethought and argued over in light of the emergent contestations over 'value' – a process, incidentally, already begun in many western countries as public service broadcasting, one of the key institutions of state modernism, is forced to face the changed circumstances emanating from social and cultural postmodernization (see e.g. Hawkins, 1997, for a good Australian reflection on these issues).

Bridging the administrative and the critical

These changed circumstances, of course, do not make it any easier for the assessor of the performance of media output. The difficulty, observes McQuail, lies in the fact that '"society", in whose interest assessment is conducted, is least likely to speak directly for itself with a single identifiable voice' (1992: 11). Indeed, in an increasingly postmodernized world the number and diversity of voices is constantly proliferating. Throughout, the developed western world especially has seen an unravelling of (illusions of a) national consensus and unitary understandings of citizenship and society in the last 30 or so years; the notion of a 'common culture' has been subverted by the emergence on the social scene of an ever greater range of identities, subjectivities and groups, emphasizing and asserting their right to cultural difference rather than sameness. The currency of notions of 'multiculturalism' is only one marker, despite the increasing power of the forces of globalization, for the irrevocable social, political and cultural pluralization of the contemporary world (Connolly, 1995; McLennan, 1995).

In such a world, the construction of a single, universal 'truth' on whose behalf any assessment of media performance (and subsequent policy formulation) can be made is highly unlikely. This drives McQuail to conclude that 'the days of unitary, normative theories are (or should be) over' (1992: 17) – a statement echoing Lyotard's (1984) famous declaration of the demise of grand-master narratives as characteristic of the postmodern condition. Does this mean then that McQuail is a postmodernist? Answering this question with a simple yes or no is perhaps not a useful exercise given the complex and controversial range of meanings the term 'postmodern' has come to connote, as we have seen. But it is certainly the case that McQuail, precisely because of his preparedness to include all perspectives and to look at things from multiple points of view, cannot escape a sense of undecidedness and indeterminacy which is so central to the (critical) postmodern sensibility (cf. Ang, 1996, Chapter 10). In a minimal sense, postmodernism can be described as 'the generalized affirmation of pluralism and heterogeneity' (McLennan, 1995: 21). From such an affirmation, McLennan further notes, comes 'the acceptance of ambivalence, hybridity and hesitation as legitimate aspects of intellectual and political endeavour today' (1995: 22). In this sense, the performance of the sponge is surprisingly closely related to a postmodern ethic, inasmuch as it is based on an openness and a deep realization of the provisional nature of all knowledge. As McLennan (1995: 23) puts it, '(p)erhaps the ultimate contribution of postmodernism is simply to loosen up that sense of intellectual "completion" [associated with modernist logic] and the rigid mental-moral set that goes along with it'.

The consequences of this, perhaps unintentionally induced, postmodern ethos for the practice of media performance assessment itself are dramatic, and it is here that McQuail shows a reluctance to go all the way (on the postmodern road). While he is acutely aware of the difficulty of setting objective performance standards, he still wants to keep faith in the possibility of social science-based, systematic and objective research in order to come to independent assessments of mass media provisions and services. Independent, that is, from 'the self-chosen goals and interests of the media, although taking account of their aims and necessary conditions of operation' (1992: 16). Securing such an independent stance from which the performance of mass media in contemporary society can be assessed and evaluated is clearly an important political aim at a time when the institutions of the media, both public and private, are becoming increasingly powerful and influential at both global and national levels. If the notion of 'the public interest' (however defined) is to remain at all relevant in the decision-making processes within these institutions, an 'independent' point of view is needed from which legitimate and authoritative discourses can be produced able to influence those processes. McQuail reckons that the deployment of social science research strategies, with their emphasis on value neutrality, the search for general outcomes, and systematic (mostly quantitative) data collection methods, provides the best instruments to 'meet the typical requirements of public policy debate, formulation, and evaluation' (1992: 17). Social science research, he continues,

> should have the best chance of communicating relevant and dependable evidence to the main parties to such debates – usually legislators, politicians, governments, 'opinion makers', the media themselves and the general public – and thus the best chance of influencing public policy or the self-chosen aims and conduct of the media themselves. (ibid.)

In this sense, the whole purpose of *Media Performance* can be seen as 'seeking to bridge the gap between normative (and thus subjective) standards and objective research' (ibid.). McQuail, in short, is trying to carve out a space for a viable 'administrative-critical' approach to research, one that combines the purposes of critique and that of policy or governance, thereby overcoming the opposition between 'administrative' and 'critical' research so famously established by Lazarsfeld.

But in the book's conclusion, McQuail remarks that with the growth and diversification of the mass media the agenda of questions about the media's performance grows longer rather than shorter – a growth, he observes, not matched by an increased capacity of research to arbitrate on these questions. And I sense that McQuail is quietly despairing of this. He notes that much of the research being undertaken is still guided by outmoded models of mass communication, based on out-of-date asssumptions of limited supply, homogeneous content and passive mass audiences. These assumptions, so deeply entrenched in the social science tradition of communication research (for which the linearity of the transmission model has been paradigmatic [Carey, 1989]), are clearly no longer adequate to describe the current, postmodern media environment. As McQuail notes: 'The problem has become, first of all, one of scale and complexity; secondly, one of assigning relative significance to the multiplicity of media supply. There are too many possible channels and sources to analyse and their relative salience is too variable and hard to assess' (1992: 312). Furthermore, he remarks that '(p)erformance research has hardly caught up with the rise of video and sound recording' and he calls for the development of problem definitions and research approaches which go beyond those 'shaped by rational-informational models appropriate to "linear" print media' (McQuail 1992: 313). 'Without progress on this', he warns, 'performance assessment will, increasingly, have a ritual character and be irrelevant to key features of public experience' (ibid.).

In the end, however, there is the clear sense of a diminished capacity, not only for the kind of 'administrative-critical' research practice McQuail advocates, but for the very idea of influencing the conduct of media institutions (which forms the rationale for the research in the first place). The ideology of the market has become increasingly hegemonic in this era of rampant economic rationalism, rapid technological change, and cultural fragmentation. Thus:

> It is probably safe to conclude . . . that direct and large-scale public intervention in media performance, on grounds of public policy becomes less rather than more likely, even if regulation of structures continues. In place of direct control, we are likely to see more reliance on self-regulation and on the informal effects of public or pressure group demands. (McQuail, 1992: 314)

The postmodern predicament

The question is what role research can play in more informal and self-regulatory forms of control over the media's performance. In asking this question I do not want to deny the indisputable fact that social research (of the empirical, systematic and 'objective' kind) is often a very useful, even indispensable bureaucratic instrument in the management and regulation of any modern institution (media institutions included), although, as I have expounded at length elsewhere (Ang, 1991), I am much more sceptical than McQuail about the effectiveness of much research in constructing agreed-upon administrative 'truths'. It is in this sense that Denis is much more reluctantly postmodern that I am.

There is at least one area in which I believe McQuail still seems to claim too much for the effectiveness of research in influencing public perception and policy. Thus he says: 'Although there is still life in the demands that media avoid harm to the young and vulnerable, especially through violence and pornography, the claim of a direct, causal connection between media and behaviour has lost credibility' (1992: 307). Yet despite the sustained debunking of such direct, causal connections between media violence and 'real' violence in decades of careful scientific research, the moral panic around media violence seems to have only increased in recent years. In this context, calls for censorship and bans have resulted in restrictive government rulings (such as the introduction of the V-chip in all television sets in the United States) in the name of a 'public interest' defined as such by highly vocal pressure groups (such as parent associations and religious groups) who, more often than not, do not care much about the complex arguments made by researchers. In other words, (calls for) intervention are still made, though not necessarily formulated through the empirically informed discourse of social science research – on the contrary, at moments of intense crisis the media are still, for better or worse, resorted to as scapegoats for all the violence and terror raging in contemporary society.

When, on a quiet Sunday in April 1996, a lone and reclusive young man, Martin Bryant, took up his shotgun and randomly gunned down 35 unsuspecting tourists and locals in a café in Tasmania, Australia, the government's response, in tandem with the public outcry and shock over the event, was increased gun control and, predictably, the curtailment of media violence. McQuail (1992: 315) argues that '[i]t is no longer feasible simply to invoke absolute value or an authority which can establish some desired condition and police subsequent performance', and that in this context 'media performance research should . . . provide the *information* which can inform public or policy choices'. But in the case of violence and the media (including sexual violence as in pornography) moral or emotive considerations can take on such highly charged meaning that the dispassionate information imparted by research seems to be reduced to irrelevance and insignificance.

Where does all this leave the project of media performance assessment as McQuail envisages it? Wouldn't all the considerations above only lead to a profound pessimism? Admirably, McQuail resists succumbing to an understandable but all too easy defeatism – in this sense, McQuail is an exemplary practitioner of Gramsci's call for a 'pessimism of the intellect and optimism of the will'. Perhaps it is precisely the performance of the sponge which makes him hold out for the possibility, if ever so modest, of some contribution to a 'better' politics of media arrangements. One key attitude he wishes to promote in this is a sense of realism, a sense of recognizing the (postmodern) realities of contemporary media culture rather than imposing lofty but unrealistic norms and expectations on it. Wryly, he notes that media critics and researchers, speaking in the name of their own more or less highminded construction of 'the public interest', often ignore 'much of what the mass media are actually doing most of the time, which is to entertain, divert and catch the eye for no particularly noble purpose or even for no purpose at all' (1992: 301). Here again, McQuail's astute awareness of the ironies of the postmodern condition – the notion that in advanced capitalist societies media production is more often than not a matter of 'show business' driven not by the intent of meaningful communication but by spectacle and display (see e.g. Baudrillard, 1983) – impinges on his perception of the (im)possibilities of media performance assessment as a critical-administrative endeavour.

In fact, so McQuail continues, given the necessity for a very large part of the media industry to operate in the so-called 'publicity model' (McQuail, 1994: 51) in which their interest is first and foremost in gaining attention for the messages and images they display, their performance is not too bad at all: for all the criticism levelled at the media from many corners of 'society', there is still a lot of 'quality' in the content and services they provide, whether these be news or television drama. This, then, is McQuail's down-to-earth, characteristically generous, and perhaps unexpectedly positive 'verdict' on the overall performance of the media today. But he is under no illusion that as an evaluatory statement this verdict will be accepted as in any sense socially satisfactory or politically effective. He even concedes that as an 'interim assessment' it 'has no great authority and certainly does not stand for all places and times' (1992: 302). As a result, he has to conclude that 'no balance of evaluation can ever be struck and assessment has to be a continuing process' (ibid.).

As a conclusion, this is as far as one can get if one is sensitive and responsive to the dilemmas and complexities of the postmodern predicament, although of course, if we are to keep the radical excesses of postmodernist thinking at bay, this conclusion itself will have to be treated as a provisional one. The prospect that assessment has to be a continuing, ongoing process should not prevent us from *making* and *voicing* particular assessments at particular moments, when the political and social circumstances call for them – this, after all, is the task of public intellectuals whether or not they deploy social science discourse to legitimize their discourse. And to a great extent it is the openmindedness and liberality of the sponge – ever receptive of what the conjunctural present calls for, even if it can absorb no more – which is best suited to the scholar's sense of social responsibility in this postmodern era, in which meaning must be fought for in the face of the rampant lack or insufficiency of meaning. It is the urgency of this struggle *for*, as well as *over* meaning which in the end, behind his commitment to science and scholarship, impassions Denis McQuail's work. As he puts it:

> The mass media themselves are organized in no postmodern spirit, whatever may be said of their content. Issues of gender definition, cultural identity, inequality, racism, environmental damage, world hunger and social chaos are examples of problems of rising salience and concern in which the media are deeply implicated, just because of their enhanced role in the organization of national and global society. (McQuail, 1994: 60)

However, while in the past modernist formulas (of reason, science, management) would have been evoked to address these persistent social problems, today the realization that '[t]he current condition is one of tension between an expanding media world and a shrinking capacity by "society" to control it' (McQuail, 1997: 40) fuels a sadder but wiser perspective. Postmodern wisdom, says Bauman (1993: 245), consists in an awareness of the fact 'that there are problems in human and social life with no good solutions, twisted trajectories that cannot be straightened up, . . . moral agonies which no reason-dictated recipes can soothe, let alone cure'. It is 'reconciled to the idea that the messiness of the human predicament is here to stay'. It is the struggle against the sense of impotence and cynicism so easily aroused by this postmodern wisdom that the world needs most as the twentieth century – the century in which the edifice of modernity reached its apex before revealing its inevitable cracks – draws to a close.

References

Ang, Ien (1991) *Desperately Seeking the Audience*. London: Routledge.

Ang, Ien (1996) 'In the realm of uncertainty: the global village and capitalist postmodernity', in I. Ang *Living Room Wars: Rethinking Media Audiences for a Postmodern World*. London: Routledge.

Baudrillard, Jean (1983) *Simulations*. New York: Semiotext(e).

Bauman, Zygmunt (1991) *Modernity and Ambivalence*. Cambridge: Polity Press.

Bauman, Zygmunt (1993) *Postmodern Ethics.* Oxford: Blackwell.

Carey, J. (1989) *Communication as Culture.* Boston, MA: Unwin Hyman.

Connolly, William (1995) *The Ethos of Pluralization.* Minneapolis: University of Minnesota Press.

Hall, Stuart (1982) 'The rediscovery of "ideology": return of the repressed in media studies', in M. Gurevitch, T. Bennett, J. Curran and S. Woollacott (eds) *Culture, Society and the Media.* London: Methuen, pp. 56–90.

Hawkins, Gay (1997) 'The ABC and the mystic writing pad', *Media International Australia*, 83 (February): 11–17.

Huyssen, Andreas (1986) *After the Great Divide.* Minneapolis: University of Minnesota Press.

Lyotard, Jean-François (1984) *The Postmodern Condition: A Report on Knowledge.* Trans. G. Bennington and B. Massumi. Minneapolis: University of Minnesota Press.

McLennan, Gregor (1995) *Pluralism.* Buckingham: Open University Press.

McQuail, Denis (1992) *Media Performance: Mass Communication and the Public Interest.* London: Sage.

McQuail, Denis (1994) *Mass Communication Theory: An Introduction*, 3rd edn. London: Sage.

McQuail, Denis (1997) 'Policy help wanted: willing and able culturalists please apply', in M. Ferguson and P. Golding (eds) *Cultural Studies in Question.* London: Sage, pp. 39–55.

III THE ETHICS OF POPULAR JOURNALISM

9

Enhancing the Civic Ideal in Television Journalism

Peter Dahlgren

The self-confidence of the Western European democracies has certainly seen better days. With economies in retreat, official political institutions moribund, and with leaders lacking compelling visions for national or transnational futures, many people are worried. They wonder if their democratic systems are capable of successfully dealing with the contemporary historical situation. A sense of having reached an impasse, a watershed in the history of democratic societies seems to be growing. Popular trust in major societal institutions is markedly low in many countries. In regard to people's involvement with the established political parties we see a continual decline, a pattern which strongly correlates with age and thus gives all the more cause for concern about the future. Particularly in comparison to the transnational corporate sector or the domain of technical innovation, the official political arenas appear stagnant.

And yet, despite these trends, we can also witness energetic involvement in many sorts of social, political, cultural and humanitarian efforts, reflecting an array of societal perspectives and political thinking. Movements, organizations, networks, and local groups of all kinds (including also anti-democratic forces) reveal widespread concern and willingness to take various forms of action, suggesting an emerging change in how politics is understood (Mulgan, 1994). Even if these social actors represent only a small minority of the populations of Western European societies, they indicate that despite the low level of inspiration from the official political realm, the capitulation to apathy or the retreat to the purely private sphere is far from total. There is still a democratic reserve on which society can draw.

The current dilemmas of late modern society in general, and their democratic systems in particular, are complex and overdetermined by many factors. And while we must be cautious not least of lapsing into an overly mediacentric understanding of the present era, the importance of the media in this problematic situation is beyond dispute. And television, as the core institution of public life in our societies, has a privileged position, as Denis McQuail (1997) argues in a recent overview of different research perspectives on the medium. What I want to explore here is the possibility that we might be able to conceptually define – and normatively encourage – a shift, or at least a complement, in the societal role television journalism might play. The trajectory of the changes I envision can be captured by the term 'the civic ideal'.

One of the important tasks for television journalism (and we must of course think in terms of a plurality of tasks) in the present context is precisely to enhance our societies' democratic capacity by helping to develop our self-confidence as citizens. A fortified civic self-confidence is no guarantee that we will solve all our dilemmas, but a civic body which has a strong sense of its own efficacy is undeniably a crucial democratic resource. Is television capable of this and can this medium, this pleasure machine, help us become better citizens? I am not sure. Is there not a contradiction between such a 'serious' goal and the (increasingly) entertainment orientation of the medium? Probably. I have no general recipes to offer – nor even concrete programme suggestions. That is better left to experienced television professionals. Yet I think it is important that we begin to discuss in a thoughtful way what a revitalized television journalism might do to help augment, even in small ways, our faith in ourselves to address the current difficulties. The discussion which follows is in three parts: first I try to specify the concept of the civic ideal, then I probe some of the relevant factors within current television journalism which might influence its implementation. I conclude with some reflections on the movement presently afoot in the United States known as 'civic journalism' or 'public journalism' and what it might mean for European television.

The civic ideal: identities and engagement

By the civic ideal I refer to the involvement of citizens in civil and political society; the civic ideal reminds us that democracy is predicated on people's participation in their society, and declining participation inevitably means a declining democracy. Clearly we need to be sociologically realistic: we cannot expect that everyone will involve themselves in some way in social or political activities outside their home. At any moment in time, those people who might be categorized as engaged citizens may well be a minority; in a democracy people must also have the right not to be involved. Yet cultural climates which systematically disinvite participation, or power constellations which ensure that involvement is marginalized in its extent and impact, will undermine democracy's potential.

In a recent collection of work they have done on political communication systems in the UK and US, Jay Blumler and Michael Gurevitch list some of the components contributing to what they call the crisis of communication for citizenship (1995: 213–14). They identify a process of depoliticization in media coverage of politics, whereby the media's focus on personalities, events and scandals coupled with politics-as-sports style of coverage dominate over substantial coverage of policies. They see a declining usefulness of political communication for citizens as the length of soundbites and visual cuts in television coverage continue to shrink. Further, the nature of media coverage coupled with the way official politics is organized have led to what they see as the growing exclusion of the public from public life. This in turn correlates with another component which the authors point to, namely public cynicism: more and more people have simply ceased to believe in the discourses of the political system, its representatives, and their rhetoric. There are many versions of this diagnosis, but the basic point is that we are witnessing a corrosion of the public sphere in the media, in particular as regards television.

Blumler and Gurevitch's perspective is that of political communication systems with its emphasis on the official political arena. The vitality of this domain is of course paramount for the health of democracy. However, in keeping with the theoretical discussions on the civil society–state–citizenship complex that have emerged in recent years (cf. Cohen and Arato, 1992; Hall, 1995; Keane, 1988; Turner, 1993) I would suggest that we go further and treat citizenship as central to both political and civil society. The development of democracy is dependent upon a productive interplay between civil society and political society/the state. A democratic state needs the continual input of democratic norms and processes from the value systems which must permeate the everyday lives of people in civil society. Civil society includes the vast terrain of domestic life, associations, organizations, social movements and other forms of sociability and collective effort outside of the state and the corporate sector. It consists, in other words, of the institutions of the everyday world where people live their lives. Such a civil society in turn needs robust institutional support and clear legal guarantees from the state if it is to thrive. As I indicated above, today we witness considerable societal involvement in this domain, not least in the form of extra-parliamentarian political activity, even if the exact extent of this involvement is difficult to specify.

Citizenship and civic communication are thus relevant for the entire social terrain, not just for the formal political arena and its elections. Democracy, in other words, is not only about official politics, but also has to do with the norms and horizons of everyday life and culture. If we take a further theoretical step or two, we can see how the notion of citizen articulates with recent work on identity politics. There has been a good deal of discussion about the processes of identity in pluralistic, multicultural societies (cf. Calhoun, 1994; Rajchman, 1995) and the notion of citizenship has been problematized around such themes as national identity (cf. Spinner, 1994) and the nature of national journalism in the era of globalization (cf. Price, 1995). What these and related work suggest to us is that citizenship must be understood not just as a formal or legal category, but also as a dimension of people's composite identities. Citizenship thus becomes one of a number of subject positions that people can negotiate and assume in given situations. We can see this in terms of a systemic necessity: if democracy is to work, people must be able to see themselves – in relevant contexts – as members and potential participants in the society to which they belong. They need to internalize and develop – at least to a minimal degree – a loyalty towards the norms and procedures of democracy.

For people to see themselves in universalistic terms as citizens of nation states is by no means in opposition to the vision of a pluralistic or multi-cultural society (I will leave aside for the moment issues of 'global citizenship', as well as the premature forecasts of the eclipse of the nation state). On the contrary, as several authors argue in a collection edited by Chantal Mouffe (1992), people's identities as citizens and their loyalty to democratic norms and procedures are a basic common ground for holding the whole enterprise together. Their citizenship becomes a minimalist cohesion which permits not only difference by subject positions such as gender and race, but also allows people to pursue different and often conflicting interests. At the same time, we should not expect or even strive for a 'one size fits all' citizenship: a pluralistic society should contain many different forms of public discourse, with many registers and inflections, and thus 'angle' citizenship in a variety of ways. In the real world there is no all-inclusive consensus on the exact components of citizenship; citizenship's specificity is often contested, which we in turn can (in our optimistic moments) view as a healthy sign. Final closure per se is not something which would serve democracy in the long run.

Thus, citizenship as a form of identity and engagement which can potentially be focused anywhere on the social terrain, not just on official politics, is a central element of the civic ideal. The civic ideal also requires that citizens have access to the information, discussions and debates they need to reflect upon current affairs in order to develop their political views. Classical journalism in liberal democracies has always defined these aspects as central to its duties. One could say that the civic ideal places a more ambitious demand on classical journalism: while it includes the traditional journalistic goals, it also emphasizes the need to actively promote citizens' identities and their social engagement.

Confronting obstacles

To suggest that television journalism might address the crisis of civic com-munication may seem odd. Television itself has often been accused of contributing to the decline of civic involvement; an argument that has recently been given a controversial American version (Putnam, 1995; see also Putnam, 1996). Without getting involved in that particular discussion, I would say that television no doubt does contribute to a retreat from the public to the private sphere, but that this need not be an automatic or total retreat. Television can also engage and mobilize. And as I indicated above, the contemporary low level of democratic participation and general societal involvement are shaped by complex forces and cannot merely be laid at television's door generally or its journalism specifically. Rather, the question is whether television can change, however slightly, and make a social difference. I would maintain that the medium has not yet lost this potential, limited though it may be. Television is a tricky medium and can do many things, including, perhaps – given the right circumstances – generating societal involvement and conveying a sense of citizenship.

To encourage television journalism to take seriously the civic ideal of enhanced citizen involvement and to try to promote it in various ways in its programming is not to propose a major revolution in television journalism. Rather, it is only to advocate that a particular dimension which is at least implicit in the commitment to public service, be given further attention, time, and resources. The civic ideal can be seen as falling within the domain of a robust public service commitment, given the inexorable link between the concept of public service and the notion of citizenship (Murdock, 1990). I am of the view that despite all the ills of the medium that we can itemize and all the institutional logic that we can mobilize to explain why television looks the way it does, there are still good programmes being made, even some quite impressive ones. Further, there are many people working in television who want nothing other than to see not only an improved performance of their medium, but also an enhancement of societal well-being. In short, there are still many broadcast journalists and producers who take the fundamental mission of public service seriously, and in the world of television this is still our best bet, despite all the obstacles.

However, there are obviously major issues to confront here. One has to do with the crises of the 1980s and 1990s. While the crises have been real, we should be careful about lapsing into a caricaturized view of public service broadcasting today as merely an enfeebled shadow of its former self. Certainly the circumstances vary between different countries, but closer inspection suggests that in many places, public service is not doing all that badly. This seems to be the perspective now emerging, for example, in the Nordic countries (cf. Søndergaard, 1996). The last decade and a half have been rather traumatic for many European public service broadcasters, and there are still large difficulties to be faced, but under the circumstances these organizations have managed fairly well to weather the storm. They still have a respectable share of the viewing audience, even if they seem to be groping to define with clarity what the actual mission of public service broadcasting is in the new situation. (And it should be recalled that even commercial stations have big financial problems; there are no guarantees for success). In short, public service television should now be able to see itself as a sturdy survivor ready to take new initiatives, to experiment with some new approaches, rather than a lame victim cautiously limping along.

Of course beyond this general state of health there lurk some more specific ongoing dilemmas, which have been an integral part of the recent crises. The notion of public service broadcasting itself is nowadays often seen as being at odds with the dominant entertainment trajectory of television in our societies, a tension amplified by the success of commercial broadcasters. Television – for producers and audiences – is increasingly about pleasure, it is argued, not about ideals which smack of paternalism, duty, effort or even social responsibility. As Ien Ang (1996) points out, public service television in Western Europe has been caught on the horns of this dilemma. They have difficulty reconciling the pleasure-seeking of real audiences with the institutional definitions of the viewer-citizens that public service is intended to serve. This dilemma is most acute precisely in the realm of journalism and current affairs programming: the traditional, 'serious' task of journalism seems increasingly at odds with the actual television practices of viewers. Even if there is a loyal core of viewers for the traditional news programmes, television is largely used as an entertainment medium by most people. Television journalism in the commercial channels is increasingly moving towards more explicitly 'popular' formats, and public service television has been developing its own, albeit somewhat more subdued, versions. Hybrid infotainment and magazine shows, tabloid news, a whole array of journalistic and quasi-journalistic talk shows, and versions of reality/reconstruction programmes have emerged in the past decade. Indeed, the distinction between journalism and non-journalism in television has become very fuzzy. Even many traditional journalism programmes have come to incorporate elements of popularization, such as increased tempo. These trends in television journalism arguably do not speak favourably for a reinvigoration of the civic ideal.

However, as I argue elsewhere (Dahlgren, 1995), popular strategies need not by definition run counter to the traditional goals of journalism; pleasure and civic usefulness need not a priori be incompatible. It is admittedly a tricky combination, and the pitfalls of the popular in terms of civic horizons are often all too apparent. Yet, given certain conditions, forms of popular television journalism can be used productively for civic goals beyond individual pleasure. Here I am thinking of the role of popular television journalism in provoking response from viewers and stimulating talk and interaction among them, a key feature for a viable public sphere. John Fiske (1989, 1992) makes such points, even if some of his claims in this context are excessive – for example, he too readily discounts the importance of the informational dimension. But he is on target in emphasizing the potential for viewer engagement: what we have seen from the more audacious popular turns in television journalism, especially on the commercial stations, is that they can be quite strong precisely on involvement. The popular formats can clearly attract and engage audiences on a large scale. They are pleasurable in many ways, and they can provoke response, stimulate the production of meaning, and enter into the popular discourses in everyday life. The basic problem is generally that the engagement that they mobilize is usually not aimed at the societal domain and the subject positions on offer do not normally coincide with the identity of citizen. The programmes normally place the viewer in a largely spectator position vis-à-vis the social world and/or position the viewer as a consumer of private pleasure.

We can on occasion see glimpses of the civic ideal in some current popular journalistic programmes. A particular interview about dealing with cancer on a talk show, a certain segment of public discussion about taxes on a studio talk show, even a sensationalist account of political corruption on a magazine show can all in various ways be important contributions. It is not so much the topics per se that convey the civic ideal, but the manner in which viewers are positioned: they are addressed as citizens who can potentially do something in the social world beyond their home, not just as spectatator-consumers. These are admittedly only glimpses – and certainly the exception – but they signal untapped potential.

If trying to go the route of the popular is a dominant trajectory, we should also be aware that popular strategies per se are no guarantee for success, either in terms of audience statistics or broader social terms. Many new programmes disappear quite rapidly; viewers are simply not captivated. More significantly, let us recall that in the crisis that Blumler and Gurevitch (1995) describe, growing public cynicism is a key feature. This cynicism is at least to a certain degree tied to the perceived debasement of public communication which follows in the wake of excessively popular (or rather, populist) strategies in television journalism. In other words, popularization does not in itself always ensure pleasure, nor does it always result even in minimal satisfaction. Moreover, serious news programmes, magazines and documentaries may be uninviting for many viewers, but there are many who do watch regularly. In Sweden, for example, each of the main newscasts on the two public service stations draws more viewers than the newscast of the commercial competitor. All this would suggest that we would be wise not to think in excessively dichotomized terms – serious or popular – in looking for possible approaches. Instead, we should keep in mind the heterogeneity of the audience and consider than any attempts to enhance the civic ideal would conceivably work with a variety of formats aimed at different target groups among viewers. Or more realistically, one could begin experimentally with a delimited target group for which a particular format is specifically developed.

'Civic journalism': lessons to be translated

The idea of promoting the civic ideal would seem to be in principle compatible with the mission and current circumstances of European public service television. As for exisiting examples, as far as I know, the only model to which such ventures could refer is the present movement of 'public journalism', or 'civic journalism', in the United States. For consistency's sake, I will use the latter term. While this requires a double translation for our purposes here – from the United States to Europe, and from the press to television, as I will discuss shortly – it is still a starting point worth looking at.

Space does not permit an extended discussion of this movement, but I will sketch some basic features. Key analytic texts on the topic are to be found in Rosen (1993, 1995) and Merrit (1995). Charity (1995) provides a practical guide to how civic journalism can be done. The movement began to take form after the 1988 presidential election, where professional self-reflection led to the conclusion that the performance of the press had reached a new all-time low and that it was time for journalism to try to develop alternative approaches. Rosen's (1995) diagnosis closely parallels that of Blumler and Gurevitch (1995), when he sounds 'alarm bells' for the press, including a 'spiritual alarm', which includes a lack of positive vision for the role of the press. He links the problems of the press to the larger dilemmas of democracy and public life.

The first step that civic journalism takes is to try to conceptually reformulate the relationship between the press and the people. Journalists are seen as having a greater responsibility for strengthening the civic culture, for rejuvenating public life. The movement is trying to build 'civic capital'. Merely 'presenting the news' is not enough. Secondly, civic journalism emphasizes establishing connections, contacts, between journalists and the communities they cover, trying to make citizens equal partners. This reorientation in journalism's norms and practices finds its expression in self-consciously different slants on news: there is an effort to focus on issues, rather than institutions, on consensus rather than conflict. There is a great effort to talk to ordinary people and not just officials, and to treat them as co-citizens, not consumers. This is expressed not least in the occasional efforts to involve citizens and journalists in an ongoing conversation about the actual aims of journalism.

The civic journalism movement is moving beyond mere positive admonishments by incorporating specific activities into its journalistic practices. To foster community connections, for example, some newspapers organize citizen focus groups, public debates and deliberative fora, where citizens can develop legislative or other recommendations and push for them in their local governments. Journalism here is moving from detachment to (what is hopefully) fair-minded participation in public life. The real core of civic journalism, however, is to be found in the over 300 projects which have been launched by newspapers. These projects can involve forms of social research, journalistic investigation, community organizing, and so on and focus on such areas as health care, education, housing and crime (see for example, Schaffer and Miller, 1995). Training for participating journalists and their papers is provided at several centres, such as the Poynter Institute and the Pew Center for Civic Journalism, and civic journalism in turn readily links up with other elements in the larger US civic movement, such as the umbrella group Civic Practices Network. Civic journalism has not surprisingly generated controversy. A number of elite newspapers such as the *New York Times* and *Washington Post* criticize the movement for engaging in boosterism, for explicit agenda-setting, and for jeopardizing the standards of objectivity in journalism. Civic journalists have of course replied that these charges are a misconception of the movement and that such claims conceal a basic refusal to take seriously the need to alter American journalism – which only serves to make the situation worse.

Could such a movement emerge in Europe? Europe comprises many political cultures with varying media circumstances. It would be difficult to say that civic journalism is a priori incompatible with any given country, given that the promotion of the civic ideal can in principle be given many varying forms of expression. Any version of civic journalism would have to be adapted to the specific historical circumstances of the country in question and its particular traditions. I would suggest that we remain open on this question until evidence suggests otherwise. Perhaps even in Europe it may more readily be developed by the press. But what about television? Is the medium by definition ill-suited for such a venture?

Television and radio journalists in the United States sometimes comment that civic journalism is merely a desperate ploy on the part of some newspapers to raise their flagging circulation figures. Alternatively, many local television stations will claim that they have always been doing civic journalism, and point to their community affairs departments, which are often separate from the news departments. However, most civic journalists would claim that the normal activities of these departments fall far short of the ideals of civic journalism. Where television has played a role it has done so in conjunction with the local press; such cooperative ventures have managed to make use of the strengths of the respective media.

Bill Silcock (1997) makes the case that there are a number of specific factors which inhibit television from involving itself in civic journalism. These have to do with, among other things, the economics and culture of the medium and the character of the journalism in television. Economically, television on the whole is doing well; there is little counterpart to the 'dying dailies', and hence little economic incentive. In terms of the medium, it is suggested that in the United States, the television public has grown too cynical to respond to any civic ideals. Also, as a television form, a civic journalism project may even appear non-professional, akin to 'open channels' where all sorts of people lacking broadcasting experience may turn up on the screen. The journalistic culture of television tends to work with short, one-off stories, and reporters with their film teams have difficulty blending among the citizens.

These are important points and should not simply be dismissed. However, it should be recalled that Silcock is describing the American situation, which means, for example, that he is talking about the economics of commercial television, where the basic criteria have to do with market success. Public service has a greater array of motivating factors. Also, it is my sense that the televisual public sphere in Europe has not yet reached the corrosive levels of cynicism observers have noted in the United States. Perhaps the biggest obstacle is the professional culture of broadcast journalism, which even in Europe has developed largely as a monological communication strategy and is normally quite socially remote from its audiences.

At the same time we should be aware that the culture of professional television journalism is in transition: the various popularization trends served to make the broadcaster/audience boundary more permeable. Despite all the problematic issues that they raise, the ubiquitous talk shows and infotainment programmes have broadened and legitimized the diversity of popular voices in the public sphere. The various 'reality television' genres, at times sordid and sensationalist, have none the less helped put many issues of the everyday world into public discourse. Another development, one waiting in the wings over the next decade, is that of digital television, which Europe (with the BBC in the forefront) as well as the United States and Japan, is hoping to launch in the next few years. While commentators often focus on the impressive quality of the picture, the real gain may well lie elsewhere: on the one hand, the digital compression of television signals can mean more channels, more specialization, more diversity for public service broadcasters. On the other hand, the possibilities for several forms of interactivity will also be made technically feasible, as television technology begins to merge with computers. How these developments will be utilized by public service broadcasters we cannot predict at present, but television journalism will undoubtedly be transformed in the process. A civic vision could help guide the changes in a beneficial direction.

Further, we should also recall that there is in Europe a tradition of local and community radio and television (cf. Jankowski et al., 1992). While the forms and circumstances of such media activities have varied greatly, this tradition is an important reference point in this context. Like the civic journalism movement in the United States, local broadcasting in Europe has largely addressed citizens' relationships to their more immediate social and political environment. These community media represent a rich and concrete legacy, one which has too often been ignored. Learning from and incorporating the experiences from these efforts would seem to be a logical step for any civic initiatives that public service television may take. Any explicit experiments in European television (and why not also radio?) to promote the civic ideal would begin precisely at the community level.

There are many lessons to be learned from the experiences of civic journalism in the US, but these have to be translated: over the Atlantic and into the non-commercial public service television framework. The difficulties should not be underestimated: real success in a given situation, for example, may mean upsetting certain constellations of power which in turn could have difficult concequences. However, the fact that there is a major movement in the US media which is commited to the civic ideal must be treated as a source of inspiration. That public service television in Western Europe is still very much alive is of course an important precondition, but the dramatic changes presently under way and those scheduled for the immediate years ahead suggest that there are opportunities to be had for experiments in civic journalism. The existing traditions of local broadcasting could be mined for useful experience. If even just a few television journalism departments in Europe could commit themselves to attempting such programming on small, introductory scales, my guess is that in a relatively short span of time the new programme genres would be developed, via trial and error, and be emulated in other countries. The possibility of launching joint ventures with some newspapers, or perhaps making use of new information technology, to generate new frameworks for media operations, and, more importantly, media–citizens relations, is tantalizing. The obstacles are sobering, but in the meantime, the question still remains: what can television do to help empower viewers as citizens and to encourage them that they might make a social and political difference?

As James Carey (1995) suggests, the struggle for the 'recovery of public life' is not a position which looks back to some golden age, but rather begins from the present with the idea of enhancing citizens' engagement with their social and political circumstances. In a dark historical time, Horkheimer, Adorno, Marcuse and their Frankfurt School colleagues saw as one of the main tasks of Critical Theory to keep alive, even if only among a few intellectuals, the vision of an alternative, a counterpoint to the historical tragedies and the emerging affirmative character of the societies they encountered. Despite all the flickering screens, and partly to some extent also because of them, we find ourselves in another kind of dark historical time. While intellectuals and other citizens need to play their critical role even today, it is imperative that television, our dominant medium, does all it can to maintain, even if only on a very limited scale, the civic ideal. Via experimental innovation in the context of a rapidly changing media landscape, television must help us maintain this vision. If television snuffs it out, today's dark times will get quite darker.

Note

I would like to thank the editors of this volume and Bill Silcock for helpful comments in the preparation of this text.

References

Ang, Ien (1996) 'The battle between television and its audiences', in *Living Room Wars*. London: Routledge, pp. 19–34.

Blumler, Jay and Gurevitch, Michael (1995) *The Crisis of Public Communication*. London: Routledge.

Calhoun, Craig (ed.) (1994) *Social Theory and the Politics of Identity*. London: Blackwell.

Carey, James W. (1995) 'The press, public opinion, and public discourse', in T.L. Glasser and C.T. Salmon (eds) *Public Opinion and the Communication of Consent*. New York: Guilford Press, pp. 403–16.

Charity, Arther (1995) *Doing Public Journalism*. New York: Guilford Press.

Cohen, Jean and Arato, Andrew (1992) *Civil Society and Political Theory*. London: MIT Press.

Dahlgren, Peter (1995) *Television and the Public Sphere*. London: Sage.

Fiske, John (1989) 'Popular news', in *Reading the Popular*. London: Unwin Hyman.

Fiske, John (1992) 'Popularity and the politics of information', in P. Dahlgren and C. Sparks (eds) *Journalism and Popular Culture*. London: Sage.

Hall, John (ed.) (1995) *Civil Society: Theory, History, Comparison*. Cambridge: Polity Press.

Jankowski, Nick, Prehn, Ole and Stappers, James (eds) (1992) *The People's Voice: Local Radio and Television in Europe*. London: John Libby.

Keane, John (1988) *Democracy and Civil Society*. London: Verso.

McQuail, Denis (1997) 'After fire – television: the past half century in broadcasting, its impact on our civilization', *Studies of Broadcasting* (Tokyo) 33: 7–36.

Merritt, Davis 'Buzz' (1995) *Public Journalism and Public Life: Why Telling the News is Not Enough*. Hillsdale, NJ: Lawrence Erlbaum.

Mouffe, Chantal (ed.) (1992) *Dimensions of Radical Democracy*. London: Verso.

Mulgan, Geoff (1994) *Politics in an Antipolitical Age*. Cambridge: Polity Press.

Murdock, Graham (1990) 'Television and citizenship: in defence of public broadcasting', in A. Tomlinson (ed.) *Consumption, Identity and Style*. London: Routledge.

Price, Monroe E. (1995) *Television, the Public Sphere and National Identity*. Oxford: Oxford University Press.

Putnam, Robert (1995) 'Bowling alone: America's declining social capital', *Journal of Democracy* 6 (1): 65–78.

Putnam, Robert (1996) 'The strange disappearance of civic America', *The American Prospect*, 24.

Rajchman, John (ed.) (1995) *The Identity in Question*. London: Routledge.

Rosen, Jay (1993) 'Community connectedness: passwords for public journalism', paper from the Poynter Institute for Media Studies, St Petersburg, FL.

Rosen, Jay (1995) *Getting the Connection Right: Public Journalism and the Troubles of the Press*. New York: Twentieth Century Fund Press.

Schaffer, Jan and Miller, Edward D. (eds) (1995) *Civic Journalism: Six Case Studies*. Washington, DC and St Petersburg, FL: Pew Center for Civic Journalism and the Poynter Institute.

Silcock, Bill (1997) 'Why television fails to embrace civic journalism', unpublished manuscript, Department of Journalism, Media and Communication, Stockholm University.

Spinner, Jeff (1994) *The Boundaries of Citizenship: Race, Ethnicity and Nationality in the Liberal State*. Baltimore and London: Johns Hopkins University Press.

Søndergaard, Henrik (1996) 'Public service after the crisis', *The Nordicom Review*, 1: 107–20.

Turner, Bryan (ed.) (1993) *Citizenship and Social Theory*. London: Sage.

10

Reality Television and Social Responsibility Theory

Jan Wieten

The screaming headline of a pamphlet printed by the Amsterdam publisher Peeter Gevaerts in the year 1597 promises its readers 'A Truthful Terrible New Tiding of Blood and Sulphur'. Reality programming and tabloid journalism have always been among us. The sensational headline points to all the aspects of the genre today, and also to the problems we have with it. It claims to be realistic, even more so than the mainstream or quality press, it relies on eyewitness reports, adds emotion to facts, and appeals to our baser instincts. This sensationalist journalism received little respect 400 years ago, as it would now. But pamphlets such as these were bestsellers, certainly compared with the first Corantos, newspapers of the educated elite rather than the people, with their emphasis on factuality rather than emotion, of which Amsterdam was to become the main publishing centre some years later.

Three and a half centuries later tabloid journalism is still the genre that influential theologians, scientists, lawyers, journalists, and publishers would most like to have vanish from the earth. Social Responsibility Theory, developed in the 1940s and 1950s, is a focal point of criticism of tabloid journalism. Looking back, the efforts of Social Responsibility theorists would seem to have been largely in vain, if we take as evidence the sweeping conquest of our television screens by the latest descendants of the pamphlet of 1597: infotainment and reality television or tabloid television.[1] I see reality television as a challenge posed to journalistic conventions and norms. It can be both a test of the normative power of Social Responsibility Theory and its descendants, such as Denis McQuail's work on media performance, and provide us with a textbook exercise in the many aspects of popular journalism, not all of them morally reprehensible. I would therefore like to take you back to the heated debates about the performance of the press in the years immediately following the Second World War, of which the idea of Social Responsibility was the most noticeable and lasting effort to make the media more responsible and accountable, and contrast this debate with the practice of reality journalism today. Consider this an exercise in relativism: our current unease with reality television is certainly not new, nor perhaps as well founded as we media scientists sometimes think.

Reality television and its making

The term 'reality television' is used to designate a variety of formats ranging from chat shows to crime reconstructions. Dutch public broadcasting's audience research department describes it as 'a program category in which truly happened, extraordinary and drastic events from the lives of ordinary people are shown' (cf. Kilborn, 1994; KLO, 1995; KLO, n.d.: 4), which reads astonishingly like the headlines used 400 years ago. Reality television shows images of victims of (natural) disasters, accidents, traffic accidents and crime in which the emotions of those involved and the often gruesome and spectacular aspects of these events are emphasized. Originally the term was reserved for direct registrations of reality without previous permission of the people involved, often using light video equipment. Later it came to include reconstructions of reality with the help of those involved, and programmes in which people are assisted by the camera in difficult situations, or simply followed by it. Emotion television, in which participants are confronted with persons, situations or events that evoke strong emotional reactions in them and among the audience, is also sometimes called reality television.

Journalistic conventions are applied in reporting. In fact the genre over-emphasizes the more traditional television journalism conventions of liveness, direct reporting of events, and staying as close as possible to 'real' reality. Those were already seen as the main features of television, as compared to film, in the earliest days of television, but have proved impossible to achieve in news reporting for technical and editorial-organizational reasons for a long time. Partly these new types of programmes are simply adaptations of existing print genres to the means and demands of commercial(ized) television. To some degree television is still the parasitic medium it has been from the beginning. Partly reality programming consists of commercial versions of existing television formats. Some reality television comes close to documentary genres, some is investigative journalism with the extra dimension of the technical possibilities of television, some reality television resembles popular television game shows. What these formats have in common is their hybrid nature, cross-cutting boundaries between public and private discourse, information and entertainment, fact and fiction. Within the genre and within one type of programme there are huge differences in the degree of professionalism, seriousness, commercialism and sensationalism.

The various reality television subgenres give their viewers different messages. The rescue, accident and disaster species stays, if anything, close to the original idea of television as reflecting reality in live images; at least it suggests that it does. The talking head of the newscaster or reporter is replaced by visuals, either real or reconstructed, that are supposed to speak for themselves. Liveness and speed are emphasized but nowness, the time dimension is not. Journalistic conventions of the classic objective news report appear to be followed. Emotion is added as part of the human condition, and is related by eyewitnesses and visuals. Real emotions and spectacular scenes are actively and consciously sought and often created. Unlike in some of the early examples of, for instance, emotion television, this is often done with more regard for the voyeurism of the audience than for the feelings of the victims of daily life the programmes (sometimes) pretend to help.

Although society is shown as more violent and dangerous than it is, the preferred reading is clear: while we live in violent times and anyone can be a victim, for law-abiding citizens the chances that they will become one are much slighter. The ultimate message is that we, as citizens, can trust that there will be caring individuals and the official services of our society such as the police, the medical profession, and the fire brigade to help us out when we need them most. The ultimate message of chat show reality programming is also pro-social rather than critical, and reflects the dominant values of society. One might argue that these values (the public's right to know for instance) are mainly invoked to give a pretence of respectability, and cover up the real (commercial) motives of the makers. Uncritical though they are, this does not, to my mind, invalidate these programmes.

Some of the newer types of consumer and crime-resolving programmes do not have this pro-social stance. They claim to adhere to the critical traditions of investigative journalism. In these programmes law-abiding citizens are often depicted as an easy prey for corrupt government and politicians, and for an impenetrable, heartless and anonymous bureaucracy as well as for individual and corporate moneygrabbers. To make this public, the rolling camera is presented as the mighty weapon that can crush even the most heartless oppressor. Arguably these programmes thus suggest that television (and specifically the programme in question) are a more populist, trustworthy and humane authority than the traditional authorities could ever be.

To conclude my description of reality television, let me give you an example. A typical reality television programme of the classic crime and accident type would look like *Special Report*, a programme of the Amsterdam local television channel AT5. This example comes from a participant observation study of the making of *Special Report* by Van de Westelaken (1996). *Special Report*'s stories about nightly Amsterdam open with hectic scenes, camera rolling, not much of an introduction, then cut to scenes of the location, the disaster itself, police, fire brigade in action, sirens screaming, victims carried away, criminals arrested, and so on. These shots are interrupted by interviews with authorities and eyewitnesses, and concluded by a final interpretation of the event by the same authorities. The items usually close with a natural visual ending such as ambulances driving off. Visuals are important, the voice-over of the reporter is factual and unobtrusive. Music is added to heighten suspense.

The use of artificial means to increase the realistic character and dramatic quality of the takes is not seen as in any way damaging the veracity of the report by the production team, according to Van de Westelaken. On the contrary, intentional shaking and trembling of the rolling camera and less than perfect images are employed to convey realness to the audience. In spite of the suggestion of directness and speed, precise references to date and time are mostly avoided in items selected or edited for *Special Report*. As spectacular and skilfully made footage may be used in the News or be sold to other stations, there is a natural drive to professionalism, and orientation on professional journalistic skills.

Interestingly, editing of the programme does not follow the inverted pyramid model, contrary to the classic rules of journalism. High-impact visuals are used at the beginning and sometimes at the end. Stories often close with tail-lights of police cars or ambulances. There is no fixed order of the items, as in the classic news genre, in the sense that the most important news comes first. Usually it is the other way round, with the most spectacular ones in the beginning and at the end or before and after a commercial break.

What may be special for the relatively inexperienced team of *Special Report* – who were not trained as journalists – and contrast with other reality television production teams not observed by Van de Westelaken, is that in the editing phase ethical norms, juridical consequences, editorial guidelines, journalistic conventions and audience expectations come into consideration quite explicitly. Faces of victims and suspects in close-up are scrambled, other means of identification are often suppressed, sometimes after discussion. A whole item may be skipped or cut short when the opposing party in a dispute is not available and when difficulties are expected because only one side was heard. Thus, even a not professionally trained, relatively inexperienced team refers to the norms and conventions of established journalism: they want to hear both sides and achieve balance. Possibly this is to lend more respectability to decisions taken on other grounds. Still, with Van de Westelaken we may conclude that established journalism, while considered dull and old-fashioned by the 'scanner' team of *Special Report*, does enjoy considerable status.

Social Responsibility Theory

Could the trend which is set by reality television be symptomatic for the direction television as a whole, or the mass media in general, is taking? In principle there are few things television (egged on by commerce and audience ratings) would not do – for 'l'audimat c'est la sanction du marché, de l'économie' as Bourdieu (1996: 78) pointed out in his recent all-out attack on television. His complaints about how the commercialized television of today trivializes everything it can lay its hands on, bear a striking resemblance to the criticism that was voiced against the commercial press in the 1940s and 1950s.

The years after the end of the Second World War were a time of feverish debate about the future of the media. They were the years not only of the

Report of the Commission on Freedom of the Press in the United States (Hutchins, 1947), but also of the first British Royal Commission on the Press, of numerous drafts for a changed legal statute of the press in France, and of the Czechoslovakian attempt to introduce a public service model for the print media, to name some of the better-known landmarks of the period. Compared to the complaints we hear today there was an added urgency to the worries about the consequences of ill-performing media. Reports such as *A Free and Responsible Press*, the Hutchins Commission report, were deeply concerned with the role of the press in periods of crisis such as the war and postwar periods. Their most urgent question – perhaps more urgently asked in Europe than elsewhere – was whether there would be one world or none. This is the dominant theme in Kingsley Martin's influential *The Press the Public Wants* of 1947, but also in the report of the Hutchins Commission and more specifically in White and Leigh's (1946) special study for the Hutchins Commission, *Peoples Speaking to Peoples*.

The world was in ruins for the second time in 25 years, heading, so it seemed, for the next catastrophe. In situations such as these the press had proved to be utterly unreliable and even irresponsible. When enlightenment was needed most, it had failed to provide it. Instead the Hearst and Northcliffe-Rothermere presses produced ultra-nationalist diatribes that added oil to the flames of ethnic antagonism, deliberately sowing hatred instead of understanding. War, sex and crime, but war above all, had been the selling topics. They were, in the view of the editor of the *New Statesman and Nation*, what could best be sold to an only half- or one-sidedly educated public (Martin, 1947: 57–8).

The American Commission on Freedom of the Press, called the Hutchins Commission, after its chairman Robert M. Hutchins, reproached the press in 1947 for emphasizing the exceptional rather than the representative, and the sensational rather than the significant, in order to attract as big an audience as possible (Hutchins, 1947: 55). Bourdieu in 1996 does the same and complains that television's only principle of selection is 'la recherche du sensationnel, du spectaculaire' (1996: 18). The Hutchins Commission blamed the economic structure of the press, the industrial organization of modern society, and the personal failure of the directors of the press for the inability to recognize the needs of a modern nation and to estimate and accept the responsibilities which those needs impose on the press. The Hutchins Commmission saw the greatest danger for society in biased international information and communication. Especially in democratic countries where foreign policies are responsive to popular majorities the press should bear the responsibility of reporting international events in such a way that they can be understood. Faults and errors of the press ceased to be 'private vagaries' and became 'public dangers' (Hutchins, 1947: 131).

In the many proposals that were made in the postwar period one basically finds two positions to remedy the evil of an irresponsible press. The first blames the profit motive, or the commercial structure of the media and of society in general, the cure for which could only be structural measures that would mitigate or completely ban the commercial character of the media. The other position understands the failure of the press primarily as the failure of individual owners, editors and journalists. In this view more editors of strong character and journalistic integrity would have made all the difference. The solution for the future, according to this position, therefore lay in better education, more professionalism and in the acceptance – or even imposition and legal enforcement of codes of conduct. The tendency in the years that followed was to move away from radical structural measures (the first position) to raising the morality of the profession and the responsibility of the individual communicator (the second position).

In the analysis of the Hutchins Commission both lines of thinking can be found, although most of the 13 recommendations of the commission to government, media and the public to improve the performance of the press, follow the second line. (The 13 recommendations have been summarized at the end of this chapter.) There is, however, a marked difference with the almost exclusively moral appeal of later publications such as Fred S. Siebert, Theodore B. Peterson and Wilbur Schramm's *Four Theories of the Press* of 1956, and Wilbur Schramm's *Responsibility in Mass Communication* of 1957, in which the full-grown Social Responsibility Theory was presented to the public, which lacked this more radical view. Though (or perhaps, because) the Social Responsibility Theory solidified into a moral appeal it has had a widespread and long-lasting influence, and so have the standards of responsible behaviour first formulated by the Hutchins Commission. Nowadays journalism education and professionalization, self-regulation by the media, media councils and ombudsmen, journalistic codes of ethics, and even public service broadcasting are often seen as direct results of the recommendations of the propagators of Social Responsibility Theory. Although that impression is not entirely correct – insofar as early examples of most of these institutions preceded the publications of the Hutchins Commission and those of Siebert, Peterson and Schramm – they nevertheless fall within the broad range of the ideas presented under the name of Social Responsibility Theory.

Whether this set of ideas has actually affected the performance of the press and whether the media have acted more responsibly since, is a question that is not as easy to answer as it may seem, when one takes for instance the first ruling in 1954 of the British General Council of the Press as a starting point. If the publication of a readership poll by the *Daily Mirror* on the question of whether Princess Margaret should be allowed to marry Captain Peter Townsend was 'contrary to the best traditions of British journalism', then the verdict on the tabloids of today should be clear (Robertson and Nicol, 1992: 522). On the other hand, if one would accept as evidence that this same *Daily Mirror* recently decided not to publish secret budget plans of the British government that were leaked to the newspaper, thereby explicitly invoking its social responsibility, who would be inclined to pass a negative judgement on the tabloids then?

Responsible reality television?

Most of the virtues of responsible journalism, as listed in Schramm's *Responsibility in Mass Communication* (1957) – truth and fairness, separation of news from comment, accuracy, objectivity, balance, reliability – bear little relationship to the realities of reality television. Yet, paradoxically, the genre's main legitimation is the principle Schramm names as the most fundamental journalistic responsibility of all: the public's right to know. This legitimation would entitle it to the same freedom and protection of its privileges as other forms of journalism, and justify most of the methods reality television employs. The makers of reality programmes decide the eternal journalistic conflict of conscience between the right to know and respect for privacy unequivocally in favour of the public's right to know. In reality in most types of programmes within the genre the entertainment value is of course of much more importance than the informational qualities.

There is an intriguing reverse side to this. In practice the claim to journalistic respectability and the need for legitimation have interesting side-effects, one of which is a degree of moderation and restraint. Together they mitigate the commercial impulse that anything which can be sold should be produced. Reality television is a genre with a low status. The urge to be respected makes its producers want to acquire the skills but also to conform to the norms of the higher-status profession that serves as an example. It is not only the work procedures of the inexperienced team of *Special Report* which I used to illustrate the making of reality television, but Social Responsibility Theory itself and a good deal of the postwar debates about how to improve the performance of the media that might be interpreted as a manifestation of a drive to respectability of a low-status profession.

Excess is also contained by pressure from outside. Unlike the traditional news genre which operates predominantly in the public sphere, reality television deals primarily with private matters of ordinary people. This does not make it less but more vulnerable to outside interference. Publications about people in public functions and about their actions are generally constitutionally and legally seen as being in the public interest, but publications resulting from intrusions into the privacy of private individuals are not. In recent years the number of complaints about trespassing and other intrusions into privacy has risen sharply (Robertson and Nicol, 1992; Záborszky-van Boxtel, 1996). Apart from this, there would also seem to be a shift from Press Councils to criminal and civil proceedings in courts of justice. This could point to a feeling among the public that Press Councils, one of the self-regulatory mechanisms of Social Responsibility, are not, or no longer, seen as effective means of undoing the wrong-doings of the media.

Although the conditions vary a lot from country to country, and I certainly do not claim to have a complete overview, courts seem generally to tend to act with a lot of restraint. Injunctions against publication are rare. In Dutch courts considerations would typically be: first of all whether the portrayed has given prior consent to be photographed, filmed or interviewed, and, if that is not the case, whether there are other circumstances that might warrant publication, depending on (1) the seriousness of the effects of the publication; (2) the seriousness of the abuse that is uncovered; (3) the available evidence for the suspicion of abuse; (4) the form of the presentation; (5) the probability that the aim of fighting the abuse might have been reached by less harmful ways for the portrayed; (6) the chance that the abuse would have become public anyway; (7) the actuality and news value of the issue (Záborszky-van Boxtel, 1996). The threat of injunctions or damages, or to take another example from reality, a government warning that legal measures against harassment by reality television crews will be considered, can cause programme makers to shy away from undertaking certain actions. Such was the case with the *Special Report* team who now make sure they keep away from ambulance personnel, who felt they had been hindered in their work by television crews. It has not, alas, resulted in making the television crews ask consent of the victims they portray.

The most commercialized forms of journalism are least likely to be affected by moral appeals. So it would seem natural that an 'ethic' of tabloid television can only be imposed from above, by the courts or by government rule. This is neither necessarily good nor necessarily bad. However, when judges are given the power to define more and more precisely the limits of acceptable behaviour in this specific area, this might have repercussions for other journalistic activities as well, and result in an unduly restricted and regulated journalistic practice in general.

Tabloid journalism and the future of social responsibility

The theory of Social Responsibility was a reaction to a crisis in the liberal ideals of progress and enlightenment brought about by the experience of two world wars. At the same time it leaned heavily on the same modernist and liberal ideas. Social Responsibility theorists were convinced there was one truth to be found and one set of democratic values to be shared. At the end of the twentieth century it has become increasingly difficult to describe the aims of communication and information in such terms as 'the presentation and clarification of the goals and values of society'. Even the common ground needed to agree to disagree seems to be missing. Media are distributors of truths, some more powerful than others, but never of The Truth. At first sight the crusade against the irresponsibility of the press undertaken 50 years ago by the founding fathers of the Social Responsibility Theory would seem to have had little or no effect. Tabloid journalism is very much alive. What is more, it now extends from the print media to television. Truth is nowhere to be found. People looking to the media for help find that news and entertainment, fact and fiction, public and private have become inextricably interwoven. Fear and anxiety might be the result for those who are confused about who is to be trusted.

Some of the complaints voiced by the Hutchins Commission seem more applicable now than they were in 1947. The concentration of power in the media and between the media has gone much further than the Commission foresaw. Commercial influence has become much stronger, even (or especially) in broadcasting. People are addressed more as consumers than as citizens. Journalists are giving in to commercial, political and audience pressures on an unprecedented scale. News, in the sense of 'a truthful, comprehensive, and intelligent account of the day's events in a context which gives them meaning' – the main focus of the Hutchins Commission – has become more and more marginal not only in a predominantly entertainment medium such as television, but also in the print media (cf. McQuail, 1992). Journalism itself is marginalized. Journalists are better trained and educated now than they were 50 years ago but this does not help much, since many of the makers of new journalistic genres such as reality television and infotainment programmes are performers and entertainers rather than trained journalists. A moral appeal to journalists nowadays would appear to be almost senseless. Should I conclude then that the Hutchins Commission has been proved wrong by history? That the Social Responsibility Theory of the press has not, nor is likely ever to become reality?

No. The picture is not altogether gloomy. Hutchins might also have found reasons to rejoice. Many of the newspapers of today are more informative and certainly more accessible than their counterparts of 50 years ago. Some come quite a bit closer to the Hutchins Commission's ideal of providing 'a forum for the exchange of comment and criticism' than their predecessors. The blurring of genres and genre conventions, and the increased room given to the personal and the emotional is not altogether bad, and some forms may have brought new audiences in contact with more relevant kinds of information about their social environment. Neither has the competition from commercial broadcasters, which most of the public broadcasting monopolies in Europe have had to endure since the 1980s, been a bad influence on the whole. It has also succeeded in many cases in awakening public broadcasting and making it more responsive to its audiences, without addressing them as consumers only.

Tabloid journalism is popular. But is it the big monster that it is sometimes made into? And is it a more and more popular genre? Even this second simple quantitative question is difficult to answer. In terms of circulation the ratio between 'serious' and 'popular' newspapers has certainly changed, but not everywhere in the same direction. Even within one country the conclusion could be negative for one period and positive for another. Reality television is a newcomer in countries which have long had public broadcasting monopolies and it has become a popular genre within a short period of time. Nevertheless, when one takes a closer look at the (Dutch) charts of most-watched programmes, the reality genre is not represented at the top. Usually reality television programmes are preceded by several sports programmes (live soccer matches in particular), a locally produced soap or two, and even one or two classic newscasts. Neither is there anything remarkable about the viewers of the rescue and crime type of reality television. They are a cross-section of the population as far as age and sex are concerned, although men and higher-educated people are overrepresented among the non-viewers and those who hate the genre. The same Dutch audience research shows that fans have a preference for entertainment, but also appreciate news and current affairs programmes. The main attraction of reality television lies in its realness and spectacularity, but much less in the possibility these programmes offer to recognize situations or identify with victims or heroes. And despite the emphasis on blood, tears and human suffering in general, fear does not play an important role in the experience of viewers (KLO, 1995).

There can be little doubt that journalism taken as a whole – both print and (radio and) television journalism – has become more popular over the last decades, and that it manifests itself in a greater diversity of formats. The verdict on these developments cannot be a simple 'good' or 'bad'. Not even when weighed against a standard derived from the Social Responsibility Theory, that media should provide the people with the information they need to make sense of the world and to take part in the public debate about issues that are relevant to them as citizens. I agree that media should play this role. And some forms of popular journalism, especially the most commercial ones, clearly fall below this standard. Other more serious forms of popular journalism have shown that there are new ways of addressing relevant issues, sometimes long-neglected ones, and have made them more accessible by establishing links between the public and the private, the rational and the emotional. (Responsible programme makers in the emotion television genre, for example, have succeeded in several instances in putting 'private' and taboo issues, such as incest and violence in the home, on the public agenda without giving in to sensationalism and voyeurism.) Should failing popular journalism then be obliged to take up serious matters in the name of social responsibility, as Dahlgren (1995) suggests? Or, alternatively, should this be left to serious journalism? Neither option is very attractive.

There is no acceptable way in which forms of popular journalism that have as their main goal to be entertainment or make a profit or both, could be held to the task of being responsible journalism. They should be what they want to be. I do not want to imply that this kind of commercial journalism should be welcomed as an improved form of journalism because its orientation on large audiences would guarantee more polysemic and less manipulative output (cf. Fiske, 1987). Even if it gives the 'people' more opportunity for resistance, that kind of resistance is not progressive by definition. Fiske's relativism itself is relative. The bottom line is that news should indeed stress its constructedness and be clear about its motives and sources, while journalists should aim at providing honest and relevant statements about reality, whatever their other or ulterior motives.

To this end, there is one extremely timely and relevant appeal in the report of the Commission on Freedom of the Press, the only one to be repeated in more or less the same form in its recommendations to government, press and public. It counsels to create new and experimental facilities in journalism. Defining, stimulating, and protecting new ways and strategies of non-profit-driven forms of both serious and popular, responsible and critical journalism will be important tasks for governments, media and civil society in the years to come. Meanwhile we might try to have a little confidence in the self-regulatory instinct of journalists in the newsroom, the impetus for which we may paradoxically provide by insisting on the low status and general inferiority of reality television as a journalistic genre.

Appendix

The 13 recommendations of the Hutchins Commision (1947) were (in abridged form):

To the Government

1. That the constitutional guarantee of the freedom of the press be recognized as including the radio and motion pictures.
2. That government facilitate new ventures, new techniques, and competition; concentration should be tolerated if necessary, if and when it benefits the public.
3. Retraction or re-statement of facts or opportunity to reply should be stimulated, instead of the libel remedy.
4. Repeal of the prohibition of expressions in favour of revolutionary change.
5. Government should inform about its policies and purposes by way of the media or on its own.

To the Press

1. The press should accept the responsibilities of being common carriers of information and discussion.
2. Finance experimental activities.
3. Engage in vigorous mutual criticism.
4. Increase competence, independence, and effectiveness of its staff.
5. The radio industry should take control of its programmes and treat advertising as newspapers do.

To the Public

1. Non-profit institutions should help supply variety, quantity and quality of press service.
2. Academic-professional centres in the field of communication should be created; broadest liberal training for journalists.
3. Independent agency to report and appraise the performance of the press.

Note

1. Only five years ago Denis McQuail could call tabloid television a 'US phenomenon' (1992: 308).

References

Bourdieu, Pierre (1996) *Sur la Télévision, suivi de l'emprise du journalisme.* Paris: Liber.

Dahlgren, Peter (1995) *Television and the Public Sphere. Citizenship, Democracy and the Media.* London: Sage.

Fiske, John (1987) *Television Culture.* London: Methuen.

Hutchins, Robert M. (1947) *Report of the Commission on Freedom of the Press. A Free and Responsible Press.* Chicago, IL: University of Chicago Press.

Kilborn, Richard (1994) 'How real can you get?: recent developments in "Reality" television', *European Journal of Communication,* 9: 421–39.

KLO (1995) *De populariteit van realiteits-televisie* [*The Popularity of Reality TV*]. Hilversum: NOS, Afdeling Kijk- en Luisteronderzoek.

KLO (n.d.) *Jaarboek 1993/1994/1995* [*Yearbook 1993/1994/1995*]. Hilversum: NOS.

Martin, Kingsley (1947) *The Press the Public Wants.* London: Hogarth Press.

McQuail, Denis (1992) *Media Performance: Mass Communication and the Public Interest.* London: Sage.

Robertson, Geoffrey and Nicol, Andrew (1992) *Media Law.* Harmondsworth: Penguin.

Schramm, Wilbur (1957) *Responsibility in Mass Communication.* New York: Harper & Row.

Siebert, Fred S., Peterson, Theodore B. and Schramm, Wilbur (1956) *Four Theories of the Press.* Urbana: University of Illinois Press.

Westelaken, H.P.J. van de (1996) 'Het Maken van Reality-TV. Een case-study' [The Making of Reality TV. A Case Study]. MA thesis, University of Amsterdam.

White, Llewellyn and Leigh, Robert D. (1946) *Peoples Speaking to Peoples.* Chicago, IL: University of Chicago Press.

Záborszky-van Boxtel, Carien (1996), 'Reality-tv en de realiteit van het recht' [Reality TV and the reality of the law], *Mediaforum,* 8 (1): 5–10.

11

The Ethics of Making Private Life Public

Liesbet van Zoonen

'I think we have a scoop', he whispered, looking around to see whether anyone could hear us. His pride was inevitable. 'About what?' I conceded. 'A big star, I can't tell here, his girlfriend has left him. He is devastated.' We had agreed to meet in one of the local coffee shops before I would take him to the university where he would lecture for a group of students about the rules and routines of the Dutch gossip and celebrity press. 'I'll show your students this week's cover; it won't be in the news stands before tomorrow.' I got excited. For a few hours, my students, myself and the editors of *Story*, the weekly for which he worked, would be the only people to know the intimate details of a famous Dutch singer's divorce. Who else would know? Why did she leave him? Who did she leave him for? 'I only hope,' he worried, 'that the other magazines won't have it.' Apparently, some weeks before, all four weeklies had had a supposed scoop on their cover about Ajax soccer talent Patrick Kluivert soon to become a father. He frowned: 'We can't have that too often; it would kill the market.' I nodded in appreciation and despite myself I got carried away and hoped with him that they would be the only one with this week's celebrity divorce.

Next day, I approached my neighbourhood news stand with vicarious excitement; what would the other three magazines have? One quick glance was enough: DIVORCE OF THE YEAR: GIRLFRIEND LEAVES MARCO BORSATO, it read on the cover of the competing magazine *Party*. And the two other Dutch celebrity magazines *Weekend* and *Privé* had not failed to pick up the rumours of his divorce either. Apart from the inevitable gloating, I felt sorry for the *Story* editor. His fantasy to have the biggest scoop of the year was only short-lived.[1]

As with their colleagues of the ordinary press, the scoop is a daily pre-occupation of gossip journalists. It will become even more important because competition in this genre is growing; journalism as a whole, driven by market forces, is becoming more and more focused on human interest and personalized stories, pushing private life into the public eye. Formerly this was the undisputed stronghold of society columns, celebrity magazines, and tabloids – the number of titles and readerships still expanding. Nowadays most newspapers and television stations have their own celebrity sections and columns, sometimes tongue-in-cheek as if to legitimate their existence, sometimes deadly serious in the process of attracting larger audiences. Television has seen the talkshow booming, a cheap genre to produce with its endless procession of ordinary people talking in public about their private affairs.

There are considerable varieties in the gossip press in different countries: the genre I will start with here is the weekly celebrity magazine such as the Dutch *Privé*, *Story* and *Weekend* which has its counterparts in the British *Hello* and *Chat* or the German *Gala*. My arguments, however, will pertain more generally to various kinds of publications (press and broadcast) on private lives. For the subjects of gossip writing, growing competition in the genre may both enlarge the already considerable burden of being in the public eye, and – on the other hand – improve possibilities for image-building. Marco Borsato, for example, did not fare too badly after the revelation of his divorce: his fanmail quadrupled and his new compact disc which appeared a month later was sold out within half an hour, breaking all previous records in the Dutch music industry – undoubtedly of course because of the quality of the songs rather than because of gossip promotion. The television industry likewise needs the gossip press to promote new programmes and stars.

The merger of private and public so typical of the celebrity community has always been the subject of fierce debate and criticism, both on the stars who are seen as selling their privacy and authenticity for commercial interests and on the journalists who are conceived as obtrusive, unscrupulous and irresponsible invaders who feel anything is permitted to get an insider's view on private lives. This whole debate rests on the idea that the distinction between public and private life is important and needs to be protected, and is part of (western) society's inalienable qualities. 'Public' and 'private' however are fairly recent historical constructions that have served to discipline us as well as give us a sense of autonomy and self. For the purpose of this chapter I will take 'private' to refer to intimate domestic or personal life, including sexual life (cf. Fraser, 1992).

The rise and fall of private life

The domestic intimate sphere of family relations is a fairly recent phenomenon inextricably tied to the gendered division of labour in modern western societies and in particular to its bourgeois and middle-class milieux. In premodern societies, neither common people nor the nobility knew such separate spheres of life. For the common man and woman production and consumption were located in the undivided household, for the nobility all of life took place in public. The waking up of Louis XVI (*le levé*) for instance, as well as his going to sleep (*le couché*) were public events for which it was a great honour to be invited.

The nineteenth century in particular saw the social construction of a separate domestic realm, resulting from the industrialization process but already propagated in the work of political philosophers such as Rousseau and firmly embedded in the puritan ideology of the Victorian age in which the private was promoted as a safe haven against the proverbial heartless world, a haven to be managed and maintained by women leaving this heartless world of public affairs to men. News media were a constitutive part of the burgeoning public world, maybe not in the eyes of contemporary sociologists like Habermas who holds them accountable for the demise of the public sphere, but definitely in the eyes of the news media and professional journalists themselves. In any case, public life in all its varieties formed the core business of the booming newspaper industry, domestic and personal life were relegated to demarcated and specialized sections in the paper or to women's magazines. Thus, the social public–private divide had its media counterpart, and media became as gendered as society itself.

A significant rupture in this order began with the rise of the Hollywood movie industry as a result of the star system of the major American film studios. Many people were as interested in the joys and sorrows of the movie stars as they were in the movies. The public function of celebrities' private lives was something that came with the job of being in the movies, music industry or television and was – with notorious exceptions like Greta Garbo – accepted and exploited by most celebrities; it increased their box office value. Their romances, parties, health, quarrels and divorces became the object of fantasy and dreams of ordinary people and produced general points of identification. The celebrity community is therefore often said to have joined the royalty in its symbolic function as the embodiment of society's norms and values. And in the United States of course without a royalty of its own, Hollywood is considered royalty itself (with the exception of the 1950s in which Hollywood was accused of being a hotbed of unamerican values).

Increasingly the celebrity community comprises people for whom private life seems to be less of a commodity than for traditional celebrities: politicians, industry leaders and sports heroes have become famous as a byproduct of their career in another field, but not by choice it seems. As a result, they are much more reluctant to exploit their private lives (although for politicians this depends on the particular political culture they operate in) and they are often seriously annoyed with publicity of their private lives. Nevertheless, celebrity status has become theirs, and considerable resources are put into handling this status, for instance in the form of media training and the construction of public images.

In addition, we have recently seen an upsurge of genres in which the private lives of ordinary people are in the centre of the public eye: the talk show being one example, reality television in most of its varieties another one. For the media then, the public/private divide seems to have vanished into one undivided spectacle of matters for public attraction. The fact that many ordinary people confess their most intimate thoughts effortlessly in talk shows and other public arenas, and the increasing use of mobile telephones in public spaces are signs that the public/private divide may be eroding in the daily lives of ordinary people too.

The pros and cons of making private life public

The 'publication' (in its literal sense of becoming public) of private life in its various forms raises a number of issues concerning the public interest and the ethical responsibility of the media which up till now have not been adequately addressed. The various labels in circulation for the genres that specialize in private lives are indicative of a general contempt and suspicion towards their ethical standards that do not allow for much debate, theorization or inspiration for the development of such standards. Gossip journalism has been labelled 'Grub Street journalism' or 'gutter journalism' and its practioners as 'the sleazy nuisance who relies on eavesdropping, intrusion and harassment as basic research methods' (Bird, 1992: 85). Gossip magazine editors have experienced the low status of gossip journalism many times, especially in the company of fellow journalists from higher-valued genres: 'They accept and even appreciate me for telling juicy stories about people they know too, but as soon as something they consider fundamental comes along they tell me I should get the coffee because I won't grasp what is going on anyway.' Although the talk show fares a little better statuswise, it has met with derogatory comments like 'exploitation of intimacy' or 'freak show' as well (Joyner-Priest, 1995).

There are indeed many examples of concrete publications of private lives in gossip magazines and talk shows that have caused irreparable and unneccessary damage to the people involved.[2] Infamous and known worldwide is the case of Colorado Senator Gary Hart who was the frontrunner for the Democratic presidential nomination in 1987 when the *Miami Herald* revealed he had had an extra-marital affair, which forced Hart out of the race. Similar allegations against candidate Bill Clinton have continued throughout his presidency, culminating in Paula Jones being allowed to bring him to court. In the 1997 British elections several Tory MPs were exposed as involved in sexual and financial scandals, one of several reasons for the annihilation of the Conservatives. A notorious case in the Netherlands concerns a witch hunt in the early 1980s against the social-democrat prime minister Joop den Uyl who allegedly abused government money for his own benefit. Later one of the journalists involved confessed that the scandal had emerged solely from the head of the right-wing executive editor of the leading gossip journal *Privé* (Van Rooyen, 1985). Ordinary people too may suffer from public scrutiny and many talk show participants have later expressed regrets because of unexpected and hostile reactions to their public appearance (*Vesuvius*, 1993).

On the other hand, private life has also become a commodity for celebrities which needs to be exploited for the advancement of their career. For politicians in the United States and the United Kingdom and increasingly in other political cultures as well, private and family life have become indispensable tools in building up a reputation of reliability, integrity and merit. Ordinary people have benefited from the therapeutical context that talk shows offer. It is precisely in that respect that gossip journalists and other communicators specializing in private lives will raise their defence when asked about their standards: 'A lot of dirty laundry is carried into our news room by the stars themselves, they are only too happy to cooperate.' Talk show producers hardly ever have to look for participants because many people register voluntarily to take part.

The fact that the publication of private life has advantages and disadvantages for the people involved should not release the 'publishers' of private lives from the responsibility to think about the limits of publishing on private lives. There is certainly debate on ethics within the professional communities of these 'publishers' – journalists and other communicators involved in making private life public – if only because they so often have to defend their work. One of the new Dutch commercial stations, SBS6, strong in reality genres, has even set up its own ethics committee to develop standards for their reality reporting. This is an exception, however. It is more usual that ethics talk takes place on 'Friday afternoon', gossip journalists say. Moreover it is usually based on emotional, ad hoc judgements of the stories concerned. Dutch gossip journalists for example claim to be very reluctant to publish a story on a celebrity having Aids, but would have no problems in writing that he has cancer. Although one intuitively can see the logic there, it is not a logic that gossip journalists themselves easily explain or rationalize. A more visible and standard rule is applied to politicians: their private performance is judged on the basis of their political standpoints, journalists say. Thus, politicians who proclaim the centrality of family life, like christian democrats and conservatives, should live up to the example, and social-democrat politicians who favour sharing community resources and finances should especially not be found with their hands in government money. Whereas these general rules direct the gossip journalists' standards towards politicians, they still do not always work the same way. Ruud Lubbers, a former Dutch prime minister in office for a record-breaking 12-year period, despite being the leader of the christian democrats, never personally proclaimed the family as society's cornerstone and thus his family life and publicized – alleged – extra-marital affairs did not cause much moral indignation (Van Zoonen, 1998a, b).

So although there are traces of ethical considerations in the professional codes of gossip journalists, the debate is not very systematic or productive and certainly has not led to a clear guideline of how to deal with people's private lives, whether they are celebrities, ordinary or just 'famous for fifteen minutes' in the words of Andy Warhol.

The ethics of making private life public

Let us *first* begin with the assertion that private lives are in the public eye and will not disappear from it any more; on the contrary it is only one of many signs that the public/private distinction itself is currently under redefinition. Therefore it is more useful to think of the implications of the new 'public private' life, to examine the intrinsic value of privacy and to explore the scope of private life in postmodern times than to condemn current trends and long for previous times (which I myself often do for that matter). Let us consider *secondly* that many people, both celebrities and ordinary people, see no problem in revealing their private lives (or having them revealed) in public. Thus, when thinking about ethics and standards, a dimension of choice and agency should be included. In addition, publishing the private lives of individuals often has a beneficial function, sometimes only for themselves, sometimes also for society at large. Thus *thirdly* when thinking about ethic and standards a dimension of functionality should be included as well. Also, and *fourthly*, there is no reason to think of publishing private life in all its varieties as other than a regular form of journalism, thus standard journalistic ethics regarding content and procedures should apply. And finally, as a *fifth* point, when thinking about ethics, a notion of power and status of the people whose private lives are publicized should be included for obvious reasons. It is easier to trash an ordinary person than a powerful industrial, just as it is easier to celebrate an already popular star than one who is over the hill.

Would it be possible that taken together these five considerations produce guidelines for ethical gossip behaviour (not necessarily a contradiction in terms)?

To begin with: the value of privacy and the scope of contemporary private life. Despite my earlier observations that many people do not seem to care much about a distinction between public and private life, the total collapse of privacy would be one bridge too far. It may be revealing for understanding the value and scope of private life to look at people who do not seem to have much of it. Take Lady Di or Fergie. Their mistake was to fall in love with British royals. Hence their every activity became prey for the British tabloids whose excessive lack of any standard regarding the confines of private life are archetypical. The lack of respect for the privacy of Di and Fergie, shown not only by the tabloids but also by the various camps within the royal family, have had devastating effects on both women, and these effects themselves have inevitably become subjects of public scrutiny. On a more mundane level, the value of some measure of privacy is often testified to by young mothers whose days are filled by the care for their children. Contemporary child health clinics, general physicians and other social institutions thus advise mothers nowadays to reserve some time for themselves in order to stay fit and friendly. Paraphrasing Thompson (1987: 126) in an observation about the value of privacy for public officials, the value of private life for all individuals is located in the possibility to sustain a conception of one's own character that is independent of one's public reputation or one's social role. Understandably, those who have lost their private lives find themselves facing the troubling question: 'Who am I, what do I want?', a question that not only haunted Princess Diana and Sarah Ferguson but which is also a well-known cry of tired mothers.

It seems obvious to conclude then that private life is necessary and valuable in order to keep a sound sense of self. But there are exceptions. Look for instance at Madonna, the pop star, a couple of years ago. In her movie *Truth or Dare*, a reportage of her music tour *Blonde Ambition*, she is accused by her lover at that time, movie star Warren Beaty, of living only in front of cameras. Beaty heaves his sigh when Madonna allows the movie crew to film her consulting her doctor for her sore throat. For Madonna herself there did not seem to be much of a difference between herself as a private person and herself as a public persona. The various Madonnas she launched throughout her career were all herself, she claimed, and why not believe that. However, critical reception of Madonna and in particular of *Truth or Dare* all focused on the lack of distinction between the 'authentic' Madonna, supposedly hidden somewhere, and Madonna the mega-star. Whereas it may have been to Madonna's rescue that she did not experience such a distinction between her private and public life and thus did not have to protect it, the search of press and public for the truth behind the image indicated a widespread belief in the public/private distinction; a belief as I have suggested in the beginning of this chapter that is crumbling. Madonna's *Truth or Dare* would definitely evoke other reactions today and it is possible that audiences would be less bothered by its perceived lack of authenticity.

Juxtaposing Diana, Sarah Ferguson and Madonna shows us that the value of privacy or the scope of private life is clearly articulated with the amount of choice individuals have in defining the limits of their private lives. Princess Di and Fergie did not seem to have any other option than not to fall in love with their respective royals; once they had done so their private lives were lived for them. Although royal persons have not chosen to be royalty, family experience and institutional support will take them through the ordeals of being public persons. But for the green in-laws that Di, Fergie or Dutch Prince Claus were, the spotlights come as unexpected hell that is difficult to handle. The spouses and partners of 'common' celebrities are in a similar position. When Dutch tennis player Richard Krajicek won Wimbledon in 1996, it was his girlfriend Daphne Deckers, a model and part-time television presenter, who – after having attracted the undivided attention of the Wimbledon off-court cameras – unpleasantly landed in the public eye. Allegedly, one of the British tabloids called its counterpart in the Netherlands, asking: 'Is there any dirt on Daphne Deckers?' With the support of a hostile ex-husband, Deckers' past was dug up by gossip journalists to discredit her relation with Krajicek, leaving her flabbergasted. 'Suddenly it is', she said some time later, 'as if you lead two lives: your own and that of the gossip press, and you can be sure they have nothing to do with each other.' Krajicek himself and other sports heroes of similar repute, of course, also did not start out their career with a vision of being in the public eye. We can assume that their sports performance instead of their public status is what drives them, the latter being a (uninteresting) byproduct for most of them.

However, if we would let 'choice' or 'agency' of the individuals involved be the only yardstick for deciding whether and what to publish about their private lives, we might end up in the rather awkward situation that we would know next to nothing about how our royals and sports (wo)men lead their lives. Undeniably an important social function of the public private life would then be lost, because whether we like it or not, societies need their heroes and villains to transpose their beliefs and worries on. Royalty and sports people obviously function as such and thus have found themselves leading two lives indeed: their own and their symbolic function which may coincide or, on a bad day, change independently from each other. Royal persons may not like their public private status but most understand their symbolic function and operate accordingly, after all noblesse oblige.

Sports people may have less of a feeling of social obligation and thus resent being public property. Movie stars, television personalities, musicians and models consider their symbolic persona as part of the job. Often it is the product of marketing and sales considerations suggested or imposed by agents and managers. When carefully constructed such an engineered public private life may operate to the benefit of their careers. Although less obviously so, this may also be the case for royalty. Many royal families have considerable state incomes, and are thus dependent on a continuing felicitous relationship with the people and its representation. Sports heroes may use their reputations for commercial purposes and start clothing labels or sell sports equipment. Media stars obviously have something to gain from being in the public eye, and nowadays many politicians have too.

When we combine these first three considerations – value of private life, agency and functionality – there appear to be different kinds of gossip subjects or celebrities: those who have little choice, such as royalty and partners of public figures but whose social function is unmistakable; those who need publicity for commercial or – increasingly – political reasons, like movie stars and politicians and who have a similar social function; and ordinary people who, voluntarily or forced, appear in the public eye. For these groups different ethical criteria may apply besides the general standards of journalistic practice.

As far as royalty is concerned, the examples of Di and Fergie are evidence of what is unethical and sometimes downright criminal. Dutch royalty has suffered less from such extreme journalistic performance, due to the different nature of the Dutch gossip press and Dutch law. Since royal persons have no choice, the only criterion for publication should be the social relevance of the story; similarly so with the partners of public figures or celebrities. In extreme cases decisions are clear: a marriage is inevitable, a photograph of a workout in the gym irrelevant. It is of course in the grey middle that debate will occur and we need a socially responsible gossip press (again a possible contradiction in terms), legislation or particularly smart public relations managers for a decent gossip press performance.

For the second category of celebrities and politicians, one would be tempted to say, for instance, that they should not complain about their private life being public property since it is in their own interest. An interesting example of this dilemma was experienced by the political leader of the Dutch liberal party, Frits Bolkestein. In 1994 he deliberately and successfully chose gossip magazines as channels for positive campaign messages involving his experiences in the Second World War, his marriage and the liberal party. A year later he was faced with the publication of two scandals involving his son allegedly abusing social security and his brother allegedly stealing a dairy barrow. It is unlikely that these affairs would have surfaced in the gossip press, if it had not been for the self-chosen celebrity status of the liberal party leader. As gossip journalists will say: 'If you can't stand the heat, stay out of the kitchen.'

Finally, ordinary people coming under public scrutiny, voluntarily or forced usually have no idea what they are in for. One would hope that ordinary people who find themselves for whatever reason in the spotlight – as a talk show guest, as the one-night stand of a celebrity, as an accident victim in a reality show, and so on – would be guided and supported in coming to terms with the impact of their 15 minutes of fame, preferably by the publishers of their private life who can be expected to know what kind of effects may be expected.

For all categories of gossip subjects – including those for whom a public private life is part of a self-chosen career path – it goes without saying that they should not be prey to unlimited digging and fishing expeditions into their private affairs. For reporting on private lives, the same standards should apply as in regular journalism (as formulated in the Code of Bordeaux, e.g. see Nordenstreng in this volume). The gossip press and its allies do not have a very reliable status in that respect. Quotes are invented or presented out of context, sources are always presented anonymously and often made up. For instance, in a story on a Dutch social democrat minister of one of the former cabinets, one of the neighbours was quoted as saying: 'It is a scandal that her party propagates energy savings and that she herself leaves the lights on all night.' Some time later, the journalist responsible for the story chucklingly admitted that he himself lives next to the minister and that he featured as 'one of the neighbours' in many stories about her. One only needs to read inside stories on gossip journalism like the shocking 1977 publication by undercover journalist Gunther Walraff on the methods of the German *Bild* Zeitung, or watch the two-hour documentary *Paparazzi* following celebrity photographers on their quest for publishable material, to be able to accumulate one example after the other of questionable journalistic methods. Precisely such examples are what has earned the genre its labels of sleaze and gutter journalism. On the other hand, an academic specialist of gossip and journalistic writing like Elizabeth Bird (1992) claims that gossip methods are structurally not very different from other journalistic forms of inquiry and writing. As in much regular journalism, for instance, a 'fact' is a 'fact' as soon as it can be attributed to a source claiming it is a fact. Thus in both forms of journalism, objectivity and accuracy are reached if one faithfully reports what was said or written by sources. Likewise, the anonymous source is a regular guest in regular journalism as the famous phrase 'sources close to the president' testifies. Bird further underlines the commonalities between tabloid or gossip journalism and regular journalism by showing how easily regular journalists switch to gossip journalism: it is not as if they have to learn a whole new profession.

But it may be that what distinguishes both forms of journalism is their ethical sensitivities: in regular journalism numerous handbooks of ethics concentrate on the definition of decent procedures and on questions of what kind of information is publishable and what not. Ethics is a standard course in all journalism curricula. As such, ethics have become a perhaps not very prominent, but at least common element in the collective consciousness of regular journalists. It is not that ethical discussions are absent among gossip journalists, rather they are not part of their collective professional identity as is the case with other kinds of journalists. For the genre to gain credibility and status, it seems imperative that a professional debate about ethical procedures and content matters comes about, geared to the specific organizational, market and audience requirements that characterize publishing about private lives.

Such a debate should focus on the four dimensions that I discussed: the value of privacy, choice, functionality and general professional standards, but it is unlikely that it will produce universal guidelines as to how and what can be published on private lives. There are different kinds of gossip subjects and from the examples given throughout this chapter, it is clear that what may be permissible in one case, is totally irresponsible in another. Context thus also makes a difference, and probably one of the most important elements of that context is the status and the power of the people whose private lives are being publicized. Celebrities and their political, royal and sports fellows increasingly have their own support staff for these matters and can be expected to direct the nature of publications to some extent. In fact, Dutch gossip journalists are already complaining that 'Dutch heroes' are more and more hiding behind their PR managers (*IQ Magazine*, 1997). It is precisely those who lack such support or experience such as, for instance, ordinary people or young and relatively unknown actors or musicians, who are dependent on the norms and values of gossip journalists and their sense of social responsibility.

Whereas it may seem naive to hope for a debate on ethics among gossip journalists that will produce a set of guidelines as part of their professional mind sets, it is not entirely unrealistic. As a result of case law, audience pressures and a new generation of journalists, Dutch gossip magazines at least are increasingly aware of the necessity that all of their stories should contain the truth to begin with. Also, the emergence of gossip in news media with a history of socially responsible reporting, may force gossip magazines to improve their standards. Although these forces and trends may be particular to the Netherlands and unlikely to result in easily applicable guidelines for the genre of reporting on private lives, one can only hope that from such day-to-day experience, a more socially responsible attitude will come about that is rooted in the professional gossip communities and that makes reading about private lives into a pleasure that one can trust is not gained at the expense of other people.

Note

1. The *Story* editor is an existing person who is an old acquaintance and who has been interviewed in the context of my research on politics and popular culture. For this project, many more gossip journalists have been interviewed who will be referred to in general in the rest of this chapter.

2. This chapter was completed before Princess Diana and Dodi Al Fayed were driven to their deaths by a drunken driver speeding to escape photographers. Had I been able to include the debate on the paparazzi and tabloid journalism that followed, the overall tenor of the chapter would not have changed, however I would have focused more on the way in which the profit-oriented media and gossip-hungry readers combine to form a deadly alliance in relation to which the paparazzi are the mercenaries rather than the instigators, and which seems to make any kind of ethical consideration subject to sales concerns (although in the aftermath some newspapers promised to raise their standards). The event also made me more aware of my probably particularly Dutch position on gossip writing which is inevitably informed by our relatively innocent and friendly gossip practices which do not compare to the British tabloids.

References

Bird, E. (1992) *For Enquiring Minds: A Cultural Study of Supermarket Tabloids*. Knoxville: University of Tennessee Press.

Fraser, N. (1992) 'Rethinking the public sphere: a contribution to the critique of actually existing democracy', in Calhoun, C. (ed.) *Habermas and the Public Sphere*. Mass: MIT Press.

IQ Magazine (1997) 'Een lief, braaf, blad', May, No. 2, p. 58.

Joyner-Priest, J. (1995) *Public Intimacies, Talk Show Participants and Tell-all TV*. Cresskill, NJ: Hampton.

Rooyen, L. van (1985) *Privé, beleef het mee*. Leiden: Batteljee en Terpstra.

Thompson, D.F. (1987) *Political Ethics and Public Office*. Cambridge: Harvard University Press.

Vesuvius (1993) Cultural talkshow, broadcast by VARA in the Netherlands.

Walraff, G, (1977) *Der Aufmacher. Der Mann der bei 'Bild' Hans Esser war*. Köln: Kiepenhauer & Witssch.

Zoonen, L. van (1998a) 'Politicians and their families in the Dutch gossip press', in L. van Zoonen and A. Sreberny-Mohammadi (eds) *Women's Politics and Communication*. New York: Hampton Press.

Zoonen, L. van (1998b) 'Finally I have my mother back! Male and female politicians in popular culture', *Harvard International Journal of Press Politics*.

12

Professional Ethics: Between Fortress Journalism and Cosmopolitan Democracy

Kaarle Nordenstreng

A decade and a half ago, in the early 1980s, I led a team which produced a document called 'International Principles of Professional Ethics in Journalism'. It was prepared and given in the name of 400,000 'working journalists in all parts of the world' at a consultative meeting of international and regional organizations of professional journalists held in Prague and Paris in 1983.[1] The document was to become a chapter in the history of global journalism, and its 10 principles even found their way to the latest edition of *Mass Communication Theory* (McQuail, 1994: 125).

These principles 'constitute the first time ever that the profession of journalism has manifested itself in a universal declaration of ethics', as I put it in a brochure promoting the document (see Nordenstreng, 1989: 250; 1995a: 124; the document is also reproduced in Cooper, 1989). Without going into detail here, let us just note that the document advocates a kind of democratic professionalism based on the people's right to true information on the one hand (Principles I and II) and a set of universal values on the other (Principle VIII: 'Respect for universal values and diversity of cultures'; Principle IX: 'Elimination of war and other great evils confronting humanity'). Thus it is not a self-centred concept of professionalism but professionalism in the service of the people and humanity. The document defines journalism as a profession with marked social responsibility (Principle III) and, along with professional integrity (Principle IV), due respect for public interest (Principle VII).

The 1983 Principles did not become a Magna Carta of global journalism.[2] Yet the document stands as a revealing reminder that at that time professional doctrines of journalism were in transition and that the ferment in the field began to bear interesting fruits 'after decades of intellectual stagnation' (Nordenstreng, 1995a: 126). Actually it was already in the 1970s, along with the process leading to the Mass Media Declaration of Unesco, that one could notice 'a great leap forward' whereby journalists became committed, not only to the old professional values of truth, etc., but also to new social and universal values of peace, etc. (Nordenstreng, 1984: 257–8).

In broad historical perspective, journalism as a profession developed over the last hundred years from various elementary forms (literature, politics,

etc.) towards professionalism dominated by technical skills and social status
– a narrow and technocratic notion which is fittingly characterized as
'fortress journalism'. However, throughout the hundred years there has also
been a countertrend towards a broader notion of professionalism, based on
international and humanitarian orientation as manifested by the 1983
Principles.[3] This trend combines global perspectives with prospects of
democracy, its latest version being the 'cosmopolitan democracy'.

Accordingly, professionalism in general, and professional ethics in particular, leads us in the field of journalism into a problematic and stimulating
terrain. I highlighted these perspectives under the title 'The journalist: a
walking paradox' in *The Democratization of Communication* (Nordenstreng,
1995a) and also as guest editor of a special issue on media ethics in the
European Journal of Communication (Nordenstreng, 1995b). This chapter
follows up these excursions by taking a look at two themes: professionalism
as a paradigm and codes of ethics as a central instrument of professionalism.
As the title suggests, I wish to expose the anti-democratic nature of professional ethics among media practitioners and thus to promote the citizens,
instead of journalists, as true masters of mass communication.

Professionalism

The evolution of professions in society has inspired a number of
sociologists – including classics such as Emile Durkheim, Talcott Parsons
and Max Weber – to theorize about the nature and significance of
professionalism. All these contributions boil down to two main strands of
thought or approaches, which can be labelled 'Functionalist' and 'neo-
Weberian', as suggested by Konttinen (1989).

The functionalist approach, in the spirit of Durkheimian integrity of
society, took the view that professions gradually occupied the place of
religion and the pre-industrial moral order in order to uphold social
harmony and balance under the new conditions of capitalist economy.
According to this view, professions with their rational and ethical standards,
collegiality and status, helped to solve the problems of the Hobbesian
pursuit of crude self-interest on the one hand, and those created by
bureaucratization on the other. Professions brought much-needed social
cohesion and new morality into the process of modernization, with scientific
specialization (Carr-Saunders and Wilson, 1933) and social service
(Marshall, 1939) as prominent characteristics of professionalism. Professionalism was seen as a positive element in a fundamentally optimistic
prospect of socio-economic development.

Diametrically opposed to such a functionalist view of professionalism
was the approach which perceived professions as bastions of narrow and
elitist interests instead of an overall societal and democratic interest. This
critical view of professionalism emerged in the 1960s, along with a number
of other similar intellectual tendencies, casting doubt on the conventional

wisdom that professions as such were functionally positive and suggesting that far from being altruistic, they served in modern society as repressive mechanisms which undermine democracy and turn active citizens into passive consumers – targets instead of sources of power. Accordingly, Illich (1973) called professions 'a form of imperialism' and wrote with others (Illich et al., 1977) a book 'disabling professions'. Likewise, Freidson (1970), Johnson (1981) and others exposed how professions turn into ideologies and how their analysis should be based on the concepts of power, control and autonomy.

This anti-functionalist view was elaborated into a true neo-Weberian approach by Giddens (1983), Larson (1977) and others by analysing the professions not only in terms of social power but above all in terms of market. Accordingly, the big question was market monopoly: 'how the professions had succeeded in gaining a monopoly position in the market of services, and how they had succeeded in closing off competitive groups which also sought the privileged position in society' (Konttinen, 1989: 175). Furthermore, developments in (post)modern societies suggested that what is crucial to professions for a market monopoly position are 'narrow intellectual techniques and a narrow specialization' (1989: 176).

Journalism as a profession fits perfectly into this overall picture. On the one hand, its evolution over the last hundred years provides a textbook example of a functionalist approach, with a surrounding ideology support-ing the profession.[4] On the other hand, reflections around media pro-fessions over the past two decades include more and more critical voices – next to those legitimizing the conventional wisdoms of the functionalist approach – and thus one can indeed speak of a democratic shift. In fact, the current debate on professionalism in journalism – with the prospects of 'information society' and its new interactive technologies – not only leads us to ask for more specialization but also invites us to question the rationale of traditional professionalism (see e.g. Bardoel, 1996).

My own approach to professionalism has evolved first along the typical route from a professional journalist's naive belief in skills-oriented competence into an academic journalism educator's more sophisticated belief in skills-plus-intellect-oriented competence. This already represented pure fortress journalism thinking, and the corresponding approach to professionalism was clearly functionalist. However, my evolution went even further – along with my involvement in the International Organization of Journalists (IOJ) and its affiliates around the world (professional and trade union organizations at the national level) – into a kind of international syndicalist's orientation based on worldwide solidarity of journalists in defence of their rights and status in society. At that stage my profes-sionalism was almost a holy concept standing for all good (from excellence of media content to honesty and freedom of communicators) against all bad (from technical ills to political repression).

However, internationalism does not only strengthen the fortress by adding foreign support to the domestic defence of political and social rights of journalists. At the same time internationalism incites a diametrically opposed tendency: to get beyond a narrow concept of professionalism into a sphere which can be called 'United Nations ideology', with values such as peace and international understanding becoming cornerstones next to the traditional values of truth, fairness, etc. Here it is no longer the media and practitioners that dominate the paradigm as the beginning and the end of professionalism. Instead, we are led to consider journalism and media just as means – instruments of universal values and principles as laid down in international humanitarian law (see e.g. Hamelink, 1994).

When a media-centred paradigm is replaced by a citizen-centred paradigm, one is also moving away from a functionalist approach to a critical (neo-Weberian) approach. I was a typical example of such a paradigm shift: the more I was acquainted with international norms and values, the less I was committed to conventional professionalism – international workers' solidarity notwithstanding. I even began to doubt the value basis of professionalism and saw it more and more as an ideological smokescreen to protect, instead of the workers' rights, the proprietors' interests. In one sense it was an ideological reorientation, with 'political' values replacing 'professional' ones. More fundamentally, however, it was a paradigm shift away from an approach which understands media and journalists as the owners of communication rights and freedoms towards a paradigm whereby it is the citizens and their civil society that should be seen as the ultimate owners of freedom of information.

This paradigm shift is highlighted by White (1995), who criticizes an individualistic ethics of media professionals and advocates that media ethics be seen as 'an integral part of the responsibility of all members of a given society for the quality of information available for collective decision-making in the society' (p. 442). I also emphasized that a self-centred fortress journalism alienated journalists from the people whom they were supposed to serve and that this professional ideology was supported by the natural inclination of journalists (and journalism students) to remain independent, thus creating a paradox whereby freedom and autonomy turned against democracy (Nordenstreng, 1995a: 118). My later remarks got ever stronger: '. . . deconstructing the conventional doctrines of professionalism as offshoots of imperialistic modernization, digested as enlightenment' (1995b: 436).

The hardening of line was obviously inspired by empirical results of case studies, notably those carried out in Sweden and Finland. A Swedish study (in fact a research programme) exposed great contradictions between the ideals and the reality of journalistic ethics (Nohrstedt and Ekström, 1994). Accordingly, critical examination of power holders proved to be only theory which did not carry on to journalistic practice; free and independent profession proved to be so highly routinized that practically no room was left for individual initiative; broad ethical norms proved to be neither broad nor stable but something that could be characterized as technocratic and opportunistic. Paradox was the concept used also by the Swedish colleagues in summarizing their results and recommending policies to bridge the gap between the ideals and the reality – mainly through internal and external media criticism (Ekström and Nohrstedt, 1996).

The Finnish case study which exposed the problems of journalistic professionalism was a large project on the role of media in Finland's entry to the European Union before the referendum on this question held in October 1994 (Kivikuru, 1996). The study demonstrated that people were quite prepared for an open and many-sided debate but the media largely missed this historical opportunity to provide a platform for a true exercise of freedom of expression. Instead of serving the civil society, journalists served the power elite – not in a vulgar and partisan way but 'professionally' by letting the elites (then mostly in favour of joining the EU) set the agenda and letting the routines shape the discourse (Mörä, 1995). In other words, the media and journalists were more or less extensions of the political and corporate powers without performing as a true 'fourth branch of government'.

Consequently, professionalism, instead of stopping such an intellectual corruption, legitimized it by providing journalists with a host of routines and cognitive conventions. And further proof of a fortress journalism is provided by the fact that the profession in Finland (in all counts among the most developed in Europe) made no use of the results of the study in its internal debate – although here we may also accuse media researchers for not pushing enough. All in all, the professionals seem to be guided by self-censorship rather than self-criticism!

Codes of ethics

In general, journalistic codes of ethics may be assessed from three angles. First, one may take a positive look by seeing them as vehicles of professionalization, as means of professional education, as instruments of consciousness-raising. Such a constructive – or naive – approach was typically taken when the first codes were introduced between the late nineteenth century and the Second World War, and it continues to be taken in the so-called developing and post-Communist countries. Second, one may take a negative look by seeing the codes of ethics as mere rhetorical devices, as deliberate window dressing and camouflage, or at best as manifestations of hypocrisy. Such a cynical approach is held today by many in the so-called western developed countries, with a marked discrepancy between the high ethical principles and the low practice of commercial media. Third, one may take an analytical look by seeing the codes as a mechanism of self-regulation, next to independent media councils and courts of honour. In this approach the codes are understood as part and parcel of a broader system of media regulation, extending from legal imperatives to cultural conventions. They are seen not just as an excuse to refrain from legislating the media but also as true means of regulating the media.

In the light of the above reflections on professionalism, there are good grounds for each of these three ways of approaching the codes, but the most important angle is opened up by the last approach: 'The message from post-Cold War Europe is clear: media must be free *and* accountable, with self-regulation an increasingly important form of "control" of the media.' (Nordenstreng, 1995b: 437). Taking a broader perspective of political science, at issue is not just journalism and the media but ultimately democracy as a system of governing society – not least the so-called civil society. Media in the contemporary world have become so vital that there are indeed good grounds to take them as a fourth branch of government – not just rhetorically but even in political theory and legal/ethical practice.[5]

Following up earlier studies in the 1970s, I initiated in 1989 an inventory of the journalistic codes of ethics adopted in the countries of the Conference on Security and Co-operation in Europe (CSCE). It was made by a graduate student (Pauli Juusela) with the assistance of the Prague-based International Journalism Institute (IJI). Based on 24 codes, the conclusion was that 'there is developing among the CSCE countries some sort of basic, universal model of journalistic codes where the accent is on truth, freedom of information, and protection of the individual' (Juusela, 1991: 1).

Since 1989–90 Europe has fundamentally changed, and therefore with another graduate student (Tiina Laitila) I made a new inventory of the codes that were valid in Europe in 1994–95. We located 31 contemporary codes adopted by journalists' associations or other bodies, notably media councils (Laitila, 1995a, 1995b). This inventory shows that most of the codes are quite fresh; over two-thirds of them were adopted in the 1990s. Many of those, such as the Polish and the Russian codes, were preceded by other codes years and decades earlier, but they were updated and revised recently in order to keep up with changing times, and more codes are in the making. Between 1995 and 1997 five new ones were completed (including Armenia and Belarus) and others are under way (including the Czech Republic). By and large we can say that there are current codes of professional ethics, adopted by journalists' own associations, in well over 30 European countries – Europe understood from the Atlantic to the Urals.[6]

As shown by Laitila, the most widely covered aspects in these codes are the journalist's accountability towards the public, his/her accountability towards the sources and referents and the protection of the journalist's integrity. Least salient of various functions of the codes is the journalist's accountability towards the state and the employers. It is significant how much emphasis is placed by the codes on the public, as well as to the sources and referents (some 60 per cent of altogether 61 provisions mentioned in the 31 codes), seen against the natural functions of protecting the integrity and status of the journalist (some 30 per cent). This means that the codes are designed not just for the selfish purpose of safeguarding the journalists' fortress but also for an idealistic purpose of serving the public interest.

An idealistic and altruistic emphasis is still present if we pick up only those provisions which are present in at least half of the European codes. This list, which could be taken as a basis for a common European code (in case there is a need to construct one), according to Laitila (1995a: 68; 1995b: 543) is as follows:

- Truthfulness in gathering and reporting information
- Freedom of expression and comment; defence of these rights
- Equality by not discriminating against anyone on the basis of his/her race, ethnicity or religion, sex, social class, profession, handicap or any other personal characteristics
- Fairness by using only straightforward means in the gathering of information
- Respect for the sources and referents and their integrity; for the copyright and laws of quoting
- Independence/integrity by refusing bribes or any other outside influence on the work; by demanding the conscience clause.

These six themes mostly represent conventional professionalism – in its less self-centred brand – except the third one (equality and non-discrimination) which has a bias on behalf of so-called ordinary people and their human rights, that is, a clear tendency away from fortress journalism. The theme of countering racial and other forms of discrimination was indeed a central element of the universal values advocated by the 1983 International Principles of Professional Ethics in Journalism. Moreover, combating racism and xenophobia in the media has become in the 1990s a common concern for journalist associations in Europe, the International Federation of Journalists (IFJ), the Council of Europe and the European Union.[7]

Although the contemporary ethics of European journalists, as reflected in the codes of ethics, still misses some aspects of the universal values of the 1983 document, the overall philosophy remains more or less the same – with a dedication to journalists' but also people's rights and a commitment to not only 'professional' but also 'political' values. This suggests quite a balanced approach to professionalism, far from the doubtful perspectives opened up by the above reflections on professionalism as such.

However, the question must be posed: what is the significance of the codes of ethics – to what extent they are put into practice in real life and to what extent they are even known among rank-and-file journalists? On both counts evidence is rather distressing, to the effect of supporting the second – negative or cynical – angle of the three outlined above. Am I then naive in taking the codes seriously; am I not inconsistent in accepting them as true readings of positive professionalism, while suspecting most other aspects of professionalism as negative building blocks of a self-centred fortress journalism?

My response to this challenge is, first, that it is worth taking the codes of ethics at face value, since they have after all been carefully elaborated and adopted by representative professional bodies. In no case should they be taken as dead letters of history, since most of them are quite recent and kept alive by periodic revisions (and by institutions such as EthicNet!). In other words, the codes do represent real and present professional thinking – however rhetorical it may be in its relation to actual practice. Secondly, the codes are invaluable as an instrument of self-reflection by helping the practitioners to understand the nature of their work and relating their practice into broader moral and ethical values. In other words, the codes serve as vehicles of sensitization or, in Paolo Freire's words, conscientization.

Conclusions

This chapter presents a narrative where professionalism arrests and codes of ethics liberate. Naturally it is a one-sided story, both ways. For example, one could choose to cast doubt on the codes of ethics and the way they are taught in schools of communication which typically prepare professionals 'more for conformity with media organizations than for creative questioning' (White, 1995: 456). One could also point out how conventional professionalism, with its routines and even protective walls, is functional and indeed much needed in countries which have moved from one socio-political system to another, with the media remaining not only free from earlier controls but also turning into a chaotic playground void of any rules.

Thus the main point is not to discover who is the hero and who the villain but to see that the concept of professional ethics contains a contradiction between media-centred professionalism and citizen-centred ethics. I suggest that it is a genuine contradiction – in the sense of a true dialectic – where both sides are vital. Still, under the contemporary conditions of the European Union, North America and the rest of the so-called western democracies, it seems to me imperative to take a critical approach to professionalism or else we let the media and journalism be taken over by anti-democratic forces.

To critically deconstruct professionalism and to promote its ethics side is just another way of joining a broader intellectual movement in defence of democracy in the contemporary world. Given regional developments such as the EU and NAFTA, and given the overall trend towards globalization – both in the real world and thinking about the world – this movement has elevated reflections about democracy from narrow national perspectives to literally worldwide perspectives. Consequently, universal values and cosmopolitan structures are back on the agenda (reminding us of the intellectual project of the anarchists in the mid nineteenth century).

Held (1993, 1995) proposes a new, 'cosmopolitan' model of democracy for the new global order composed of diverse networks of power under a UN umbrella, instead of nation states of the Westphalian order. This model fits perfectly with the perspectives of universal values for communication ethics raised by Christians and Traber (1997).

In this context, the one and a half decade old International Principles of Professional Ethics in Journalism appear quite up to date. Despite counter-trends, more and more journalists and their national and international organizations seem to have learned the lesson that professional ethics, with codes and councils as its instruments, supports media autonomy and self-regulation instead of inviting controls from the outside. Moreover, practitioners increasingly recognize that only an anti-intellectual may claim total autonomy in society, free from any accountability. A revealing statement was given by the same coalition of worldwide journalists' organizations that had earlier issued the International Principles (Nordenstreng, 1993: 105; 1995a: 126):

> We wish to reiterate the principal view that the operation of the mass media should be determined primarily by the practice of professional journalism supported by the idea of a free and responsible press.

> We acknowledge the fact that the role played by information and communication in national as well as international spheres has become more and more prominent during the past decade, with a growing responsibility being placed upon the mass media and journalists. This calls, increasingly, for professional autonomy of journalists as well as a measure of public accountability.

By and large, professional ethics as a concept and a project – by practitioners and media scholars alike – can be seen as a component of a still broader concept and project: the normative theories of the media.[8] Like professional ethics, normative theories also seek to raise consciousness and

> may not only serve as vehicles of conservative indoctrination but can also be made to sensitize media policymakers and professionals to acknowledge their own dependencies. . . . Thus normative theories are justified, not as affirmative instruments to strengthen the prevailing ideology . . . but as emancipating instruments to stand back from the prevailing ideology. (Nordenstreng, 1997a: 107)

Notes

1. The meeting was hosted by the Prague-based International Organization of Journalists (IOJ) which at the time was the largest non-governmental organization in the field of journalism (I was its President at the time). One of the outside experts who examined this document at the draft stage was Denis McQuail, who was also very helpful in polishing the English of the text.

2. The Principles became a hostage of two developments. First, the controversy around the New World Information and Communication Order (NWICO) also politicized the discourse on journalism ethics, as shown by the history of the Symposium on the Mass Media Declaration of Unesco (Nordenstreng, 1993). Secondly, the political changes in Eastern Europe paralysed the IOJ and turned Unesco around in its approach to NWICO (Nordenstreng, 1997b).

3. The international movement of journalists was shaped a hundred years ago, in the 1890s, during a dynamic period of nationalist media development and growing international contacts, notably through the telegraph. To be precise, the first international conference of 'press people' was organized in Antwerp in July 1893. I began to work on the history of the international movement of journalists when I was still IOJ President (leading to two volumes of *Useful*

Recollections), and currently I am about to complete a book on the hundred years of the international journalist (with Ulf Jonas Bjoerk and others).

4. A historical review of the professionalization of journalists by Svennik Hoyer and Epp Lauk, with an extensive bibliography, is included in the forthcoming book referred to in note 3 above.

5. The Finnish discussion among constitutional lawyers has indeed generated a proposal (by Professor Emeritus Kauko Sipponen) that the traditional three estates (legislative, executive and judiciary) be complemented by such contemporary forces as trade unions, market forces – and the mass media.

6. The texts of all these codes (translated into English) are now stored in an electronic databank called 'EthicNet' and operated at The University of Tampere, Department of Journalism and Mass Communication (see http://www.uta.fi/ethicnet/).

7. The Council of Europe commissioned in 1995 a comparative study on codes of ethics dealing with media and intolerance from the Department of Journalism and Mass Communication at the University of Tampere. Its report is included in the same publication that reproduces the bulk of Tiina Laitila's Master's thesis (Laitila, 1995a). The IFJ for its part has launched a prize for tolerance in journalism, supported by the European Commission, the Council of Europe and Europe's leading broadcasters and publishers. The prize is given at the annual European Media Forum, to celebrate 21 March – the European Day Against Racism.

8. Denis McQuail has joined me, Clifford Christians, Theodore Glasser and Robert White in an attempt to rewrite the classic *Four Theories of the Press*. For details, see Nordenstreng, 1997a.

References

Bardoel, Jo (1996) 'Beyond journalism: a profession between information society and civil society', *European Journal of Communication* 11 (3): 283–302.

Carr-Saunders, A.M. and Wilson, P.A. (1933) *The Professions*. Oxford: Clarendon Press.

Cooper, Thomas W. (ed.) (1989) *Communication Ethics and Global Change*. White Plains, NY: Longman.

Christians, Clifford and Traber, Michael (eds) (1997) *Communication Ethics and Universal Values*. Thousand Oaks, CA: Sage.

Ekström, Mats and Nohrstedt, Stig Arne (1996) *Journalistikens etiska problem* [*The Ethical Problem of Journalism*]. Smedjebacken: Högskolan i Örebro.

Freidson, E. (1970) *Professional Dominance: The Social Structure of Medical Care*. New York: Atherton Press.

Giddens, Anthony (1983) *The Class Struggle of the Advanced Societies*. London: Hutchinson.

Hamelink, Cees J. (1994) *The Politics of World Communication: A Human Rights Perspective*. London: Sage.

Held, David (ed.) (1993) *Prospects for Democracy: North, South, East, West*. Stanford, CA: Stanford University Press.

Held, David (1995) *Democracy and the Global Order: From the Modern State to Cosmopolitan Governance*. Padstow: Polity Press.

Illich, Ivan (1973) 'The professions as a form of imperialism', *New Society* 13 (September): 633–5.

Illich, I., Zola I.K., McKnight, J., Caplan, J. and Shaiken, H. (1977) *Disabling Professions*. London: Marion Boyards.

Johnson, T. (1981) *Professions and Power*. Hong Kong: Macmillan.

Juusela, Pauli (1991) *Journalistic Codes of Ethics in the CSCE Countries*. University of Tampere: Publications of the Department of Journalism and Mass Communication, Series B 31.

Kivikuru, Ullamaija (ed.) (1996) *Kansa Euromyllyssä. Journalismi, kampanjat ja kansalaisen mediamaisemat Suomen EU-jäsenyysprosessissa* [*People in Euro Mill. Journalism, Campaigns and Citizens' Mediascapes in the Finnish EU Membership Process*]. Helsinki: University of Helsinki Press.

Konttinen, Esa (1989) *Harmonian takuumiehiä vai etuoikeuksien monopolisteja? Professioiden sosiologian funktionalistisen ja uusweberiläisen valtasuuntauksen tarkastelua* [*Guarantees of Social Harmony or Monopolies of Privileges? Functionalist and Neo-Weberian Approaches in the Sociology of Professions*]. University of Jyväskylä: Publications of the Department of Sociology, no. 45.

Laitila, Tiina (1995a) 'Codes of ethics in Europe', in Kaarle Nordenstreng (ed.) *Reports on Media Ethics in Europe*. University of Tampere: Publications of the Department of Journalism and Mass Communication, Series B 41, pp. 23–79.

Laitila, Tiina (1995b) 'Journalistic codes of ethics in Europe', *European Journal of Communication* 10 (4): 527–44.

Larson, Magali Sarfatti (1977) *The Rise of Professionalism: A Sociological Analysis*. Berkeley and Los Angeles: University of California Press.

Marshall, T.H. (1939) 'The recent history of professionalism in relation to social structure and social policy', *The Canadian Journal of Political Science* V (Feb.–Nov.): 325–40.

McQuail, Denis (1994) *Mass Communication Theory: An Introduction*, 3rd edn. London: Sage. (1st edn, 1983.)

Mörä, Tuomo (1995) 'EU-agendan synty joukkoviestimissä' [Beyond the EU agenda in the Finnish mass media], *Politiikka* 4: 227–37.

Nohrstedt, Stig Arne and Ekström, Mats (1994) *Ideal och verklighet: nyhetsjournalistikens etik i praktiken* [*Ideal and Reality: Ethics of News Journalism in Practice*]. Kungälv: Högskolan i Örebro, Göteborgs Universitet och Mitthögskolan i Sundsvall.

Nordenstreng, Kaarle (1984) *The Mass Media Declaration of UNESCO*. Norwood, NJ: Ablex.

Nordenstreng, Kaarle (1989) 'Historical highlights', in Kaarle Nordenstreng and Hifzi Topuz (eds) *Journalist: Status, Rights and Responsibilities*. Prague: International Organization of Journalists, pp. 247–60.

Nordenstreng, Kaarle (1993) 'The story and lesson of a symposium', in George Gerbner, Hamid Mowlana and Kaarle Nordenstreng (eds) *The Global Media Debate: Its Rise, Fall and Renewal*. Norwood, NJ: Ablex, pp. 99–107.

Nordenstreng, Kaarle (1995a) 'The journalist: a walking paradox', in Philip Lee (ed.) *The Democratization of Communication*. Cardiff: University of Wales Press, pp. 114–29.

Nordenstreng, Kaarle (1995b) 'Introduction: a state of the art', *European Journal of Communication* 10 (4): 435–9.

Nordenstreng, Kaarle (1997a) 'Beyond the Four Theories of the Press', in Jan Servaes and Rico Lie (eds) *Media and Politics in Transition: Cultural Identity in the Age of Globalization*. Louvain, Belgium: ACCO Publishers, pp. 97–109.

Nordenstreng, Kaarle (1997b) 'The context: great media debate', in Richard Vincent, Kaarle Nordenstreng and Michael Traber (eds) *Towards Equity in Global Communication: MacBride Update*. Cresskill, NJ: Hampton Press.

White, Robert A. (1995) 'From codes of ethics to public cultural truth', *European Journal of Communication* 10 (4): 441–59.

IV THE POLITICS OF POPULAR CULTURE

13

Stories of Violence and the Public Interest

George Gerbner

Most of what we know, or think we know, we have never personally experienced. We live in a world erected by the stories we hear and see and tell. Unlocking incredible riches through imagery and words, conjuring up the unseen through art, creating towering works of imagination and fact through science, poetry, song, tales, reports and laws – that is the true magic of human life. Through that magic we live in a world much wider than the threats and gratifications of the immediate physical environment, which is the world of other species.

Stories socialize us into roles of gender, age, class, vocation and lifestyle, and offer models of conformity or targets for rebellion. They weave the seamless web of the cultural environment that cultivates most of what we think, what we do, and how we conduct our affairs.

The story-telling process used to be hand-crafted, home-made, community-inspired. Now it is mostly mass-produced and policy-driven. It is the end result of a complex manufacturing and marketing process. It both defines and then addresses the public interest. This situation calls for a new diagnosis and a new prescription.

The stories that animate our cultural environment have three distinct but related functions. These functions are (1) to reveal how things work; (2) to describe what things are; and (3) to tell us what to do about them. Stories of the first kind, revealing how things work, illuminate the all-important but invisible relationships and hidden dynamics of life. Fairy tales, novels, plays, comics, cartoons, and other forms of creative imagination and imagery are the basic building blocks of human understanding. They show complex causality by presenting imaginary action in total situations, coming to some conclusion that has a moral purpose and a social function. You do not have to believe the 'facts' of Little Red Riding Hood to grasp the notion that big bad 'wolves' victimize old women and trick little girls –

a lesson in gender roles, fear, and power. Stories of this kind build from infancy on the fantasy we call reality. I do not suggest that the revelations are false, which they may or may not be, but that they are synthetic, selective, often mythical, and always socially constructed.

Stories of the second kind depict what things are. These are descriptions, depictions, expositions, reports abstracted from total situations and filled in with 'facts' the fantasies conjured up by stories of the first kind. They are the presumably factual accounts, the chronicles of the past and the news of today. Stories of what things are may confirm or deny some conception of how things work. Their high 'facticity' (i.e. correspondence to actual events presumed to exist independently of the story) gives them special status in political theory and often in law. They give emphasis and credibility to selected parts of each society's fantasies of reality. They convey information about finance, weddings, crime, lotteries, terrorists, and so on. They alert us to certain interests, threats, opportunities and challenges.

Stories of the third kind tell us what to do. These are stories of value and choice. They present things, behaviours or styles of life as desirable (or undesirable), propose ways to obtain (or avoid) them, and the price to be paid for attainment (or failure). They are instructions, laws, regulations, cautionary tales, commands, slogans, sermons, and exhortations. Today most of them are called commercials and other advertising messages and images we see and hear every day. Stories of the third kind clinch the lessons of the first two and turn them into action. They typically present an objective to be sought or to be avoided, and offer a product, service, candidate, institution or action purported to help attain or avoid it. The lessons of fictitious Little Red Riding Hood and her more realistic sequels prominent in everyday news and entertainment not only teach lessons of vulnerability, mistrust and dependence but also help sell burglar alarms, more jails and executions promised to enhance security (which they rarely do), and other ways to adjust to a structure of power.

Ideally, the three kinds of stories check and balance each other. But in a commercially driven culture, stories of the third kind pay for most of the first two. That creates a coherent cultural environment whose overall function is to provide a hospitable and effective context for stories that sell. With the coming of the electronic age, that cultural environment is increasingly monopolized, homogenized and globalized. We must then look at the historic course of our journey to see what this new age means for us and for the public interest.

The industrial and electronic revolutions

For the longest time in human history, stories were told only face to face. A community was defined by the rituals, mythologies and imageries held in common. All useful knowledge was encapsulated in aphorisms and legends, proverbs and tales, incantations and ceremonies. Writing was rare and holy, forbidden for slaves. Laboriously inscribed manuscripts conferred sacred power to their interpreters, the priests and ministers. As a sixteenth-century scribe put it:

Those who observe the codices,
Those who recite them.
Those who noisily turn the pages of illustrated manuscripts.
Those who have possession of the black and red ink and that which is
    pictured;
they lead us, they guide us, they tell us the way.

State and church ruled in a symbiotic relationship of mutual dependence and tension. State, composed of feudal nobles, was the economic, military and political order; church its cultural arm.

The industrial revolution changed all that. One of the first machines stamping out standardized artefacts was the printing press. Its product, the book, was a prerequisite for all the other upheavals to come. Printing begins the industrialization of story-telling, arguably the most profound transformation in the humanization process. The book could be given to all who could read, requiring education and creating a new literate class of people. Readers could now interpret the book (at first the Bible) for themselves, breaking the monopoly of priestly interpreters and ushering in the Reformation. When the printing press was hooked up to the steam engine the industrialization of story-telling shifted into high gear. Rapid publication and mass transport created a new form of consciousness: modern mass publics. Publics are loose aggregations of people who share some common consciousness of how things work, what things are, and what ought to be done – but never meet face-to-face. That was never before possible.

Stories could now be sent – often smuggled – across hitherto impenetrable or closely guarded boundaries of time, space and status. The book lifts people from their traditional moorings as the industrial revolution uproots them from their local communities and cultures. They can now get off the land and go to work in far-away ports, factories and continents, and have with them a packet of common consciousness – the book or journal, and later the motion picture (silent at first) – wherever they go.

Publics, created by such publication, are necessary for the formation of individual and group identities in the new urban environment, as the different classes and regional, religious and ethnic groups try to maintain some sense of distinct integrity and also to live together with some degree of cooperation with other groups. Publics are the basic units of self-government. They make it possible to elect or select representatives to an assembly trying to reconcile diverse interests. The maintenance and integrity of multiple publics makes self-government feasible for large, complex, and diverse national communities. People engage in long and costly struggles to be free to create and share stories that fit the reality of competing and often conflicting values and interests. Most of our assumptions about human development and political plurality and choice are rooted in the print era.

The second great transformation, the electronic revolution, ushers in the telecommunications era. Its mainstream, television, is superimposed upon and reorganizes print-based culture. Unlike the industrial revolution, the new upheaval does not uproot people from their homes but transports them in their homes. It re-tribalizes modern society. It challenges and changes the role of both church and education in the new culture. For the first time in human history, children are born into homes where mass-produced stories can reach them on average more than seven hours a day. Most waking hours, and often dreams, are filled with these stories. The stories do not come from their families, schools, churches, neighbourhoods, and often not even from their native countries, or, in fact, from anyone with anything relevant to tell. They come from small groups of distant conglomerates with something to sell.

The cultural environment in which we live becomes the byproduct of marketing. The historic nexus of state and church is replaced by the new symbiotic relationship of state and television. The 'state' itself is the twin institution of elected public government and selected private corporate government, ruling in the legal, military and economic domains. Media, its cultural arm, is dominated by the private establishment, despite its use of the public airways. Giant industries discharge their messages into the mainstream of common consciousness. Channels proliferate and new technologies pervade home and office while mergers and bottom-line pressures shrink creative alternatives and reduce diversity of content. These changes may appear to be broadening local, parochial horizons, but they also mean a homogenization of outlooks and limitation of alternatives. For media professionals, the changes mean fewer opportunities and greater compulsions to present life in saleable packages. Creative artists, scientists, humanists can still explore and enlighten and occasionally even challenge, but, increasingly, their stories must fit marketing strategies and priorities.

Viewing commercials is 'work' performed by audiences in exchange for 'free' news and entertainment. But, in fact, we pay dearly through a surcharge added to the price of every advertised product that goes to subsidize commercial media, and through allowing advertising expenditures to be a tax-deductible business expense. These give-aways of public moneys for private purposes further erode the diversity of the cultural mainstream. Broadcasting is the most concentrated, homogenized, and globalized medium. The top 100 US advertisers pay for two-thirds of all network television. Four networks, allied to giant transnational corporations – our private 'Ministry of Culture' – control the bulk of production and distribution, and shape the cultural mainstream. Other interests, religious or educational, minority views, and the potential of any challenge to dominant perspectives, lose ground with every merger.

Formula-driven assembly-line produced programmes increasingly dominate the airways. The formulas themselves reflect the structure of power that produces them and function to preserve and enhance that structure of power. Perhaps the leading example of such story functions is violence. It is a good example of how the system works; it is also an indication of the magnitude and nature of its challenge to the public interest.

Stories of violence

Humankind may have had more bloodthirsty eras, but none as filled with images of crime and violence as the present. While violent crime rates remain essentially flat or decline, news of crime surges to new highs. Violence is a demonstration of power. Armies conquer, states impose their will, persons use violence to intimidate. Violence is always a complex scenario of victims as well as victors and a wide range of needs, circumstances, justifications and motivations.

Media violence is a symbolic show of force serving many of the same functions more cheaply and of course entertainingly. It shows who can get away with what against whom. This show-and-tell is a staple of all storytelling. It cultivates a sense of command and a calculus of vulnerability. It shapes society's pecking order. It makes some people act like majorities and others like minorities. The perennial debate about media violence, made trendy by the very fears it generates, brought forth a remarkable array of obfuscations from all sides and levels of the political spectrum. Most of the public discourse, conducted through and shaped by the media themselves, persists in asking the questions reflecting, amplifying, and exploiting media-driven anxieties and interests: Does media violence incite real-life violence? Is it a product of freedom of expression, therefore in the public interest? If so, is its regulation a form of censorship? But the issues are much more fundamental than parental advisories, V-chips, labelling, or simple controls. They deal with the structural connections between television violence, marketing imperatives and social controls. The questions we will address are: What is the difference between television and other media violence? What drives television violence? What are its consequences for human development, the public interest and the distribution of power?

US television networks doubled the time given to crime coverage between 1992 and 1993. *TV Guide*'s survey of 13 August 1994 also showed a steep increase in stories of violence, especially in local television news. Monitoring by the Des Moines (Iowa) Register (27 March 1994) illustrated how crime and violence skew news priorities. Of the six top stories on Des Moines evening newscasts during February 1994, one out of four (118 stories) dealt with crime and violence. By comparison, 27 featured business, 17 dealt with government, 15 reported about racial relations, and two were stories about the schools. A University of Miami study of local television news found that time devoted to crime ranged from 23 to 50 per cent (averaging 32 per cent) while violent crime in the city remained constant, involving less that one-tenth of one per cent of the population.

A study by Robert Entman for the Chicago Council on Urban Affairs found not only that local news shows are dominated by vivid images of violence, but that 'a high percentage of African-Americans and Latinos are shown as victimizers of society, and few as social helpers', contributing to a sense of fear and distrust (that our own research diagnosed as the 'mean world syndrome'), and to the notion that 'the inner city is dominated by dangerous and irresponsible minorities' (Entman, 1994). Another study of homicide news reporting found that only one of three actual homicides was reported, and that the most likely to be selected were those in which the victims were white rather than black or Latino, contrary to the actual crime statistics. University of Pennsylvania sociologist Elijah Anderson also noted in the November 1994 issue of *Philadelphia Magazine* that media portrayals of crime and violence involving blacks and the resulting demonization of black males, becomes a major reason for 'white flight'. In fact, however, African-American men, not whites, are the most likely to be the victims of violence.

Our Cultural Indicators study of local news on Philadelphia television found that crime and/or violence items usually lead the newscast and pre-empt any balanced coverage of the city. Furthermore, 80 per cent of crime and violence reported on Philadelphia local news was not even local to the city. It is as if a quota were imposed on the editorial staff to fill from wherever they can. It is also the cheapest way to fill the time. We also found that whites are more likely to be reported when they are the victims and African-Americans are more likely to be reported when they are the perpetrators. Black-on-white crime is less frequent but more newsworthy than any other combination. The percentage of prime time television dramatic programmes with overt physical violence was 58 in 1974, 73 in 1984, and 75 in 1994. The saturation of violent scenes was five per hour in 1974, five per hour in 1984, and five per hour in 1994 – unchanged. In Saturday morning children's programmes scenes of violence occur between 20 and 25 times per hour. They are sugar-coated with humour, to be sure; that makes the pill of power easier to swallow.

Violence is, of course, a legitimate and even necessary news and dramatic feature to show the tragic costs of deadly compulsions. However, such tragic sense of violence has been swamped by 'happy violence' produced on the television dramatic assembly line. 'Happy violence' is cool, swift and painless, and always leads to a happy ending. Far from Shakespeare or the Bible, it occurs five times per hour, designed to deliver the audience to the next commercial in a receptive mood. Action movies cash in on the trend. Robocop's first rampage for law and order killed 32 people. *Robocop 2* slaughtered 81. The sick movie *Death Wish* claimed nine victims. In the sequel, the 'bleeding heart liberal' turned vigilante disposed of 52. *Rambo: First Blood* rambled through Southeast Asia leaving 62 corpses. *Rambo III* visited Afghanistan killing 106. *Godfather I* produced 12 corpses, *Godfather*

II put away 18 and *Godfather III* killed no less than 53. The daredevil cop in the original *Die Hard* saved the day with a modest 18 dead. *Die Hard 2* achieved a phenomenal body count of 264.

Violence is a demonstration of power. Its principal lesson is to show quickly and dramatically who can get away with what against whom. That exercise defines majority might and minority risk. It shows one's place in the societal pecking order. The role of violence in the media mainstream of television emerges from our analysis of prime time network programmes monitored since 1967. Women play one out of three characters in drama, one out of six in the news. Young people comprise one-third and old persons one-fifth of their actual proportions of the population. Most other minorities are even more underrepresented. Most of the groups that are underrepresented are also those who suffer the worst fate. The typical viewer of prime time television drama sees, every week, an average of 21 criminals arrayed against an army of 41 public and private law enforcers. Crime and violence engage more characters than all other occupations combined. About one out of three speaking parts, and more than half of all major characters, are involved in violence either as victims or as victimizers, or both.

We calculated the violence 'pecking order' by counting the number of victims for every ten perpetrators of violence. That 'risk ratio' expresses the 'price' groups of characters pay for committing violence. We found that overall average risk ratio (the number of victims per ten perpetrators) is 12. But the ratio for women is 17, for lower-class characters is 19, for elderly characters is 20, and for women of colour is 22. In other words, minority groups tend to pay a higher price for their show of force than do the majorities.

Our surveys show that heavy viewers express a greater sense of apprehension and vulnerability than do light viewers in the same groups. Heavy viewers are more likely than comparable groups of light viewers to overestimate their chances of involvement in violence; to believe that their neighbourhoods are unsafe; to state that fear of crime is a very serious personal problem; and to assume that crime is rising, regardless of the facts of the case. Heavy viewers are also more likely to buy new locks, watchdogs, and guns 'for protection' (thus becoming the major cause of handgun violence). Moreover, viewers who see members of their own group underrepresented but overvictimized develop an even greater sense of apprehension and mistrust. Insecure, angry, mistrustful people may be prone to violence but are even more likely to be dependent on authority and susceptible to deceptively simple, strong, hard-line postures and appeals.

Violence and corporate imperatives

Media violence is not a reflection of creative freedom, viewer preference, or crime statistics. It is the byproduct of a manufacturing and marketing process. The real problem of television violence reflects structural trends toward concentration, conglomeration and globalization in media industries and the marketing pressures fuelling those trends. Concentration of ownership denies access to new entries and to alternative perspectives. Having fewer buyers for their products forces the remaining 'content providers' deeper into deficit financing. As a consequence, most television and movie producers cannot break even on the domestic market. They are forced into video and foreign sales to make a profit. Therefore, they need a dramatic ingredient that requires no translation, 'speaks action' in any language, and fits any culture. That ingredient is violence.

Our analysis shows that violence dominates US exports. We compared 250 US programmes exported to 10 countries with 111 programmes shown in the US during the same year. Violence was the main theme of 40 per cent of home-shown and 49 per cent of exported programmes. Crime/action series comprised 17 per cent of home-shown and 46 per cent of exported programmes. NAFTA and GATT dumps even more mayhem on the world in the name of 'free trade'.

Far from reflecting creative freedom, the strategy wastes talent, restricts freedom and chills originality. Production companies emphasizing alternative approaches to conflict, like Globalvision, Inc., G-W Associates and Future Wave, have difficulty selling their product. Concentration of ownership brings streamlining of production, economies of scale, and emphasis on dramatic ingredients most suitable for aggressive international promotion. Cross-media conglomeration and 'synergy' means that ownership of product in one medium can be used, reviewed, promoted, and marketed in other media 'in house'. It means less competition, fewer alternative voices, greater emphasis on formulas that saturate more markets at a lower cost per viewer. Privatization of formerly public service broadcasting around the world means production and distribution of even more of the same type of product.

Not the least of the consequences is the damage done to dramatic originality and integrity. Arbitrarily contrived violence is inserted into formula-driven programmes according to market conditions, not dramatic need. If dramatic integrity and creativity are not valid reasons for most violent scenes, neither is the industry's chief rationale – public appeal. To be sure, some highly popular films and programmes are violent, but by no means most. In fact, violent programming is not especially popular either with viewers or, as we shall see, with broadcasters who are responsible to the public as licence holders. Why, then, does a public relations-conscious and politically sophisticated industry persist in risking domestic backlash and international embarrassment for its perennially violent fare? The answer is that violence travels well.

There is no free market on television. Expensive and risky production requires the pooling of large resources and even larger distribution capabilities. That is (and will continue to be) the main reason for networks and other forms of consolidation and conglomeration. The oligopolies that dominate the market can set the price of production so low that most producers barely break even on the domestic market. They are forced on to the world market and all forms of syndication, including cable and video sales worldwide, to make a profit. Syndicators demand 'action' (the code word for violence) because it 'travels well around the world,' said the producer of *Die Hard 2*. 'Everyone understands an action movie. If I tell a joke, you may not get it but if a bullet goes through the window, we all know how to hit the floor, no matter the language.' (Graphic sex also travels well and is second to violence, but it runs into many more inhibitions and restrictions around the world.)

The usual rationalization that media violence 'gives the public what it wants' is disingenuous. The public rarely gets a fair choice in which all elements but violence, including placement, headline, promotion, air time, celebrity value, treatment, and so on, are equal. Economic analysis and trade press reports indicate that in the media marketing formula of cost per thousand (readers or viewers delivered to the advertiser), cost weighs as heavily in the balance as the audience side of the equation. There is no evidence that, cost and other factors being equal, violence per se gives audiences 'what they want'. As the trade paper *Broadcasting & Cable* editorialized on 20 September 1993 (p. 66), 'the most popular programming is hardly violent as anyone with a passing knowledge of Nielsen ratings will tell you'.

Indeed. We compared the ratings of over 100 violent and the same number of non-violent shows aired at the same time on network television. The average Nielsen rating of the violent sample was 11.1; the rating for the non-violent sample was 13.8. The share of viewing households in the violent and non-violent samples, respectively, was 18.9 and 22.5. The non-violent sample was more highly rated than the violent sample for each of the five periods studied. The amount and consistency of violence further increased the unpopularity gap.

There is no evidence that, other factors being equal, violence per se is giving most viewers, countries and citizens 'what they want'. On the contrary, the evidence is that most people suffer the violence inflicted on them with diminishing tolerance. Organizations of creative workers in media, health professionals, law enforcement agencies, and virtually all other media-oriented professional and citizen groups have come out against television violence. A March 1985 Harris survey showed that 78 per cent disapprove of violence they see on television. In a *Times–Mirror* national poll in 1993, 80 per cent said entertainment violence was 'harmful' to society, compared with 64 per cent in 1983. Local broadcasters, legally responsible for what goes on the air, also oppose the overkill and complain about loss of control. *Electronic Media* reported on 2 August 1993 that in its own survey of 100 general managers, three out of four said there is too much needless violence on television and 57 per cent would like to have 'more input on program content decisions'. A US *News & World Report* survey published on 30 April 1994 found that 59 per cent of media workers saw entertainment violence as a serious problem.

Citizen action

There is a liberating alternative. It exists in various forms in all democratic countries. It is an independent citizen voice in cultural policy-making. More freedom from inequitable and intimidating marketing formulas, and a greater diversity of sources of support, are the effective and acceptable ways to increase diversity of content. That is also the democratic way to reduce media violence to its valid role and reasonable proportions. The liberating alternative requires citizen action. No other force can provide the broad support needed for loosening the global marketing noose around the necks of producers, writers, directors, actors and journalists. More freedom, not more censorship, is the effective and acceptable way to reduce television violence to its legitimate role and proportion. The role of Congress, if any, is to turn its anti-trust and civil rights oversight on the centralized and globalized industrial structures and marketing strategies that impose violence on creative people in many cultures, and foist it on the children of the world.

The Cultural Environment Movement was launched in response to this challenge. CEM's Founding Convention was held in St Louis, Missouri, 15–17 March 1996. It was the most diverse international assembly of leaders and activists in the field of culture and communication that has ever met. The 261 participants debated and approved a People's Communication Charter, the Viewer's Declaration of Independence, and developed recommendations for action. The new approach of the CEM involves:

- Building a new coalition involving media councils worldwide; teachers, students and parents; groups concerned with children, youth and ageing; women's groups; religious and minority organizations; educational, health, environmental, legal, and other professional associations; consumer groups and agencies; associations of creative workers in the media and in the arts and sciences; independent computer network organizers and other organizations and individuals committed to broadening the freedom and diversity of communication.
- Opposing domination and working to abolish existing concentration of ownership and censorship (both of and by media), public or private. It involves extending rights, facilities, and influence to interests and perspectives other than the most powerful and profitable. It means involving in cultural decision-making the less affluent and more vulnerable groups, including the marginalized, neglected, abused, exploited, physically or mentally disabled, young and old, women, minorities, poor people, recent immigrants – all those most in need of a decent role and a voice in a freer cultural environment.

- Seeking out and cooperating with cultural liberation forces of all countries working for the integrity and independence of their own decision-making and against cultural domination and invasion. Learning from countries that have already opened their media to the democratic process. Helping local movements, including those in the most dependent and vulnerable countries of Latin America, Asia, and Africa (and also in Eastern Europe and the former Soviet Republics), to invest in their own cultural development; opposing aggressive foreign ownership and coercive trade policies that make such development more difficult.
- Supporting journalists, artists, writers, actors, directors and other creative workers struggling for more freedom from having to present life as a commodity designed for a market of consumers. Working with guilds, caucuses, labour and other groups for diversity in employment and in media content. Supporting media and cultural organizations addressing significant but neglected needs, sensibilities, and interests.
- Promoting media literacy, media awareness, critical viewing and reading, and other media education efforts as a fresh approach to the liberal arts and an essential educational objective on every level. Collecting, publicizing and disseminating information, research and evaluation about relevant programmes, services, curricula, and teaching materials. Helping to organize educational and parents' groups demanding pre-service and in-service teacher training in media analysis, already required in the schools of Australia, Canada and Great Britain.
- Placing cultural policy issues on the social-political agenda. Supporting, and, if necessary, organizing local and national media councils, study groups, citizen groups, minority and professional groups and other forums of public discussion, policy development, representation and action. Not waiting for a blueprint but creating and experimenting with ways of community and citizen participation in local, national and international media policy-making. Sharing experiences, lessons, and recommendations and gradually moving toward a realistic democratic agenda.

The condition of the physical environment may determine how long our species survives. But it is the cultural environment that affects the quality of survival. We need to begin the long process of diversifying, pacifying, democratizing and humanizing the story-telling process that shapes the mainstream of the cultural environment in which we live and into which our children are born.

Note

For information, write to CEM, PO Box 31847, Philadelphia, PA 19104, USA. e-mail: CEM@libertynet.org   Fax: 215 387 1560.

References

Auletta, Ken (1993) 'What they won't do', *The New Yorker*, 17 May, pp. 45–6.
Entman, Robert M. (1994) 'Violence on television news: news and "reality" programming in Chicago', a report commissioned and realeased by the Chicago Council on Urban Affairs.
Gerbner, George, Mowlana, Hamid and Schiller, Herbert (eds) (1996) *Invisible Crises: What Conglomerate Media Control Means for America and the World.* Boulder, CO: Westview Press.

14

Sports Reporting: Race, Difference and Identity

Andrew Tudor

Sport is about difference. The difference, of course, between winners and losers, but also between the skills of individuals, the styles in which people play the game, the character and distinctive attributes of teams. So we have league tables, medal counts, height/weight statistics, record times, speeds, goals and points scored, numbers of home runs, touchdowns, sets, matches and series. *Homo ludens* is nothing if not competitive, and there is a massive worldwide apparatus dedicated to recording and reporting that competition. This apparatus – let us think of it as 'sports reporting' in all its manifestations – documents difference. Its raison d'être is to present, narrate and celebrate the differential achievements and distinctive characteristics of sport and sports people.

But this is not all. Sport is also about identity, for how else can there be difference if there are no identities to differentiate one from the other? Identities of individuals, obviously – sport is constructed as a world of game-playing subjects ('I play therefore I am') – but also of teams, clubs, whole nations. To narrate a sporting event is to articulate the conjunction where difference and identity meet, to render intelligible not just the differential skills on display but also the identities in whose service such skills are harnessed. Historically, of course, sporting activities were often grounded in identities of locale: village versus village, club versus club, city versus city. But as sport (and sports reporting) has traversed the boundaries of nation states, and as the media through which that reporting flows have become global, conceptions of difference/identity have been drawn from increasingly diverse sources. Whatever it may have been in the past, sport in the age of television has become a spectacle on which is mounted an extraordinary array of naturalized discourses of identity and difference.

Here I want to reflect upon only a small part of that process, homing in on the play of race, nationalism and xenophobia in sports reporting. Although my concern with this question will be mainly judgemental, focusing upon the adequacy of British media performance (McQuail, 1992) in relation to such matters, my interest has a history which will bear a little elucidation since it casts some light on the more general issues. In 1974 I was one of a group of researchers engaged in examining various aspects of the television coverage of the football World Cup of that year (Buscombe, 1975). This was, I believe, the first time anyone had sought to look systematically at television coverage of a worldwide sporting event of this kind, and my particular task was to analyse the various 'support pro-grammes' (panel discussions, expert analysis, 'story-so-far' compilations) which took up about 30 per cent of the World Cup air-time across the two main British channels. Three clear themes arose from my work. One was the way in which the medium itself created and sustained tele-experts in central roles – television 'superstars' as I mischievously described them. A second theme (relatively undeveloped in the published material) related to the narrative and characterization needs of the coverage, the pressures of story-telling. And third, most striking to me at the time in that it proved far more significant than I had expected, the remarkable dependence of both commentators and 'experts' alike on a shorthand system based on ethnically derived stereotypes.

It might be said that I should have expected no less, that the entrenched racism of British culture in the early 1970s was apparent enough. It might also be said that – like many white 'liberal' observers – I liked to think that 'things were getting better,' that racism, both attitudinal and institutional, was on the wane. Those would indeed be pertinent observations on my views of the time, but I shall not rehearse here the material that changed my thinking (Tudor, 1975, 1981). Suffice to say that the television World Cup discourse proved to be deeply imbued with 'national character' contrasts, at least some of which incorporated strong racial (if not racist) elements. Subsequently, other researchers examined the World Cup compe-titions that followed at four-yearly intervals, also encountering a degree of ethnic and national stereotyping, though often conceptualizing it with more sophistication than I had (see, for example, Blain et al., 1993; Nowell-Smith, 1979; Sugden and Tomlinson, 1994; Tomlinson and Whannel, 1986; Wren-Lewis and Clarke, 1983). In 1990 I returned to World Cup coverage with a view to repeating the 1974 analysis. This involved further developing the themes encountered in 1974 as well as picking up on the facts that several African teams would appear in the competition for the first time in 1990 and that black players more generally had become increasingly prominent in European football. The Italia '90 competition, therefore, seemed likely to cast additional light on the ethnic dimensions of sports reporting.

So it proved. Elsewhere (Tudor, 1992) I have reported at some length on both the racially inspired patronizing tone applied to, for example, Cameroon footballers, and, not unrelated, on the powerfully xenophobic sense of 'them and us' that informed English television's view of the England team and its opponents. Let me use the Cameroon case here to illustrate the general point. In the typical language of television sports reporting Cameroon players were – until the fact of their success in the competition necessitated revision – 'happy-go-lucky', tended to 'get excited', were 'innocent', 'over-enthusiastic', 'naive' and 'carefree'. Reasonable enough descriptions, you might think, until they are placed in the context of white culture's stereotypical views of black Africans, frameworks which were generated in the experience of slavery and colonialism. Against that background, innocence, naivety and the rest, fall into place as part of a discourse of inherent superiority of white over black and of Europe over Africa. There is not as big a gap as we might like to think between such descriptions as these and the rolling-eyed, deferential, simple-minded black stereotype personified, for example, in the characters that Stepin Fetchit played in 1930s films. These are simple souls, the discourse tells us, uncivilized, not caught up in the reflective awareness of white life, happily at one with nature. In Cameroon, one commentator observed, they played 'barefoot in the jungle' (jungle, of course, is itself a heavily laden term with a long history of popular cultural association with primitivism) while another, on seeing a television shot of a T-shirt autographed by the Cameroon team, expressed surprise that 'they can all sign their names'.

Lazy journalists and the way things are

Out of such materials, then, was one blatant form of difference constructed. There were others, of course, most of them part of the process of sustaining 'our' identity, at least as that was understood by English television commentators. All drew upon well-established discourses of ethnicity, race, and national character to provide both a vocabulary and a taken-for-granted framework of comparison. What is going on in such television narration is that the materials of sports reporting are being drawn from beyond the domain of sport itself. One mapping of difference is superimposed upon another such that the activity of sport is understood as emblematic of racial and national differences. This is not to suggest that sports reporters and football commentators are overtly racist – though, as in all areas of life, the sports-related institutions surely have their share of those espousing racist views. It is, rather, to claim that the discourses routinely applied to football (and, indeed, to sport more generally) have forms of racism written into them. This is what Stuart Hall (1990: 13) calls inferential racism: 'those apparently naturalized representations of events and situations relating to race, whether "factual" or "fictional", which have racist premises and propositions inscribed in them as a set of unquestioned assumptions'. Although we can certainly find overt racism in media representations, inferential racism, he observes, 'is more widespread – and in many ways, more insidious, because it is largely invisible even to those who formulate the world in its terms' (ibid.).

If this is so – and it would be hard to deny, whether in sports reporting or media representations more generally – then it means that here, as elsewhere, the media play a significant role in circulating and therefore legitimating such discourses. Or, to put it the other way around, where media accounts embody racist presuppositions, that process of naturalized repetition is itself an essential element in the reproduction of such views. In general terms, then, there is reason to suggest that sports reporting is culpable (though not alone) in sustaining patterns of inferential racism, since the kinds of discursive practices which I and others have observed in English football reporting are also found elsewhere in sports coverage. Not always with football's high media profile, of course, but common enough nonetheless. However, culpability and liability are not always the same. Can we also hold our media liable in this matter, or – as it is so often when the media are blamed for social failings – would that be pernicious scape-goating? What defences might be mounted to the charge that sports reporting plays a significant role in sustaining racist views?

Broadly, I believe, there are three typical defences: the 'lazy journalism' defence; the 'reflecting society' defence; and the 'yes, but things are improving' defence. Let us consider each in turn. The heart of the 'lazy journalism' defence is the claim that what is at issue does not involve the reproduction of a racist discourse, but is simply an unfortunate byproduct of poor-quality, unreflective journalism. In other words, the problem, if problem it be, is a consequence of particular failings rather than collective sentiments; it is individual rather than cultural. So, when television commentary on the opening ceremony of the 1990 World Cup refers, as it did, to the 'natural sense of rhythm' of the black African women featuring in the parade, this is simply a failure of one journalist to recognize the current limits of permissible stereotyping. Or, as was often the case during the 1980s when black footballers were becoming increasingly prominent in English football, where tabloid newspaper sub-editors have constant resort to headlines of the 'black pearl', 'black diamond', 'black flash' form, this is really no more than thoughtless laziness on their part, easy word-play for everyday entertainment.

Such a defence might be plausible were it not for the fact that this kind of usage has been all too common and therefore difficult to dismiss as a product of isolated, individual errors of judgement. The redundant addition of an ethnic qualifier – black being the most frequent – was a systematic feature of newspaper sports reporting in England until very recently. Not, it must be said, in the context of an attempt to grapple with problems of racism in sport (on which much of the media tend to be conspicuously silent, as I shall suggest later) but simply as part and parcel of defining individuals in racial terms. In context, the 'black' adds nothing to the reporting other than a gratuitous and, to at least some of those thus described, an offensive designation of difference. It reflects a tacit frame-work of ethnic reference, its very routineness betraying its status as part of a system of discourse rather than an accidental product of poor-quality journalism. Such naturalized use of qualifiers imported from other discursive systems is never a matter of individual error – it is always symptomatic of a wider, more culturally diffused 'way of seeing'.

In claiming that, of course, I am beginning to blur the line between the first two defences, at least in as much as consideration of the 'lazy journalism' position leads inevitably back to the role of the social and cultural context within which sports reporting operates. So does sports reporting usage simply reflect conditions in the larger society, as the second defence suggests? At one level, of course, the answer is an unproblematic yes. What complicates things is the term 'simply': the implicit claim that media usage can be defended on the grounds that it does no more than reflect prevailing social circumstances. For it does not simply reflect the socio-cultural environment; it also articulates it, selects from it, amplifies it, and spreads its terms far and wide through the social fabric. That role carries with it certain ethical responsibilities which cannot be wished away in the claim that sports reporting is doing no more than 'speaking the language' of the ordinary sports fan. Like all versions of 'giving the public what it wants' this view mistakenly presumes a homogeneous public and, in consequence, promotes a kind of cultural tyranny of the alleged majority. Given these terms, it is hardly surprising that popular sports reporting in the tabloid press, which is especially prone to appeal to crude populist assumptions, tends to deploy gross concepts of (national) identity and concomitant designations of difference.

None of which is to suggest that the media are somehow more guilty of inferential racism than are the population at large. The claim is, rather, that because of their position as the conduit through which flows so much of our public discourse, the media should be much more aware of their responsibilities in these respects. Of course there is racism in the wider society. Of course there is racism within the institutions of sport and among sports spectators. But none of that offers any defence for the use of those ethnically based referential frameworks which have been so common in sports reporting. If it is an abrogation of our responsibility as members of a community for us to lay the blame for our failings at the door of the media, as indeed it is, so it is equally an abrogation of responsibility on the part of the media to claim that they are merely reflecting public views and giving the public what it wants. For the media and the community are inextricably intertwined in the use and articulation of frameworks for comprehending the everyday world.

'All that racism stuff'

Even so, the argument might run, things are improving. Overt and inferential racism are not as common as they once were in sport and in sports reporting. There has been progress. This is the third defence, of course, and much the strongest in that it concedes that there has been and perhaps still is a problem, but argues that broadcasting institutions, newspapers, and sporting organizations have all sought to discharge their responsibilities more seriously in recent years. I have mixed feelings about this claim. It is certainly true that ethnic stereotyping was much less common in English television's coverage of the 1994 World Cup than it was in 1990, although it is also true that crass 'national character' designations (especially of 'the Germans' who occupy a special place in the repertoire of English negative stereotypes) were notable in television coverage of the England-based Euro '96 competition and positively glaring in the tabloid press. Much depends on how long a view one takes. In a programme broadcast on Channel Four in 1991, *Great Britain United,* many British black footballers attested both to the racism that they had experienced and to their sense that there clearly had been improvement since the 1970s when some of them had begun their careers. That older patterns of inferential racism survived, however, was amply demonstrated in an interview with the Chairman of one football club (Ron Noades of Crystal Palace) who opined that while black players had great pace and were great athletes, not 'many can read the game', they could 'play with the ball in front of them – when it's behind them it's chaos' and in 'midwinter in England you need a few of the white hard men to carry the artistic black players through'. As Whannel (1992: 129) notes, it was an interesting development that these views met widespread newspaper condemnation, even in some of the tabloids.

Nevertheless, I am not entirely convinced that the undoubted steps that have been taken are as far-reaching as all that, or that they are very much a product of a new sense of responsibility in media coverage. After all, one important factor in undercutting racism in British sport has been the sheer range and level of success achieved by black players and athletes. Another, especially in football, has been the emergence of grass-roots anti-racist organizations which have done much to promote change. This has also been fostered by at least some elements within the game. At the club where I watch football regularly, Leeds United, there is much less racist abuse to be heard than was the case in the 1980s, a considerable success on the part of both the club and the supporters' anti-racism campaign. This, it should be noted, in a city where the cricket ground is deservedly notorious for its appalling crowd behaviour. Even so, ask any English football supporter or player and they will tell you that racist insults are still part of the game both on and off the pitch. Yet watch football on television, listen to commentary on the radio, read the football reports in the press, and you could be forgiven for thinking that the issue of race was no longer relevant, that it had simply gone away.

In a sense, of course, it has, in as much as while British media coverage of sport is often xenophobic in its construction of international difference, it now appears to have developed a 'hear no evil, see no evil' response to issues of racism in domestic sport. Though there have been public denials, it is widely believed – and for good reason – that television coverage of football has adopted a policy of ignoring or, if that proves impossible, down-playing any racist incidents. There have even been occasions when no amount of manipulation of the broadcast volume of crowd sounds can disguise the fact of, for instance, mass 'jungle noises' being directed at particular black players. Television commentators and 'experts' routinely do not remark upon such events. The rationale for this attitude of judicial ignorance is that one should not afford publicity to such behaviour since that is precisely what the delinquents in question want. That policy was developed in the context of so-called 'football hooliganism' in the 1980s, and while it may make sense in those circumstances, it is not clear that it best serves the cause of anti-racism where that is the issue. It is at least arguable that such a policy serves to suppress awareness of racism in sport and, therefore, encourage the belief that there is no longer a real problem.

Even as I write (early 1997) some force is lent to that suggestion by British media coverage of a high-profile accusation by one top player that he had been subjected to racist abuse by another. Although some of the 'serious' press have used this as an occasion to run stories on racism in sport, it is notable that the broadcast media have been much more cautious. While that may be quite intelligible in the context of possible legal action, it is also consistent with their more general 'hands-off' approach to race-related sports stories. The tone of the broadcast media's response was perhaps well caught by a presenter on BBC radio's *Sports Report* pro-gramme who, while discussing with an interviewee the possible impact of the accusations on the players involved, used the throwaway phrase 'all that racism stuff'. It is not that he was condoning racism – the journalist concerned is probably as anti-racist as any other – it is, rather, that attending to racism in British sports reporting has been rendered peripheral by a mixture of complacency about how much improvement there has been and a policy of turning a blind eye in the hope that lack of publicity will make such uncomfortable, extra-sporting problems go away.

My judgement, then, on the third defence (there have been problems, but things have improved) is mixed. Things have improved, both in sports reporting and sport itself. But they have not improved to the degree that journalism can be any less vigilant in monitoring its own role in sustaining inferential racism, nor does a policy of ignoring or minimizing incidents of racism in sporting events suggest a well-thought-out view of the role of sports coverage in relation to the larger context of sporting culture. The discourses of difference in British culture (and, surely, in most European societies as well) are deeply pervaded by racist assumptions, and the British media and British sports organizations do not like to have that drawn to their attention. Keep race and politics out of sport, runs the familiar chorus, as if sport or any other social institution could somehow be rendered immune from divisions and problems faced by the larger society. Yet sports reporting itself is profoundly guilty of importing extraneous conceptions of difference into its representations of sport, even to the extent of building coverage around them.

Discourses of difference

Take national identity, for example, a designation of difference which often draws upon unacknowledged racist presuppositions. On the night that

England played West Germany in the 1990 World Cup, television coverage reached an apotheosis of all things English. 'It is this sort of night that draws us all together' observed the ITV commentator, a form of celebratory nationalism which has been employed by many a journalist seeking an angle on all manner of international competition. Samuel Johnson famously suggested that 'patriotism is the last refuge of a scoundrel'. Faced with modern sports reporting, he might well have observed that conceptions of national identity are the first refuge of journalistic scoundrels, all too eager to tap into the wellspring from which flows our culture's illusory sense of shared sentiment and purpose. As Benedict Anderson (1991) has argued so eloquently in the context of the rise of nationalism, we live in 'imagined communities' – nations of the mind complete with selective histories and constructed rituals. In modern societies the spectacle of international sport has come to play a striking role in articulating the 'naturalness', the pre-given solidity of our imagined communities, and thus in what Blain et al. (1993: 18) call 'the daily reconstitution of cultures'. This is, of course, an achievement managed in and through ideology, and one which depends upon our media to no small degree.

It also depends crucially on manipulating difference, which has to be suppressed within the imagined community and emphasized beyond its boundaries. There must be an Other – better still, Others – in contradistinction to whom the community can sustain its identity, but Otherness must also be made invisible where it might divide those who are ensnared in the community's web of illusions. This is where race, difference and identity come together, albeit uneasily, in sports reporting's modern rendering of international sport as spectacle. It is also the locus, in England at least, of the most remarkably blunt articulations of xenophobia. During the 1980s and 1990s we have become accustomed to a powerful anti-European strand in English public debate. This is arguably more a consequence of a generalized xenophobic nationalism than of 'reasoned' opposition to specific European policies, and, if that is so, sports reporting has certainly played its role in articulating and circulating the cultural frameworks which make the political discourse viable. Its dependence on concepts of Otherness at a variety of levels provide terms within which a populist language of difference and identity may be constructed. If, as Castells (1996: 3) observes, 'in a world of global flows of wealth, power, and images, the search for identity, collective or individual, ascribed or constructed, becomes the fundamental source of social meaning', sports reporting and other popular cultural discourses of difference are constant contributors to that process.

Must we simply accept, then, that a globally communicated intolerance is the price to be paid for late modernity's crises of identity? Of course not, neither macroscopically in terms of the trajectory of international politics, nor microscopically in terms of the typical frameworks within which our cultures encourage us to conceptualize identity and difference. As far as British media performance is concerned, there is still every opportunity to recover from the drift toward discourses which, however indirectly, feed intolerance in sports reporting and elsewhere. But the first stage in such a recovery is to recognize that there is a problem. To recognize that racism remains a significant if unevenly distributed feature of contemporary sport and sports reporting. To recognize that to combat it requires that it is openly attended to, not swept under the carpet in the cause of 'good taste' or uncontroversial coverage. To recognize, furthermore, that the assertive nationalism routinely deployed in sports reporting draws upon the same kind of crass differentiation and prejudices which structure racist discourse. And to recognize also that sports reporting is not, cannot be, an innocent bearer of factual messages, but inevitably plays a crucial role in constructing our ways of understanding the events on which it purports merely to report. When television or radio commentators use highly charged concepts of difference and identity in mediating sport – most obviously those relating to race and nation – they do so to provide effortless involvement for audiences, but at the risk of giving sustenance to divisive and unacceptable attitudes and behaviour. Although complexities of context mean that there are no easy solutions – we cannot simply legislate for acceptable sports reporting, provide a straightforward code for journalists' behaviour – we do have the right to demand that our broadcasters and print journalists recognize and respond to the dangers that go hand in hand with any attempt to frame sport within larger discourses of difference, especially those revolving around the frequently linked ideas of race and national identity.

Race, difference, identity. The three key terms of my discussion interlock with each other in the practice of sports reporting. What is construed as difference at one level – racial differences in domestic sport, say – is suppressed in the cause of collective identity at another. And that collective identity itself depends on exclusion and stereotyping of precisely the form, if not always the substance, that shapes the familiar patterns of racism. At every level, then, the common factor is intolerance of Otherness, and, at its most general, sports reporting tends to assume that its audience has a 'natural' allegiance to those who 'fly the flag' of the nation state, be they representative national teams, clubs in international competitions, or drivers of Formula One racing cars. By juggling the discourses of difference and identity at these various levels, sports reporters meet the narrative and emotional demands of story-telling, routinely applying frameworks which encourage the relocation of sporting spectacle into extra-sporting discourses of difference. In this way the incessant jingoism of sports reporting feeds the imagined community's insatiable appetite for intolerance, its need for Others against whom its own identity can always be reforged. There is, I believe, a price to pay for that, and it is paid not by those who promulgate such material on our television screens and in our newspapers. It is paid by those who become the hapless victims of a culture which, in consequence, is always willing to sacrifice 'Them' in order that we can become 'Us'.

References

Anderson, B. (1991) *Imagined Communities: Reflections on the Origin and Spread of Nationalism.* London: Verso.

Blain, N., Boyle, R. and O'Donnell, H. (1993) *Sport and National Identity in the European Media.* Leicester: Leicester University Press.

Buscombe, E. (ed.) (1975) *Football on Television.* London: British Film Institute.

Castells, M. (1996) *The Rise of the Network Society.* Oxford: Blackwell.

Hall, S. (1990) 'The whites of their eyes: racist ideologies and the media', in M. Alvarado and J. Thompson (eds) *The Media Reader.* London: BFI Publishing, pp. 7–23.

McQuail, D. (1992) *Media Performance: Mass Communication and the Public Interest.* London: Sage.

Nowell-Smith, G. (1979) 'Television – football – the world', *Screen* 19 (4): 45–59.

Sugden, J. and Tomlinson, A. (eds) (1994) *Hosts and Champions: Soccer Cultures, National Identities and the USA World Cup.* Aldershot: Arena.

Tomlinson, A. and Whannel, G. (eds) (1986) *Off the Ball: the Football World Cup.* London: Pluto Press.

Tudor, A. (1975) 'The panels', in E. Buscombe (ed.) *Football on Television.* London: British Film Institute, pp. 54–65.

Tudor, A. (1981) 'The panels', in T. Bennett, S. Boyd-Bowman, C. Mercer and J. Woollacott (eds) *Popular Television and Film.* London: British Film Institute/Open University Press, pp. 150–8.

Tudor, A. (1992) 'Them and us: story and stereotype in TV World Cup coverage', *European Journal of Communication* 7: 391–413.

Whannel, G. (1992) *Fields in Vision: Television Sport and Cultural Transformation.* London: Routledge.

Wren-Lewis, J. and Clarke, A. (1983) 'The World Cup – a political football', *Theory, Culture and Society* 1 (3): 123–32.

15

Cultural Citizenship and Popular Fiction

Joke Hermes

California in the 1970s: a group of women manage to capture a rapist and exact retribution by stapling him to a tree by the balls. . . .[1] Feminist victory over patriarchal manhood in what came to be known as the feminist detective (a subgenre in women's crime fiction): politics and text come together seamlessly in a genre with a high degree of moral besides political deliberation. Which is also, interestingly, one of the most popular book fiction genres for women. To what ends may women go to better their position and chances in a hierarchically gendered society? How to stop both real and symbolic violence? These are the questions women investigators are faced with, besides needing romance, sex, adventure, friends and an income.

The feminist detective makes clear that popular culture is more than mere entertainment: women's rights, violence, economic inequality, justice and the public interest are important issues in the books. The same goes for other popular culture genres: the political and moral importance of popular music, for instance, have been pointed out by musicians and academics alike. Mir Wermuth (1994) claims that the anger and emotions expressed in a music genre such as hip hop (or rap) is a political as well as a cultural expression of rage and impotence. Apart from analysing its homophobic, sexist and violent lyrics, it is important to see contemporary black dance music as a forum for the exploration of suitable attitudes and answers in response to existing societal values and repression. Rap like other black music genres is a political arena, however problematical we may find its texts. Rap reflects the everyday life world of American black inner-city youth. In effect, rap may be a gateway to citizenship, however uncouth its language.

Other popular culture theorists have argued similar theses for genres such as the quiz show (Fiske, 1990) and soap opera (Ang, 1985). The quiz show, it can be argued following John Fiske, allows its (mostly female) spectators to rewrite the patriarchal contract. Women's boisterous and loud behaviour in front of the set and in the studio audience counter the code imposed on girls and women to be well-behaved, restrained and to not raise their voice. Also the quiz show allows for the deployment of a 'feminine', relational and intuitive knowledge (Fiske, 1990: 143) in the public space of television when it comes to, for example *Perfect Match* (Australian show), or *I'm*

Sorry (Dutch show). Consumer knowledge, often down-graded as materialist, unpolitical and narrow-minded, is given its due as a viable and respectable frame of reference. Like the quiz show, the soap opera – implicitly – revalues forms of knowledge usually coded 'feminine' and thus virtually worthless, and offers a criticism of prevailing high culture standards and the cultural power system they are part of.

Obviously, the cultural criticism implicit in the audience's appreciation of popular genres is hardly political behaviour in a narrow sense. Understandably, therefore, conventional thinkers have had trouble condoning John Fiske's claim that the pleasures of the quiz show may liberate women from their husbands' economic power (1990) and should be considered a 'resisting pleasure'. Likewise with his even more audacious claim that understanding the popular should lead us to recognize its dimension of 'semiotic democracy' (Fiske, 1991). I find Fiske's work inspiring if not always entirely convincing. Fiske's strategy is to translate popular culture into argumentation and critique. Such a strategy is doomed. Popular cultural genres will always fall short of modernist political theory's rationalist standards. Rather than translate popular culture into another frame of reference, it should first and foremost be respected for its own qualities. In as far as Fiske also implies that politics should be defined as broadly as possible, I could not agree more. That will allow us to give credit to popular culture's strengths when it comes to commitment and engagement.

The cultural as entry to citizenship

The political value of popular culture is to be found in its contribution to citizenship. Essentially citizenship – in the sense of individuals' and social groups' commitment to the common good (or public interest) – is the basis and the prerequisite for a functioning democratic system. Regrettably, the common good or the public interest defy concrete and long-lasting definition. The highly abstract notions we have agreed on, such as the integrity of the body or the right to free speech, necessitate continuing interpretation through debate and discussion. Ideally such discussion is not restricted to experts and closed institutions, such as parliaments, the courts or the world of science, but remains part of our everyday life world.

The media, and especially the press, have long claimed their privileged role and duty as forum for this type of discussion and debate. Journalists like to feel they are the 'watchdogs of democracy'; television and radio shows claim they provide space and ammunition for public discussion. To ensure that journalism can perform this important task a set of routines, rules and codes have come into existence over time. Their aim has been to free journalism as much as possible from the shackles of commercialism. Journalists should not try to please audiences or sell advertisments, they have a public duty to perform. Other (governmental) aims to ensure that the watchdog will be able to perform have been to protect accessibility and pluriformity as much as possible. Journalistic routine has evolved in this spirit, with quality journalism leading the way for a truthful and unbiased reporting based on an absolute separation of fact and fiction. Popular culture, of course, deals in fiction, and worse still, will mingle fact and fiction to a great extent. But it is, as we know, a fiction in itself that factual news genres and fictional popular genres are not related. Journalists' news values too are 'just those values that any storyteller uses in creating a tale' (Bird and Dardenne, 1988: 73). Popular culture is not that far removed from democracy's alleged core genres such as journalism.

The question for media theory is whether it wants to stick with its modernist prejudices and the exclusion of many from debating the public interest or whether it truly wishes to generate as broad and good a public debate as possible. In the latter case, media theory would do well to recognize the political potential within the heart of popular culture. The core issue is whether we will continue to understand debate as the exchange of rational arguments, or whether we will come to an understanding that foregrounds commitment and engagement. Because that, as Dahlgren points out in Chapter 9, is precisely the power of popular cultural genres.

If we can agree then for the moment that there might be more to popular culture than meets the modernist eye, we need a more precise view of citizenship and of the public interest as well, in order for me to show how 'cultural citizenship' is not the contradiction in terms it might appear to be. The concept refers to the crucial and positive potential of popular fiction genres and the domain of the cultural in general for many non-dominant groups' interpretative frameworks and community-building. Apart from commitment to a common good, citizenship can thus be understood as 'a set of practices which constitute individuals as competent members of a community' (Turner, 1994: 159). Of old the community in question was the national culture. However, in pluriform, fragmented contemporary society the nation state can hardly be seen as a unified forum or community. Under outside pressures of the globalization of culture (by ever-expanding communication and information networks), and by inside pressures from the new social movements and from new groups of citizens such as labour migrants, national culture has lost its unifying compelling force. What then is citizenship in postmodern society?

First of all, citizenship should be redefined as sets (plural) of practices that constitute individuals as competent members of sets of different and sometimes overlapping communities one of which should ideally constitute the national (political) culture. National cultures could, following this argument, be defined along procedural rather than substantial lines. That is to say that rather than try to define once and for all of what elements a national culture consists, it would be wise to understand the strengths (and weaknesses) of a national heritage in terms of how specific achievements were brought about, whether these achievements concern the right to vote, social security or architectural masterpieces. Thus rather than defend substance, for instance by insisting on a never-changing canon of great literary works, it is preferable to stress openness and flexibility and to recognize that today's criteria might close off parts of that very heritage that we will appreciate in another 20 years' time. That therefore the open and flexible procedure is the key value that needs to be upheld.

Citizenship also needs to be understood as intrinsically mediated practices, whether by actual contact between community members (mediated by specific jargons or languages) or by the use of or participation in media-centred (sub)cultures that constitute us as competent members of the communities in question. Because citizenship cannot be defined as the membership of one community only, there is room for a broad orientation and inclusion of core democratic values, without necessarily excluding other views and ideas, coming from other (interpretive) communities. Individuals can be competent participants in different communities fully aware that codes or ideologies clash but not particularly concerned about this – since we are all adept to 'do in Rome as the Romans do'.

Obviously then my argument leads me to state that citizenship nowadays not only concerns our relation to democratic government but also to 'society' in a much wider sense. As Dahlgren (1995: 146) has shown, citizenship relates not only to the directly political and social, but also to identity formation, personal identification, emotional evaluation, and so on. Our sense of commitment and belonging, essential to who we feel we are, is also essential to citizenship. Given the abstract nature of today's government, allegiance to our national communities as they are is channelled through highly diverse practices, surely some of which are popular cultural practices. The open, only marginally organized, non-coercive structure of popular culture (good music, a second-hand novel, a left-over magazine are to be had anywhere) is highly attractive, especially to those who lack the cultural capital or competence to engage with democratic practice at a more political and abstract level. And, I might add, to those who feel disengaged from and cynical about political practice in its current male-dominated, competitive form.

Popular culture is typically unorderly and unattractive from a modernist point of view; creative and inspiring, however, when seen from a postmodern orientation. Especially when democratic government and community-building are seen as complex endeavours that benefit by, nay, even need central fictions. Thus, even though popular culture is never the domain of administrative politics, of voting and decision-making, it may provide the grounding for a citizen-identity. It may reinforce the emotions and utopias out of which a sense of community is built. As readers of popular fiction genres we may come to see new truths, see venues for change, or develop a critical stance. I will illustrate this in the next section, where I will discuss a much read (and also a personal favourite) genre: the women's crime novel. My basic assumption is that a set of texts will invite its readers to rethink and possibly revalue moral issues and, by implication, the public interest. This is not a question of any one genre purveying one simple message but rather of an ongoing discussion that can be recognized in the themes that crop up time and time again in that particular genre. 'Cultural' citizenship, then, is not our new hope for flagging interest in and enthusiasm for the formal procedures of established democratic institutions. Reading fiction may however sharpen our democratic abilities and appetite and constitute us as worthy partakers in debates that are vital for democracy.

Utopia and women's crime writing

I am a fan of the feminist detective. I like gutsy feminist private investigators who will tackle basically anything from the church to other forms of organized crime, the shipping or insurance business, to family relations turned sour; who will stand their 'woman' in a fight if it comes to that. Quite a few of my favourite heroines are no longer spring chickens (V.I. is now over 40, as is Anna Pigeon, as is Pam Sweet's heroine Cat O'Connel; Sandra Scoppetone's Lauren Laurano is going grey), often they are lesbians, usually they get by on small incomes but manage to live pleasurable lives anyhow. They cannot be defined in terms of their intimate relationships alone. They are not primarily somebody's wife or mother. Of course they have close friends that are important to them, such as V.I. Warshawski's friend Lotty (Warshawski is a creation of Sara Paretsky); Stoner McTavish (by Sara Dreher) has her aunt and her friend and partner in a travel agency; Anna Pigeon, park ranger (by Nevada Barr) has her sister Molly who is a psychiatrist in New York. Some have partners, such as Lauren Laurano's Kip. These women keep an important part of what feminism is alive: it is the creation of new forms of womanhood and of new relations between women, as friends, lovers and caregivers, neither necessarily gay nor heterosexual. The feminist detective puts a resolute end to any naturalized roles for women.

Cut loose (by chance or by their own doing) of the ties of family and kinship, the heroines of the feminist detective are free to operate on their own. In her article 'Friendless orphans' Nicole Décuré (1994) agrees that we can find a feminist dream here: to be freed of the needs of others and of taking care of them (the orphan). The relative friendlessness, of course, also makes the protagonist more available for romantic liaisons, another important attraction of this particular (sub)genre. I do not agree with Décuré that the idealistic feminist p.i. is absolutely without friends. I think it is the case that feminists portray a realistic version of the place and importance of friendship in one's life: precisely not a stifling tie, or a huge obligation – however important loyalty between friends is. Décuré points out that many authors of the family-free heroines are themselves portrayed on backflaps as reassuringly committed in relationships, including children and pets. This I would like to see as strengthening the dialogic nature of the genre of women's crime fiction as a platform for discussion: several options are given, it is made clear that choices are involved in how one lives one's life. Curious – in this light – is the detail that quite a few woman investigators have animals: V.I. has her dog Peppy, Anna Pigeon has her cat Piedmont and so on and on . . . A woman's best friend is her cat/dog?

A second important trait of the feminist detective is humour. Humour is almost by definition at someone's expense. By implication self-mockery or self-derision is one of the few forms available to such a politically conscientious genre as the feminist detective, as is the sharp retort to overbearing males. V.I. Warshawski, for example, never uses her full name when dealing with work contacts. She is addressed as V.I. (Vic for friends). When asked what V.I. stands for (Victoria Iphigeneia), she either makes a quip, or says: my first names, and leaves it at that. Both putting offensive others in their place and a certain degree of self-reflexivity are the mark of the feminist detective.

> 'Who the hell are you?' 'My name's V.I. Warshawski. I'm a private investigator and I'm looking into Peter Thayer's death.' I handed him a business card. 'You? You're no more a detective than I am a ballet dancer.' 'I'd like to see you in tights and a tutu', I commented, pulling out the plastic-encased photostat of my private investigator's license. (Sara Paretsky, *Indemnity Only*, 1982, the first V.I. Warshawski novel, p. 260)

Some fictive figures go to such lengths in self-depreciation that it is unclear whether they should be counted as feminist – a little self-respect would seem to be essential to a feminist sense of self. Especially likeable is Nevada Barr's park ranger Anna Pigeon and her sense of humour. Anna is widowed and around 40. After losing Zach, her husband, Anna starts a new career law-keeping in the wilderness. In the four novels published to date she has become an ex-alcoholic. There are affairs with (younger) men and a developing relationship with FBI agent Frederick Stanton. Anna is a real person with her strengths and her weaknesses. Her nice sense of humour is especially obvious in the regular telephone calls with her sister (Dr Molly Pigeon, psychiatrist in New York):

> 'Tell me a story', Anna said into the mouthpiece. 'I've had a real bad day.' 'What kind of story?' Molly asked. 'One where all the bad guys die?' 'One where nobody dies and the girl gets Robert Redford.' 'Is this a New York story, or do they live happily ever after?' (*A Superior Death*, 1994: 80. The New York reference is to Anna Pigeon's dead husband, who was killed by a cab in a car accident.)

And in the bandying about with other women, such as with her friend Christina and her five-year-old daughter Alison:

> Ally bounded up on the opposite side of the bed. 'Smell me, Aunt Anna.' [Anna has had a fight with the bad guy – a woman – while deep-sea diving and has contracted nitrogen narcosis, diver disease. She is recovering in hospital.] Anna grabbed the little girl by the ears and smelled deeply on the top of her head. 'Hmmmm . . . What is that divine scent you're wearing?' She sniffed again. 'Rotting squirrel guts? No . . .' Ally squirmed and giggled. '"Eau de Roadkill?" No . . . I've got it! "Essence of Dog Vomit".' Ally squealed with delight. 'For heaven's sake,' Christina sighed, 'Ally will be completely beyond redemption by

the time she's old enough to drive.' 'You must be ladylike or the boys won't like you,' Anna intoned ominously. 'No more bat-dung hair mousse.' 'Boys. Ish.' Ally tossed her head with such disdain that Anna and her mother laughed. (Also from Nevada Barr, *A Superior Death*. The second Anna Pigeon mystery, 1994, pp. 295–6)

I read these humorous exchanges which lighten up stories of suspense that contain quite a bit of violence and threat, as attempts at politically correct humour. This does not sound all that funny of course. But it does bear contemplation. Contrary to the common put-down of feminism – those women have no sense of humour – women (and feminists of course) have always used humour in much the same way they use gossip: as a means to settle symbolic scores and turn the scales on the powerful – men, employers and so on. It is, as Patricia Meyer Spacks says of gossip '. . . a crucial means of self-expression, a crucial form of solidarity' (1986: 5). And it is a characteristic mark of the feminist detective.

The utopia that binds the feminist detective as a subgenre (whether we are considering the more old-fashioned amateur detective, or the more modern paid investigator) has to do with women having the strength to settle their own scores, and finding the humour to reflect on their own powers and the demands that others make of them. Humour is also the means to take the sting out of the set of norms binding women into a corset not of their own making. The mainstream women's thriller offers a far less clear picture of what utopia for women might look like. They do, however, tend to perceive the drama of combining the incompatible roles of 'woman' and 'professional' much more clearly and thus provide an incentive to fight against the dishonest restrictions put on women trying to make it in a man's world.

Mainstream women's thrillers are the feminist detective's counterpart. They are more often American rather than British, Australian or Canadian, they picture women as successful law enforcers, lawyers, judges or medical examiners but they also problematize successful professionality for women. The feminist detective novel differs from the thriller in that the detective is a more disinterested figure, even if she sustains injuries and has to fight her way through to the conclusion. Sara Paretsky's V.I. Warshawski or Nevada Barr's Anna Pigeon are fighters, never victims. Although they might from time to time indulge in self-criticism they basically feel suited to their jobs.

Mainstream women's thrillers are not necessarily less feminist than the feminist detective, in the sense that they do not measure up to the feminist project. But they are different. For example they totally lack the overly didactic tone that earlier feminist detectives certainly had (such as the Pam Nillsen novels by Barbara Wilson or Val McDermid's Lindsay Gordon detectives – McDermid remedied this in her 1990s Kate Brannigan novels). The mainstream women's thriller hardly ever features lesbian protagonists. The heroine/victim earns a good salary and she is often romantically involved with a successful male, who may or may not be the bad guy. Some of them remind me forcibly of the gothic novel, popular in the 1970s, situated in the nineteenth century, in which young women set out to be governesses to the children of German counts with whom they fall in love but whom they also start to suspect of evil-doing. The counts usually turn out to have jealous twins, who are unmasked and all is well that ends well, after having given the reader a good fright.

Less romance, more scares and frightful murders by psychopaths make up the mainstream women's thriller such as written by Mary Higgins Clark. What makes them interesting is the fact that the female protagonist is both a successful woman in her own right and a woman punished, or so it would seem, because of her professional identity. As if femininity and professionality cannot happily combine. The mainstream women's thriller in fact attempts to unravel the psychological and emotional ramifications of woman-as-professional in a tight spot. In the feminist detective novel this would be reported as thoughts and observations of the heroine which sets limits to the depth of these reflections. As does the ironical slant in much of these books. Carrie Blue, heroine of the women's thriller *Don't Talk to Strangers* (Bethany Campbell, 1996) on the contrary, does not use (or need) the distance irony can provide. She regards both her professional endeavours and the slowly developing romance between her and her boss Hayden Ivanovich with honesty, while the author makes clear this honesty is made possible by the liminal period Carrie Blue's life has entered (children grown up; back to school, to start a new professional life). Arguably this construction gives more opportunity for identification than the tough and humorous p.i. style in the feminist detective. I personally rather dislike the heroine being 'the object of persecution and the discoverer of its source' (Craig and Cadogan, 1981: 236), even if I appreciate that many women will immediately recognize (more mundane) varieties of this scenario.

All in all, we can conclude that contemporary women's crime writing offers elements of a feminist utopia and ongoing criticism of the hurdles women face in their march towards full social and civic participation. But the huge number of books published as women's crime fiction do not have the form of a political tract. They contribute to building a sense of what is needed where sex, justice, humour and professionality are concerned. Since the market for women's crime fiction is well established (women have always, that is since the end of the nineteenth century, been successful writers of crime fiction and have created successful heroines, see Bargainnier, 1980, Introduction), and since neither supply nor demand are monopolized, it can be argued that readers have some control over which authors or types of storyline are contracted by the publishers. By preferring some authors over others, by continuing to buy feminist detective stories from small publishing houses, readers express their preference to come back, over and over again, to these particular themes and also encourage the big publishers to contract feminist authors. One may conclude from this that readers of Anglo-American and German crime fiction (the big markets for this genre) recognize and enjoy the themes they are offered. The numerous Internet lists devoted to women's crime writing further confirms this conclusion as do the magazines published by women's crime readers clubs in Australia and the United States.

A particular case in point are the discussions over the sex scenes. The books take relatively a lot of trouble over writing good sex scenes from a woman's point of view. Again, though implicitly, women's crime writing offers a critique of dominant, mostly 'hetero-sexist', male-dominated codes of representation in popular genres. Interestingly, this sexual dimension especially is much bickered about on Internet discussion lists and in such publications as the Melbourne *Sisters in Crime Newsletter* and *Ariadne Forum*.[2] The bickering is alternately about whether 'lesbians do it better' or about the importance of love scenes in what should according to some be 'whodunnits' (still others arguing they should be 'whydunnits'). From the perspective of citizenship and the public interest, this discussion comes close to the classic ideal of uncoerced open debate about the best possible life for all in society. Not only do many of the heroines in women's crime try to change established institutions, which make them the moral figures I am interested in, readers of women's crime writing engage in lively discussion about what they feel comes closest to the core of their lives and lifestyles.

Cultural citizenship and the performance of fiction genres

The feminist detective novel successfully passed through its 1970s didactic phase. For the power of popular fiction is not to hand out rational argumentation. These days, it offers examples of women's lives and lifestyles. Sometimes shocking or accusatory, more often humorous and engaged. The feminist detective is an extra-mural course in good citizenship and in how to cope with an unjust and unequal world without giving up or giving in. As readers we share in the utopias and practical wisdom of these novels. Many readers do not confine themselves to either the feminist detective or the mainstream women's thriller when they want to read women's crime fiction. The mainstream women's thriller is less flippant than the feminist detective and closer to the horrors of societal power struggle. It calls forth the problems and dangers women face in making careers, to then assuage them. In remarkably different ways, then, these (sub)genres in their own way contribute to (women's) citizenship. They make clear that citizenship is an exercise in respecting the other's perspective, opinions and feelings, fed by one's competence as a member of (highly) different (interpretive) communities.

I have shown how citizenship can be understood as a mediated practice, for example as a reader community. Reading women's crime fiction can be understood as constituting a person as a competent member, not only of the reader communities of mainstream women's crime fiction and the feminist detective but also of the national-political community at large. Being a crime fiction reader belonging to different interpretive communities builds the broad orientation and critical perspective that produces a sense of belonging and commitment to liberal-western democracy as an integral part of one's identity, as well as respect for differences of outlook and opinion. The meting out of justice and of criticism in equal measures is standard fare in this particular fiction genre. But it also presents a dream, utopian vistas of a better world, without which allegiance to the national-political community could not be reinforced. Fiction genres, then, are integrally part of the functioning of western democracy. When we discuss media, citizenship and the public interest, we tend to use limited (and usually implicit) notions of media performance. This is a shame, especially in relation to the crucial and positive potential of popular fiction genres and the domain of the cultural in general for many non-dominant groups' interpretative frameworks and community-building. Much energy has been spent on analysing the harmful and sexist qualities of popular genres. Now it is time to understand how their users may benefit by their choice of popular literatures, musics and other forms. The women's movement is a case in point. Many types of media content have been generated by feminists, ranging from flyers and political tracts to songs, autobiographies and literary novels. Book genres have always been important carriers of feminist messages. Books are and were easily produced, distributed unproblematically via bookshops or via alternative channels such as the infrastructure of the movement, writing can be combined with other types of work and women have a long tradition both of being readers and writers of books. The felicitous combination of tradition, technology and distribution may make a media form especially suitable for specific social groups – whether we are talking books when it comes to the women's movement, music genres for the black movement or videotapes for migrant groups (see e.g. Lee and Heup Cho, 1990). Other media forms, and particularly those favoured by media and political theory for political communication, such as the quality press, are often far less accessible and have less status and attraction for group members.

Notes

Many thanks to Pieter Hilhorst, Liesbet van Zoonen and Kees Brants. And to Jillian Trezise and Lorraine Barrow, Dominique Peters, Irene Costera Meijer and Ute Bechdolf for books, tips and good talks about women's crime fiction.

1. In order to portray the feminist detective as a moral figure and as a figure inspiring moral and political debate, it was perhaps unnecessary to start by briefly describing any man's worst nightmare. After all, Inspector Morse has been approved by the influential journal, *Feminist Review*, as a man who combines a deep sense of morality with the ability to nurture (besides having traditional paternal qualities). In short, Morse is a feminist (Thomas, 1995: 8–9). This ungloved approach was to demonstrate what women today, in huge numbers, like to read, even if most novels following *Angel Dance* (from which the rape revenge extract came) did not go quite as far in their meting out of justice. *Angel Dance* was written by M.F. Beal and published by a small New York feminist publisher, Daughters, in 1977.

2. *Ariadne Forum der Frauenkrimi Almanach* is a journal published by the German left-wing publishing house Argument that was the first and is still the biggest force behind the feminist Krimi, making Germany the only big non-English market for these novels.

References

Ang, Ien (1985) *Watching Dallas. Soap Opera and the Melodramatic Imagination*. London and New York: Methuen.

Bargainnier, Earl (ed.) (1980) *10 Women of Mystery*. Bowling Green: Bowling Green State University Press.

Bird, S. Elizabeth and Dardenne, Robert W. (1988) 'Myth, chronicle, and story: exploring the narrative qualities of news', in James W. Carey (ed.) *Media, Myths and Narratives: Television and the Press*. London: Sage, pp. 67–86.

Craig, Patricia and Cadogan, Mary (1981) *The Lady Investigates: Women Detectives and Spies in Fiction*. London: Victor Gollancz.

Dahlgren, Peter (1995) *Television and the Public Sphere*. London: Sage.

Décuré, Nicole (1994) 'Friendless orphans: family relationships in women's crime fiction', *Phoebe* 6 (1): 27–41.

Fiske, John (1990) 'Women and quiz shows: consumerism, patriarchy and resisting pleasures', in Mary-Ellen Brown (ed.) *Television and Women's Culture: The Politics of the Popular*. London: Sage, pp. 134–43.

Fiske, John (1991) 'Postmodernism and television', in James Curran and Michael Gurevitch (eds) *Mass Media and Society*. London: Edward Arnold.

Lee, Minu and Heup Cho, Chong (1990) 'Women watching together: an ethnographic study of Korean soap opera fans in the US', *Cultural Studies* 4 (1): 30–44.

Meyer Spacks, Patricia (1986) *Gossip*. Chicago and London: University of Chicago Press.

Thomas, Lyn (1995) 'In love with Inspector Morse: feminist subculture and quality television', *Feminist Review* 51: 1–25.

Turner, Bryan S. (1994) 'Postmodern culture/modern citizens', in Bart van Steenbergen (ed.) *The Condition of Citizenship*. London: Sage, pp. 153–68.

Wermuth, Mir (1994) 'Bubbelen voor Pinko's en Vanilla's. Etniciteit en seksualiteit in zwarte dansmuziek', *Tijdschrift voor Vrouwenstudies 57*, 15 (1): 63–78.

V BACK TO THE FUTURE

16

With the Benefit of Hindsight: Old Nightmares and New Dreams

Kees Brants

The strainer of the past, an old Chinese saying goes, only lets the sun shine. If one asks older people to reflect on the neighbourhood they live in, one is bound to get a litany about the sort of people that have recently moved in, the loud-mouthed youth that is roaming the streets and the sense of community that has long gone and been replaced by a sense of fear (about crime) or cynicism (about whether they are taken seriously). No, then the 'good old days', when we knew our neighbours, when it was safe to go out and living there was still *gezellig*, that Dutch word which captures so well the mixture of cosiness and warmth, belonging and pleasantness. The sun always shines on the summers of our youth, the British version of the Chinese saying goes.

Likewise, it is not difficult to find people who will idealize the 'good old days' of broadcasting, full of interesting, high-quality series and documentaries, and television hosts not chosen for their showy presentation, but for their capacity to make sense of the complicated. At the same time they will complain about 'those lousy TV-programmes' that fill our screens today. And certainly in Western Europe, one is quick to point an angry finger at 'those new TV-stations' that 'go for the cheap' and have dragged in their commercial wake the traditional public broadcasters. 'Americanization' is another accusatory label. One might disagree about its exact meaning (ranging from sitcoms with 'canned laughter' to highlighting people's sex life in political communication), but it is definitely bad.

Leaving aside the question whether we can relive history objectively, the chapters in this book discuss the media issues of the twentieth century in liberal democracies against a historically informed background; and occasionally the sun of the past shines exuberantly among the clouds. They also try to capture questions posed as to the media's responsibilities in the twenty-first century; and the weather forecast can be changeable. On the whole, three themes seem to guide the discussions: do we have to worry about the role of mass media in democracy, do we need regulation of media content and practice and if so, how much, and what is the media's role vis-à-vis the public? In the answers we often find much doom and gloom about past and present, which is almost reminiscent of the *fin de siècle* feeling at the turn of the last century, but also contributions with a sense of relativism and optimism.

One way or the other, the authors in this book have related to Denis McQuail's seminal work on mass communication, the public interest, the normative and policy issues that have come out of a media landscape in turmoil and issues surrounding the question of the media's performance in democracies and for the public good (McQuail, 1992). Different authors have summarized different regulatory and moral issues which have more or less dominated the policy debate in, say, the last 25 years. It will be useful to see if we will take them along into the next century or whether they will be the remnants of a bygone era.

Nightmares, past and present

Conveniently (but certainly not surprisingly) McQuail himself has summarized policy issues into those he thinks will fade away, stay or become new and burning. He locates, in the mid twentieth century, three broad themes in most liberal democracies, the oldest being that of national security and the maintenance of public order expressed in government powers to supply or withhold information or even to censor, under conditions of emergency and 'in the national interest' (ibid.: 32). At the end of *Media Performance* (1992: 311), the extreme form government control can take – mass manipulation and propaganda – is considered one of the fading issues. Propaganda in the blunt form we have come to know it has certainly disappeared in liberal democracies, but I wonder whether Peter Golding (Chapter 2) will agree with the disappearance of the issue itself. His 'public relations state' is much more refined, but still aimed at constructing consent as a way of maintaining order. The fact that the new Labour government in the UK has shelved a Freedom of Information Bill, which they promised when still in opposition, is significant in this respect.

Secondly, there was the theme of press freedom or what we would now call communication freedom, animated both by fear of state control and by the perceived dangers of large commercial monopolies. This touches on two problems. In the first place, the paradox of so-called freedom *from* and freedom *of*: communication freedom from state interference is probably best guaranteed through (financial – in the form of subsidies – and regulatory – in the form of universal service and access) provisions by that same state. In the second place, the question whether the possible effects of media monopolies are an issue for cultural policy (and thus ask for some form of content regulation vis-à-vis equity, balance and diversity) or industrial policy (and thus guaranteeing competition and access via regulations such as anti-trust laws). Judging from the multiplicity of channels and the new potential of telecommunications, it is not surprising, on the one hand, that according to McQuail the universal provision of basic service is a fading issue. On the other hand, he sees (with others in this book) that this raises new problems for equality. In spite of the potential for communication media to help equalize the quality of life in a modern society, cultural and informational inequality, notably but not only for minorities, still exists, caused by social and economic inequality.

Lastly, the potential moral and cultural impact of media, especially on the young and otherwise vulnerable, has been another subject of normative debate and a basis for regulation and self-regulation. With both the growing interest in and offer of entertainment, series and serials, and the recognition of popular culture as such, it is not surprising to find 'mass (low taste) culture' a fading issue according to McQuail. Of a different nature and magnitude is the concern about pornography and violence, especially from commercial television stations. This is still prevalent, however much there seems to be an increasing market for such programmes. Governments have always felt a need to regulate or warn against such content. The American V-chip discussion which has crossed the Atlantic is only one example, reality television and the portrayal of crime and its victims another. Joining Blumler (1992), McQuail (1992: 310) sees competition for audiences leading to increased media sensationalism with largely negative implications for the cultural and informational quality of the performance of the media. Moreover, ethical standards will be placed under severe strain where these conflict with commercial goals. It is thus surprising that McQuail considers the portrayal of violence and crime to be one of his fading issues. Gerbner (Chapter 13) and Blumler would probably not agree.

A recurring nightmare of a different order for several of the authors in this book (and for McQuail as well) is the decline of public broadcasting. They have, in the last 10–15 years, seen the public service ideal and its 'translation' in broadcasting go down the drain. With it, they feel, are drowning the quality and diversity of television programmes, the citizen orientation and balanced politicization in informational genres, and a sense of the public interest being linked to a civic ideal. In other words: the cultural-pedagogic logic, as the cornerstone of the European model of broadcasting, is rapidly disintegrating. And in its place comes a hybrid mixture of the informational and the entertaining, quality and pulp.

Perhaps gloomier than McQuail's is also the picture, in Europe as well as North America, that often accompanies the description of the new multichannel and multimedia reality. The abundance of channels and other traditional and electronic media outlets has resulted in (to summarize in an arbitrary way by throwing many countries in the same basket): entertainment holding the front seat and penetrating all pores of informational television; news 'shows' (as the word indicates) dominated by the intrusive camera and the sensation-prone reporter; much 'recycling' of old films and series; the duplication of formats that proved to be successful, to the detriment of originality; quantitatively more to choose from but qualitatively more of the same; more murders at prime time; an ambiguous picture of the multicultural society but unashamed unambiguity as regards 'the inner city being dominated by dangerous and irresponsible minorities'; a widening gap between information rich and poor; a shift from cultural primacy, with emphasis on cultural heritage and human rights, to economic primacy in which the market decides by itself and the unobstructed trade of goods and services is the liberal state's 'pet project'.

In the wake of such sombre predicaments, new technologies and communication facilities are treated with suspicion. They might have been accompanied by euphoria about consumer choice, interactivity and democratic potential, but access is limited to a small elite that will get all the more information-rich. Moreover, technological applications have resulted in an explosion of such extremes as violent videogames, child pornography on the Internet, exploitation of privacy, interactive chat boxes in which people can produce a cacophony of noise while hiding behind faked identities, set-top boxes (for digital television) which not only allow for more choice (of the recycled and the duplicated) but also for controlling what people are watching and for registering what their interests are. It is a picture of an electronic leisure park where Big Brother watches, or where at least industry is given the chance to bombard consumers with the direct mail they did not ask for. One could be carried away by such an emotional, self-sketched, latter-day Hieronymus Boschian triptych Temple of Doom.

Between politics and pleasure

Postmodernist authors in this book have a different story to tell about the changes of broadcasting, journalistic performance in public and private spheres, and citizens caught between politics and popular culture. They see a confirmation of a new societal arrangement in which the grand narratives are replaced by a multitude of little stories, ideological certainties by fragmented constructions and struggles over meaning. Quality, for example, one of the pillars of the public broadcasting ideal, is seen more as a social construction with enormous political and policy implications than as an objective, measurable phenomenon. Communication rights should also include the right to cultural difference, to appreciate, for that matter, soaps or sports.

The plight of public broadcasting organizations in the postmodern discourse is seen as marking the end of cultural-pedagogic paternalism, in which the broadcasters were less interested in what the public wanted and more in quibbling about what they – supposedly – needed. The assumption of a polysemy of readings is not only a radical break with the implicit hypodermic needle thinking which legitimized much media regulation, but it tries to lift audiences above the amorphous category of consumers which we find with both Frankfurter Schule and mass society theorists. Instead the public is defined as active, information- and fun-seeking. In taking the pleasure of popular culture seriously, postmodernists do not exclude civic journalism and the existence of a civic ideal. They state, however, and accept, that not everyone is a political animal, eager to join a discursive exchange in the public sphere; that Habermassian dream which might well be the application of a historic construction of *herrschaftsfreie Kommunikation* which can only be imagined under perfect conditions (Habermas, 1981).

While modernists and postmodernists might even agree on many a joyful moment they spent in front of the television in the 'good old days', they have different opinions on how to evaluate the present and certainly disagree about the future. On the one side we find the forecasters of a (further) decline of the values and qualities which have guided public broadcasting in the past and changes to the detriment of journalistic practice, developments which leave little room for something like the public interest. Governments, following a neo-liberal logic, are more and more keeping their distance which will lead to a US-style of television and tabloid journalism. Programmes will become commercial in the double sense in which that label is used today: they are easy to digest and aimed at making money. The journalistic approach will favour sensationalism, scandal and human interest, while from an ethical point of view the 'blood soaked' ambulance chasers and the 'gutter gang' of gossip journalism have no morals other than the rule of the 'buck'. That image is, to say the least, questioned on the other side. Moreover, quality as such is 'problematized' and the pleasure of popular culture recognized.

This modernist–postmodernist divide is often framed in polar positions and in dichotomies which freeze arguments in undisputable and closed discourses. In spite of the middle positions and openmindedness to be found in this book, many believe either in regulation or in the market; it is cultural versus economic primacy, or people-centredness versus market-centredness, quality or quantity (quantity of course equalling pulp), the public as a different sphere from the private, rationality versus subjectivity or emotion, fact against fiction, pleasure as incompatible with seriousness, etc. Two dichotomies are, I believe, basic, closely related, as well as problematic here. And although they are usually discussed in relation to television, they could easily refer to the distinction between the so-called serious and popular press/journalism too. First, the opposing positions described so eloquently by John Corner (1991) as the public knowledge and the popular culture project. In these two separate 'domains' audiences have – and this is the second dichotomy – different roles to play: that of citizens and that of consumers respectively. The distinction not only refers to scientific interest in different television genres and their respective viewers (to put it bluntly: citizens watch the news and consumers soaps), but particularly to the position one takes vis-à-vis that 'cultural-pedagogic logic', one's vision of television's role in society in general and in democracy in particular.

In the public knowledge project the emphasis is on being informed by television's representation of reality in news and current affairs programmes. The viewer is seen as a citizen who, by watching, builds up rational knowledge which enables him to make sense of the world and actively participate in the public sphere, a discursive, opinion-forming domain. Regulation of free access to information, diversity of content and affordable universal service in media relate to this project. Here television is about information and whereas watching can be fun too, that is for the other part of the 'little grey cells', the 'affective alter ego' (Dahlgren, 1995: 38) or for different people all together, in one word: for consumers. Empirically citizen and consumer can be one and the same person, normatively they are not.

The consumer belongs to the realm of the popular culture project, where the focus is on entertainment and fiction, and where questions of pleasure and taste take predominance. Any labelling of audiences as entities that do (or should, in the case of citizens) watch certain kinds of programmes, is of course a contextual construction (Ang 1991). Broadcasters and politicians construct, depending on their respective interests and aims, types of audiences which have or should have different interests and needs. Some authors in this book try to overcome the polarity of consumer interest and citizen roles, either by defining citizenship as a dimension of people's composite identities and thus rejecting any unitary conception of it, or by radically breaking with the public–private distinction and thus taking the affect of the consumer as seriously as the cognitive of the citizen.

Such a position makes it possible to take the analysis of the competitive and converging media-reality of infotainment, talk shows and tabloid journalism, beyond the defensive and into another domain of the normative. Because, in spite of all the differences put forward in this summary of polarities, almost all the authors seem to agree, one way or the other, that there has to be some ethical hat-rack to hang one's worries and uncertainties on. The non-commitment, if not inherent in then at least lurking around the corner of postmodernity, is felt to turn a blind eye to and shy away from responsibility.

Ethical and policy issues are here to stay. As enduring and new issues for the next century McQuail (1992: 331) names: bridging information and culture gaps; securing political involvement; maintaining creativity, independence and diversity; social solidarity and minority rights; cultural autonomy and identity. All touch on the role of media in democracies, be it in sometimes conflicting ways. Bridging gaps and enhancing social solidarity and minority rights are necessary conditions, but not a guarantee, for political involvement. Maintaining creativity, diversity and independence as well as enabling cultural autonomy and identity recognizes citizenship in relation to people's composite identities and thus might help our self-confidence as citizens. But by constantly recomposing themselves along lines of taste and consumption, people's media use will individuate increasingly and allow for escaping information and political content, instead of promoting their social engagement as a result of which they could internalize and develop loyalty to the norms and procedures of democracy.

Implicitly or explicitly the media's role in democracy and its relation to a participating public is at the heart of the media-regulation debate. And it is here that democracy seems to have a problem.

The democratic dream

Television as a pleasure machine and popular journalism are often considered at odds with the media's expected role in democracy, because politics is serious business and media are supposed to play an intermediary role between the decisions of the political actors and the electorate. In the traditional idea of direct democracy in the Greek city states, all (free and male) citizens participated actively in political debate and opinion formation and were obliged to fulfil political tasks by rotation. This horizontal form of democracy thus relied on the direct participation of the citizens themselves in the excercise of power; the small scale of the polity of course allowing for the practicality of it. Since the French Revolution democracy is indirect and vertical, in that there is delegation of power of the people to elected representatives. In what we have come to understand the public sphere to be, however – a space between decision-making and the private domain – opinions are formed in discursive debate. Ideally, the issues raised there are picked up and put on the agenda within the decision-making domain.

Habermas (1962) has sketched how in the eighteenth and nineteenth centuries media performed both as platform, educated informers and passers-on for the bourgeoisie deliberating in the tea and coffee houses of Britain's and France's capitals. Under industrial capitalism the mass media, having to serve an ever greater and dispersed audience, became a basis for consumption rather than for discussion. Publicity, Habermas claims, turned into public relations and journalism lost its critical role. Moreover, in the modern world the ends and values of democracy have been translated into the shape of liberal democratic values emphasizing tolerance and respect for *individual* rights rather than the civic virtue of the ancient Greeks.

The sometimes nostalgic but also selective references to Greece and other historic periods come partly from a realization that, as we enter the twenty-first century, society is in a state of flux and democracy suffers from a sort of mid-life crisis. The causes are often summarized as: *globalization* (multinational corporations not hindered by national boundaries, more trans- and supra-national political organization, the nation state not being self-evident any more, worldwide processes of migration), *individualization* (elevation of personal aspirations and expectations, single-issue awareness and strength of new social movements as the bearers of change and efficacy), *fragmentation* (of identities and of traditional arrangements around family, neighbourhood, community, recognition of the gendered and ethnic realities of multisexual and multicultural society), *depoliticiza-tion* (declining belief in the makeability of society and of political ideology as its 'cement', in rationality and the blessing of scientific discovery, growing cynicism towards policies, politics and politicians).

The way democracy as a system works nowadays, with the emphasis on accountability and individual rights, is called *thin democracy*, because of its weak view of citizenship and low esteem of and destructive effect on participation (Barber, 1984; cf. Curtin, 1997). The idea of strong democracy is reminiscent of a Tocquevillean view of civil society, comprised of citizens and associations. But with citizens individualizing and fragmenting and the 'associations' only covering limited domains of society, the need for civil society to include other spheres as well grows. Democracy, as Dahlgren (Chapter 9) rightfully points out, is not 'just about official politics, but also has to do with the norms and horizons of everyday life and culture'. Civil society should then include social movements (playing a publicly visible role in our life world) and the vast terrain of domestic life (playing a publicly less visible role) too. This, consequently, also means that the traditional divide between the public and the private sphere is not self-evident any more.

Let me give two examples where the traditional public–private divide and top-down approach has broken down and participation has revitalized. The first, the talk show, is often discarded as a non-informative example of infotainment within the popular culture project. The second, the Internet, although very much used as a toy and for industrial applications, has been hailed for its potential contribution to participatory democracy and thus fits within traditional conceptions of the public knowledge project.

Infotainment and other virtual values

One can have one's doubts about many an example of the talk show – if one can catch them all under one umbrella – as a new public platform for both public and private concerns. It can contribute to civil society, albeit that the genre is problematic too. First and foremost, talk shows tend to evade the critical and as such are often considered an easy platform for politicians. They can, while hardly being seriously interrupted, polish their image before an audience not much interested in politics. President Clinton for that reason preferred to talk to news shows and in European countries we find this trend too. Secondly, talk shows of the topical kind tend to attract and go for the exhibitionist in many a person. If the talk show is to be part of an entertaining and at the same time consciousness-raising public sphere, there is a responsibility for the host too which compares with the role of the civic journalist. S/he is not the Peeping Tom but the prudent 'co-citizen', not the top-down informer from the public knowledge project, but the bottom-up provider of a platform for 'experience-based experts' instead of just officials. For many 'ordinary people' – and minorities are a notable example – this is the only public space where they can address a wider audience with the sort of issues they deem relevant and confront dominant political discourse with common sense (Leurdijk, 1997).

The problem with the talk show is that the issues raised rarely reach the decision-making sphere, let alone the political agenda. This is probably inherent in infotainment. Partly because the chat show with pseudo-spontaneous celebrities has degraded the other, debating and audience-discussion type talk show, partly because it does not take itself seriously, the genre is disregarded as a potentially expressive forum of public issues. Whereas it is a discursive public sphere and does initiate debate and participation.

If the talk show is one example of a bottom-up approach and partici-patory enterprise, the interactive potential that new media and the Internet in particular have unleashed is another. Most applications of information and communication technology (ICT) in relation to democracy are usually of an instrumental kind. They are generally top-down and aimed at improving the existing representative democracy, for instance by opening up public information systems and access to politicians. Only very few ICT applications go for a more interactive use, active democracy and decision makers and the public sharing responsibility. The PEN project in Santa Monica, USA, the City Card project in Bologna, Italy, and some Digital Cities in the Netherlands are examples of these non-hierarchical, bottom-up and voluntary networks, where everybody is welcome to raise issues, participate in debate with complete strangers and put information on the network (Brants, 1996).

These examples and their often substantive public participation point to a revitalization of social structures, albeit in virtual communities. Ideally, with the notion of socializing democracy, citizens share in the responsibility of decision-making and thus turning politics into an Athenian-style co-production. In practice, however, politicians feel uncomfortable with the different role they have to play in such a challenging direct democracy. And where, on the one hand, discussion groups can function as an alternative discursive public sphere, the issues raised are, on the other hand, not automatically picked up in the decision-making sphere. The strength of the voluntary nature of many of these networks is also their weakness: no one is committed to the outcome.

At the same time, where ICT applications are hailed as potential new forums for electronic or tele-democracy, particularly the Internet raises new and familiar ethical and regulatory issues. First in relation to access. In spite of its user-friendliness and local tariffs, much ICT is a costly affair which will exclude many from its use – notably third world countries, and the poor and ethnic minorities in the rich world. For the Internet to be a truly democratic new medium it should be treated as a public service, its access, availability and affordability guaranteed by government. The trend in most liberal democracies is of course towards governments retreating and deregulating, certainly where it concerns issues of universal service. Success or failure is left very much to the market. Not so in relation to the second regulatory issue, that of content. Pornography, racist and nazi propaganda, copyright, violent games, moral and property right issues in general seem to trigger more government intervention; albeit not always as rigorously with regard to every issue, and differently in different countries. Regulation of content has been commonplace in the first phase of new (electronic) media, but tight policing of the Internet because of its anarchistic nature might kill off its virtual democratic potential. A press model of regulation is desirable.

Finally, it is claimed that the Internet will make the profession of journalist obsolete. Now that people can consult a vast array of sources themselves, citizens are not dependent on journalistic selection criteria any more. This assumption is of course based on a questionable notion of the public actively and consciously searching for (politically relevant) information themselves. Also, Bardoel (1996) claims that in a situation of information abundance and targeted political communication, the critical and selective role of journalists is needed more than ever. Leaving aside Habermas' claim that journalism lost its critical role long ago, Bardoel argues from a cultural-pedagogic ideal that does not do justice to the activity and insights of audiences themselves – who might prefer journalistic intervention and selection for reasons other than guidance. All in all there seems not much reason to demonize the Internet for this reason.

Talk shows and the Internet, *bien étonnés de se trouver ensemble*, both point to a redefinition of the public–private divide and a revitalization and extension of the traditional citizen. In the talk show not only is popular culture taken seriously, but also McQuail's central theme of equality. With all its limitations and hybridizations, the platform allows for the traditionally excluded to voice opinions. The interactive and democracy-related applications of the Internet have, on the one hand, set in motion an issue attention cycle: content regulation is back on the agenda. On the other hand, if access is more widely guaranteed, the Internet can be a plaything for active participation. Democracy should be fun too.

References

Ang, I. (1991) *Desperately Seeking the Audience*. London: Routledge.

Barber, B. (1984) *Strong Democracy. Participatory Politics for a New Age*. Berkeley, CA: University of California Press.

Bardoel, J. (1996) 'Beyond journalism: a profession between information society and civil society', *European Journal of Communication* 11 (3): 283–302.

Blumler, J.G. (1992) *Television and the Public Interest*. London: Sage.

Brants, K. (1996) 'Policing democracy: communication freedom in the age of Internet', *Javnost/The Public* 3 (1): 57–71.

Corner, J. (1991) 'Meaning, genre and context: the problematics of "Public Knowledge" in the new audience studies', in J. Curran and M. Gurevitch (eds) *Mass Media and Society*. London: Edward Arnold, pp. 267–84.

Curtin, D.M. (1997) *Postnational Democracy: The European Union in Search of a Political Philosophy*. Inaugural lecture, University of Utrecht.

Dahlgren, P. (1995) *Television and the Public Sphere. Citizenship, Democracy and the Media.* London: Sage.

Habermas, J. (1962) *Strukturwandel der Oeffentlichkeit.* Neuwied and Berlin: Luchterhand.

Habermas, J. (1981) *Theorie des Kommunikativen Handelns I und II.* Frankfurt am Main: Suhrkamp.

Leurdijk, A. (1997) 'Common sense versus political discourse: debating racism and multicultural society in Dutch talk shows', *European Journal of Communication* 12 (2): 147–68.

McQuail, D. (1992) *Media Performance: Mass Communication and the Public Interest.* London: Sage.

Index